hp

شكرًا

谢谢

謝謝您

Děkujeme vám

Mange tak

Vielen Dank

Σας ευχαριστούμε

Thank You

GRACIAS

Kiitos

Merci

תודה

Köszönjük

Grazie

ありがとう

감사합니다

Hartelijk dank

Takk

Dziękujemy

Obrigado

Спасибо

Tack

Teşekkür Ederiz

Child with tablet in a school bus in Hong Kong, 2015

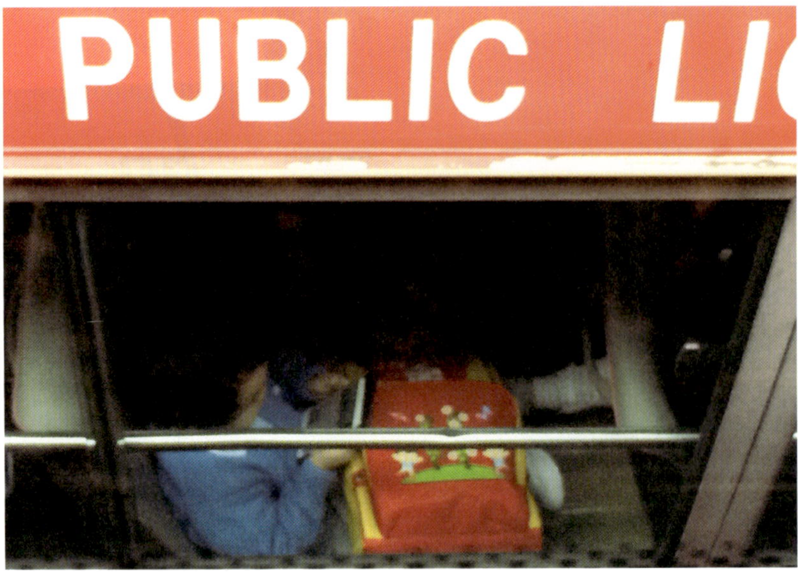

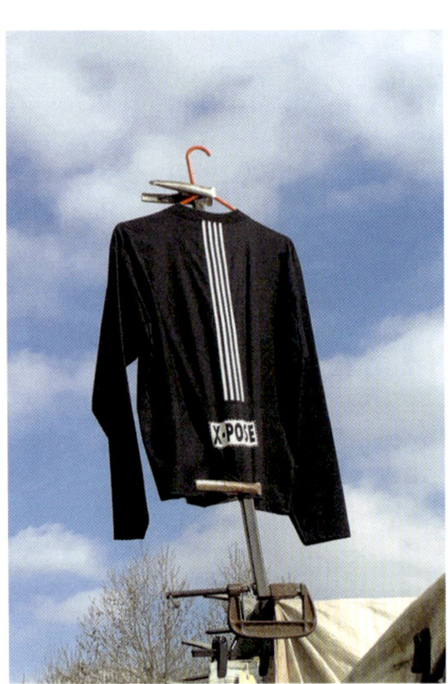

X-POSE, T-shirt featured at Whitechapel Road market, London, 2019

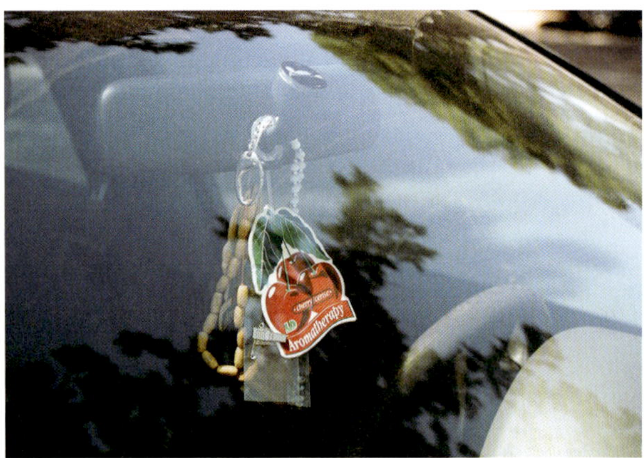

Tree-shaped air freshener labelled “Aromatherapy” and wooden prayer chains in a car in Jerusalem, 2012

Details of Colosseum, 2020, labelled T-shirts, ceiling supporters, hangers, clamps, Zabriskie Point, Geneva, 2020. Exhibition views: Matheline Marmy

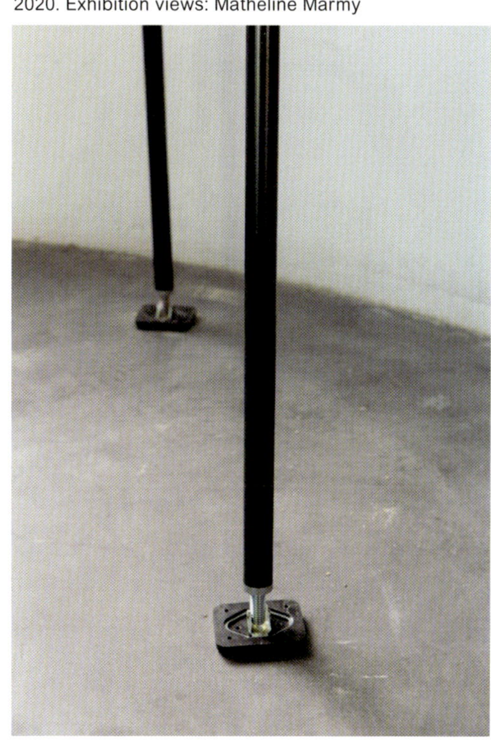

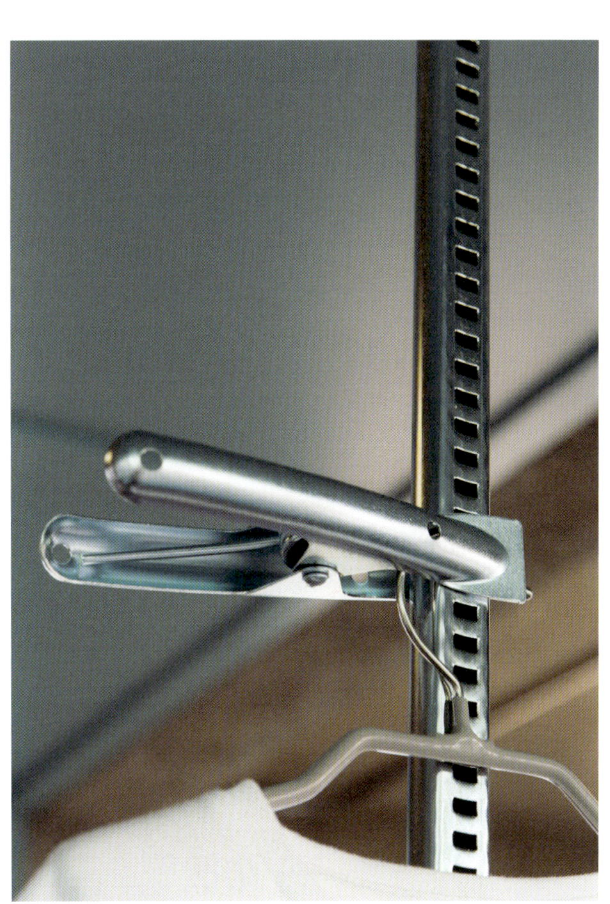

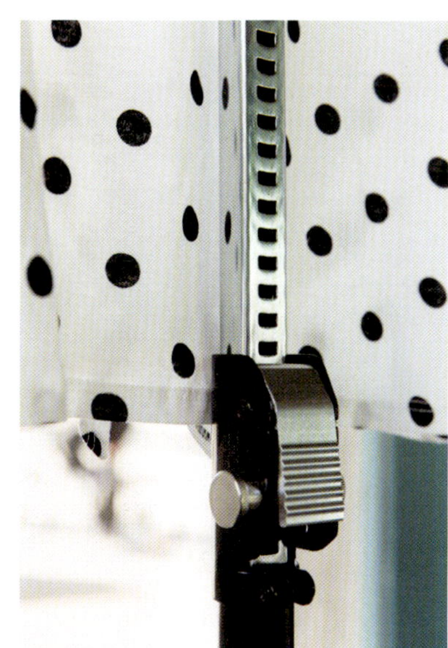

Imprint on a children's T-shirt, acquired in a department store in Switzerland during the summer of 2020. Image: Matheline Marmy

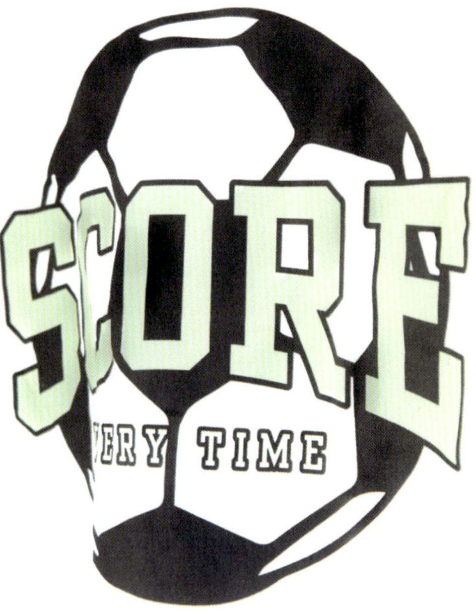

Detail of <u>Colosseum</u>, 2020, labelled T-shirts, ceiling supporters, hangers, clamps, Zabriskie Point, Geneva, 2020. Exhibition view: Matheline Marmy

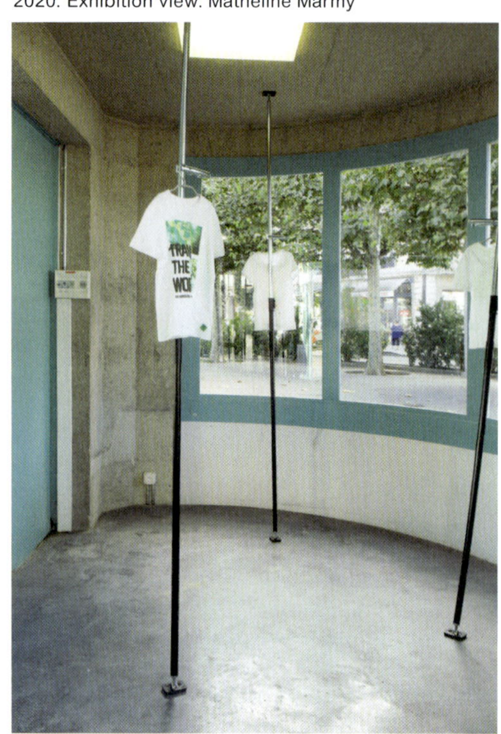

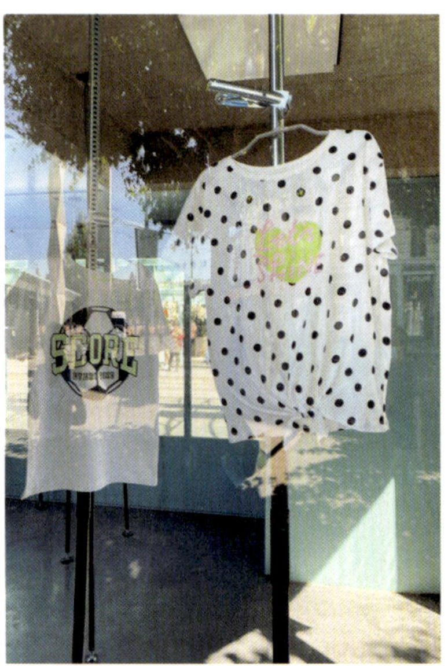

Detail of <u>Colosseum</u>, 2020, labelled T-shirts, ceiling supporters, hangers, clamps, Zabriskie Point, Geneva, 2020. Exhibition view: Matheline Marmy

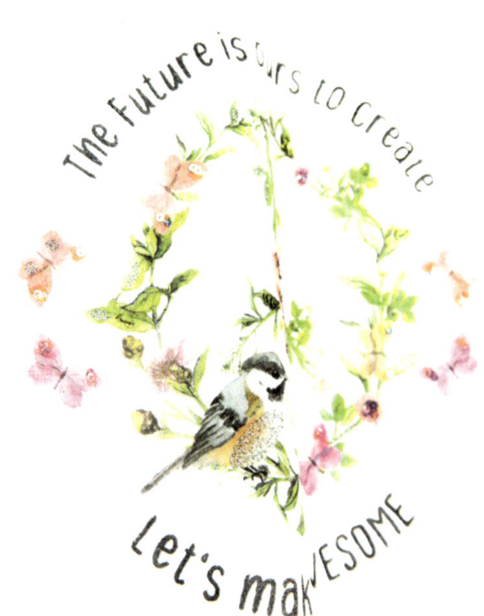

Imprint on a children's T-shirt, acquired in a department store in Switzerland during the summer of 2020. Image: Matheline Marmy

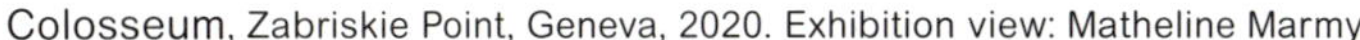
Colosseum, Zabriskie Point, Geneva, 2020. Exhibition view: Matheline Marmy

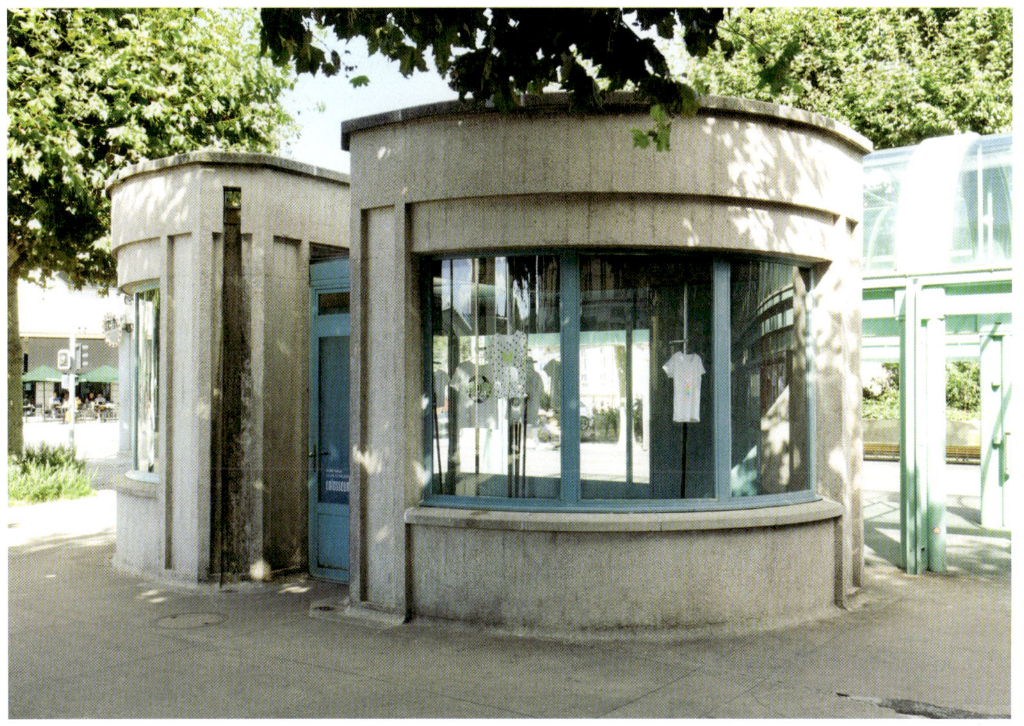

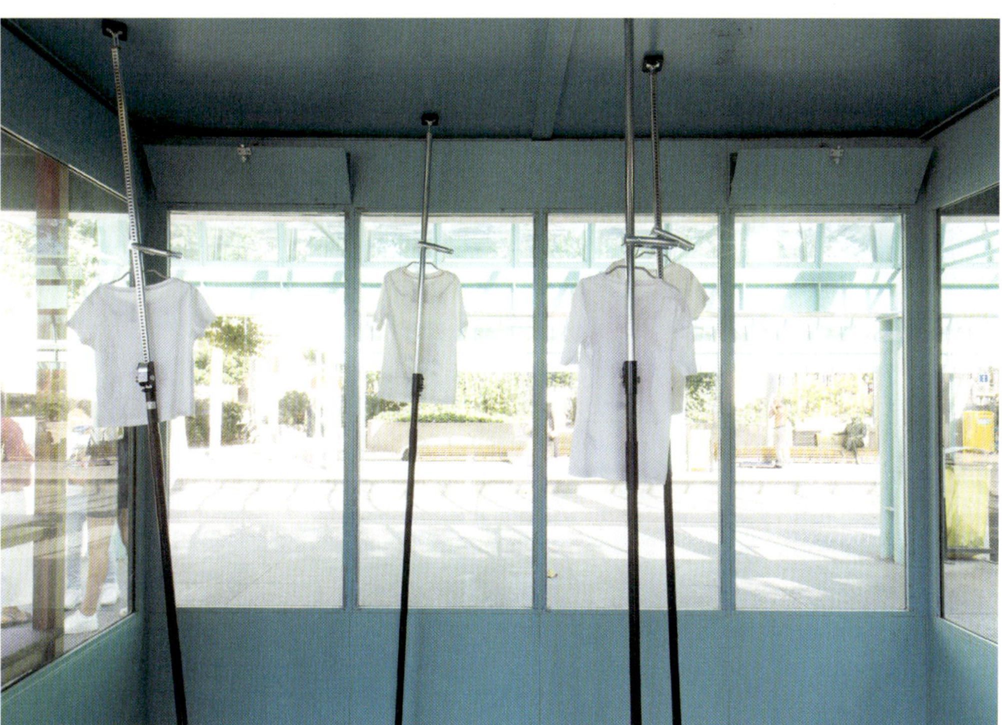

Detail of Colosseum, 2020, labelled T-shirts, ceiling supporters, hangers, clamps, Zabriskie Point, Geneva, 2020. Exhibition view: Matheline Marmy

Colosseum, Zabriskie Point, Geneva, 2020.
Exhibition views: Matheline Marmy

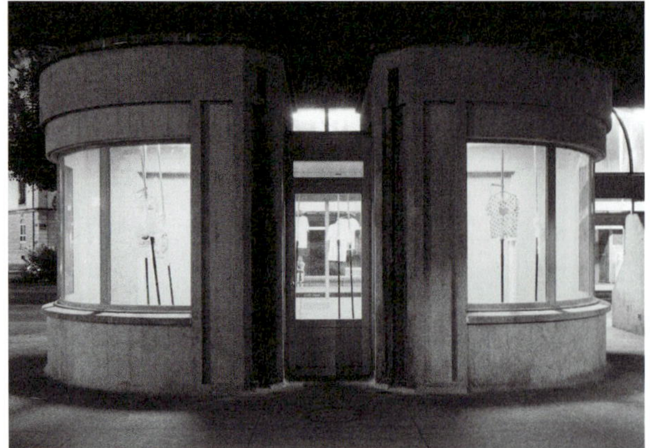

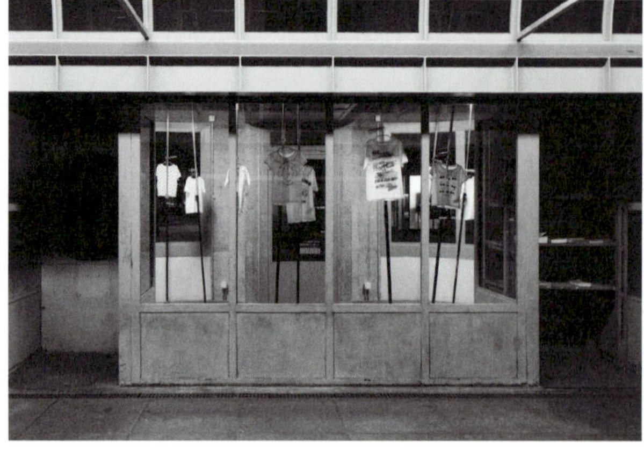

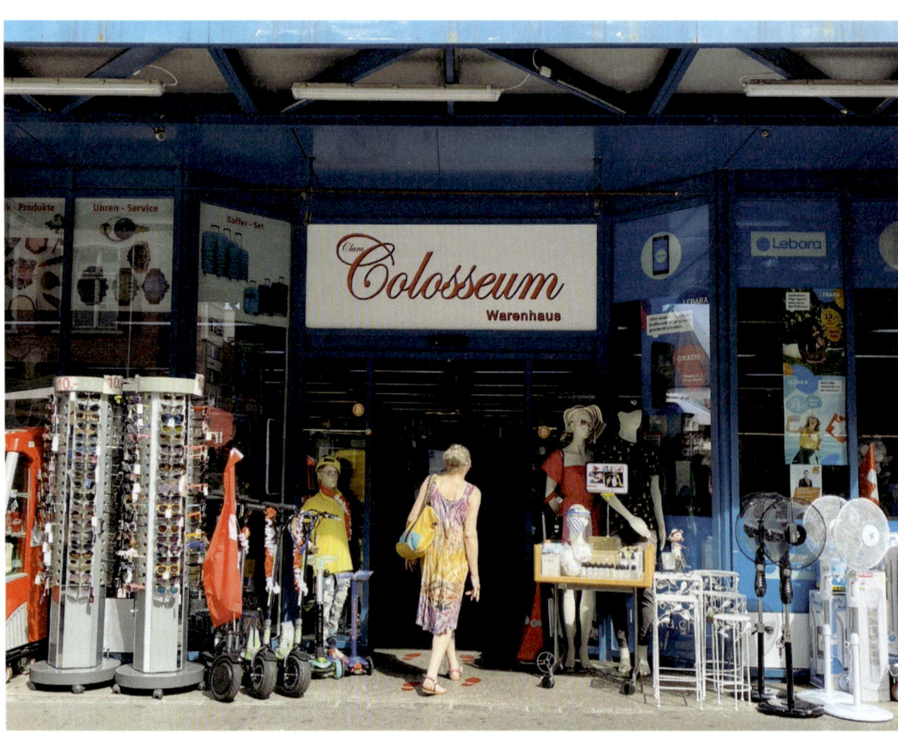

Colosseum Warenhaus on Clarastrasse, Basel, 2020

Detail of Colosseum, 2020, labelled T-shirts, ceiling supporters, hangers, clamps, Zabriskie Point, Geneva, 2020. Exhibition view: Matheline Marmy

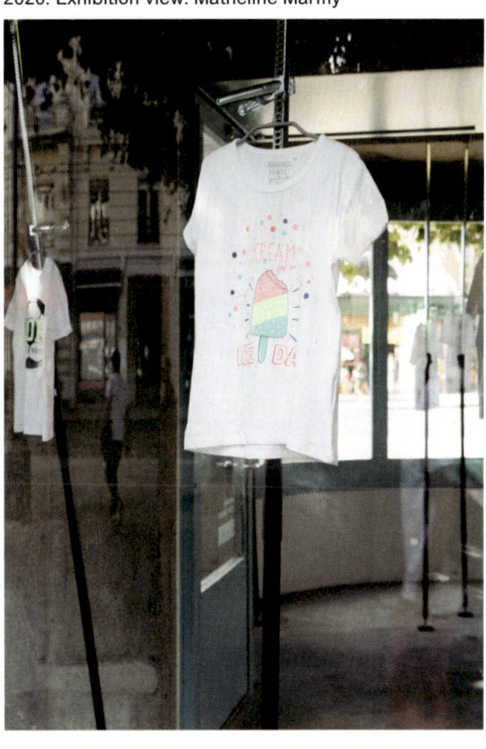

Imprint on a children's T-shirt, acquired in a department store in Switzerland during the summer of 2020. Image: Matheline Marmy

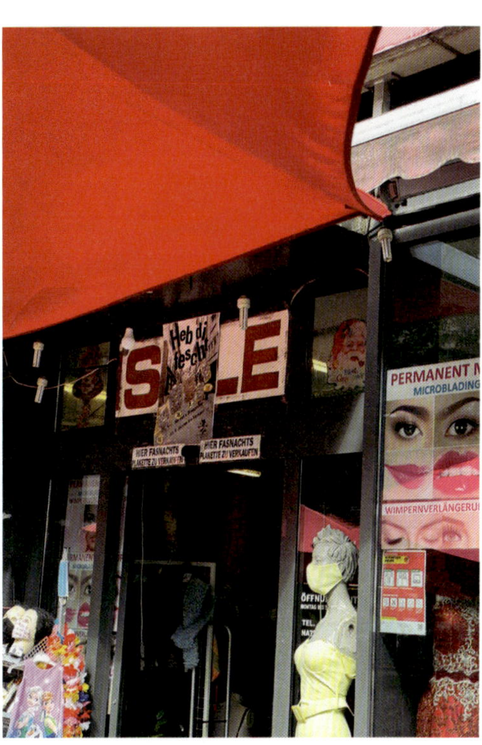

Glow & Glory department store on Clarastrasse, Basel, 2020

Google street view in Tel Aviv-Jaffa (research for
Blue White High, 2013/2017), accessed May, 2021

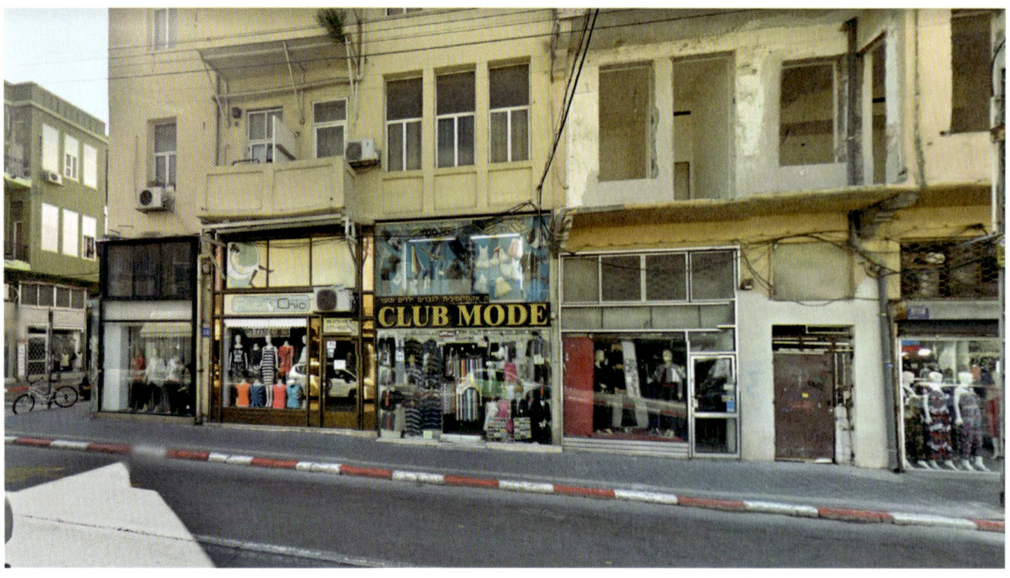

8

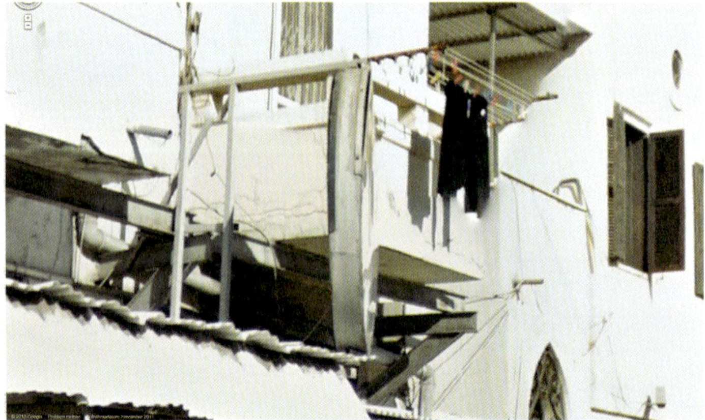

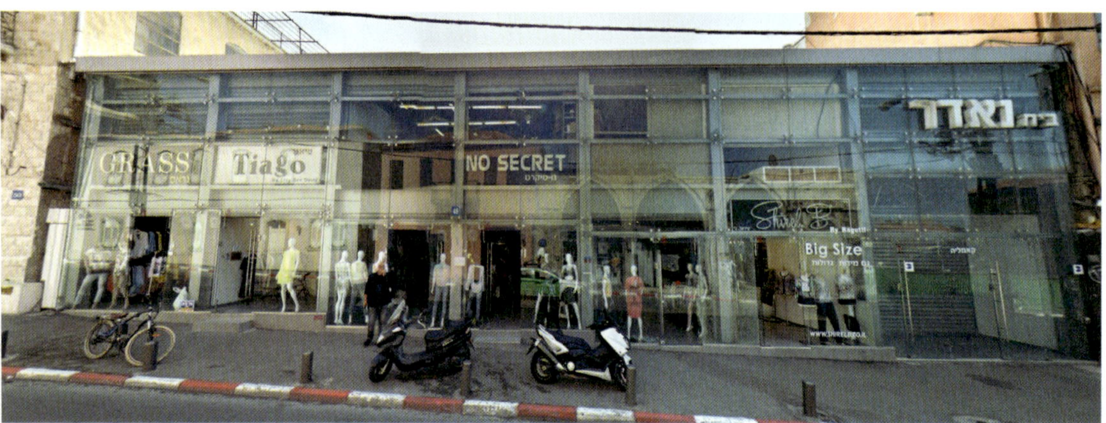

Google street view, detail of a shop display in Ajami, Jaffa, accessed January, 2013
Google street view in Tel Aviv-Jaffa (research for Blue White High, 2013/2017), accessed May, 2021

Google street views in Tel Aviv-Jaffa (research for <u>Blue White High</u>, 2013/2017), accessed November, 2012

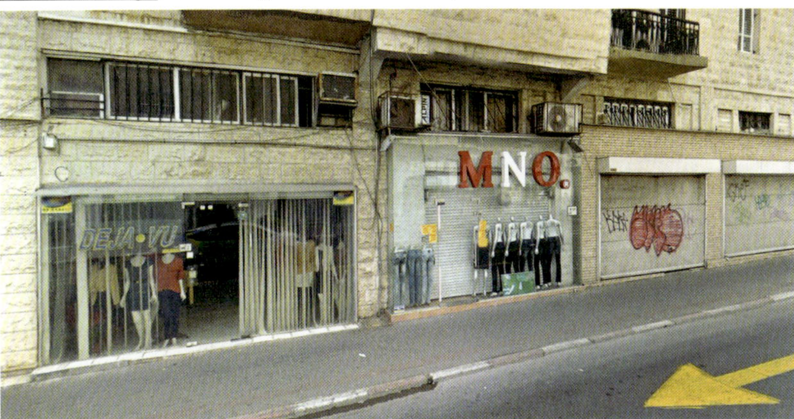

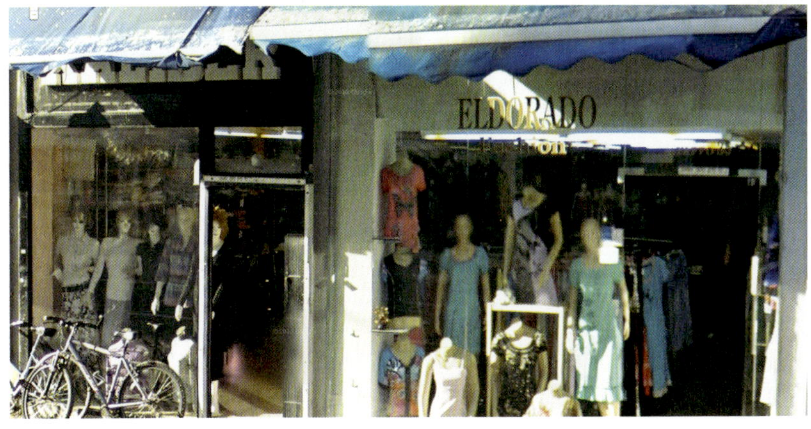

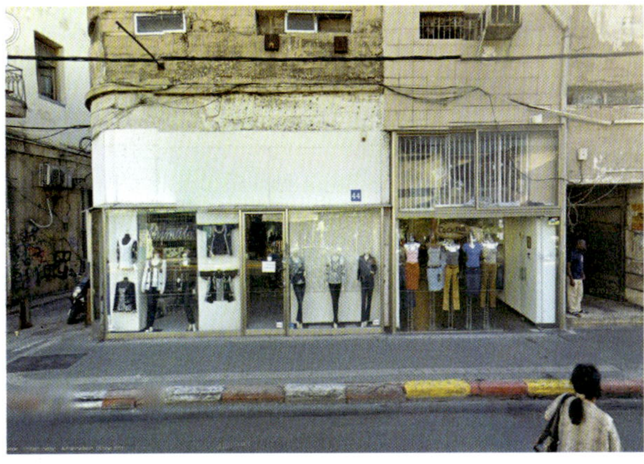

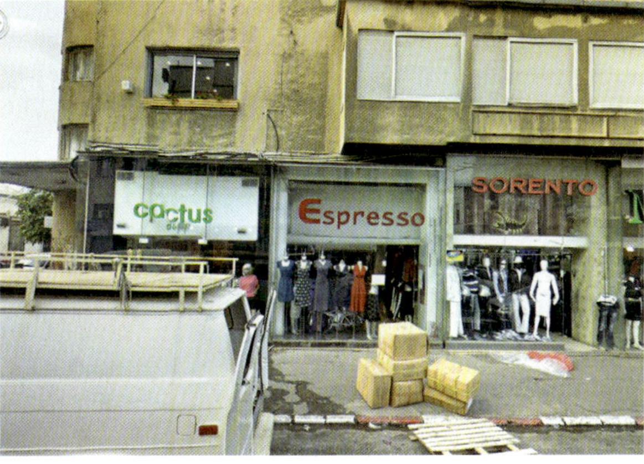

Google street views in Tel Aviv-Jaffa (research for Blue White High, 2013/2017), accessed May, 2021

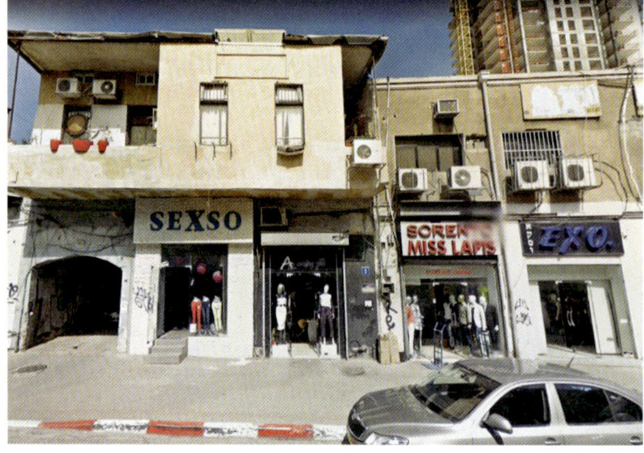

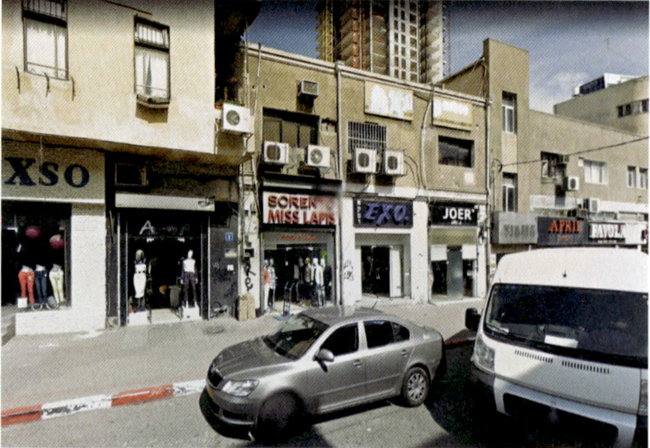

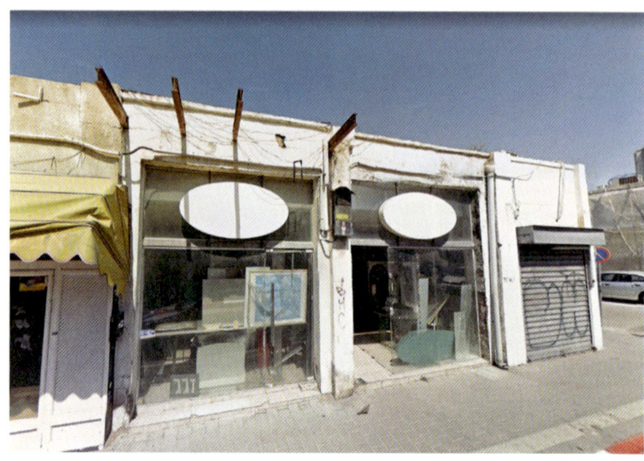

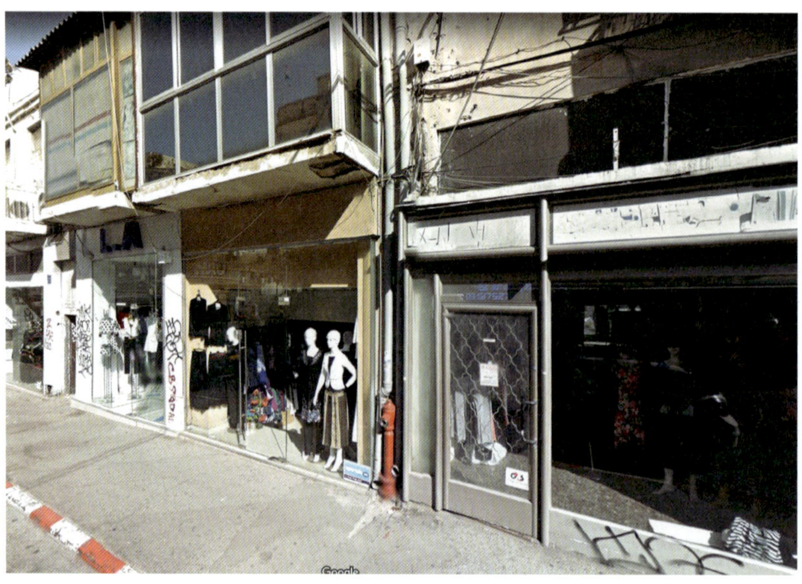

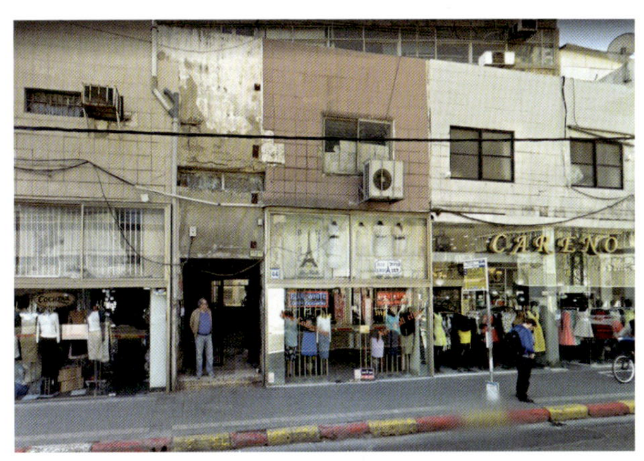
CARENO

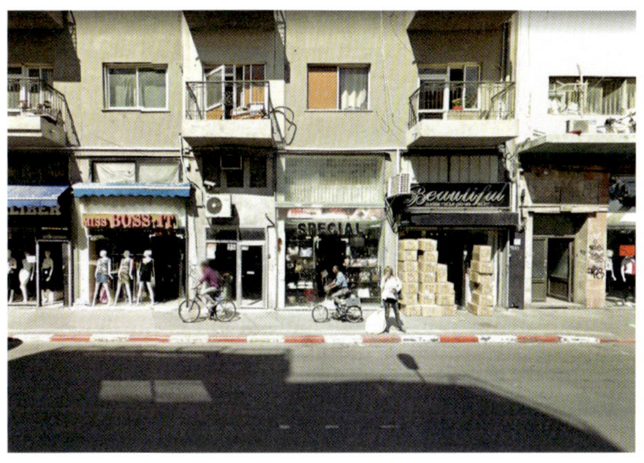
SPECIAL
Beautiful

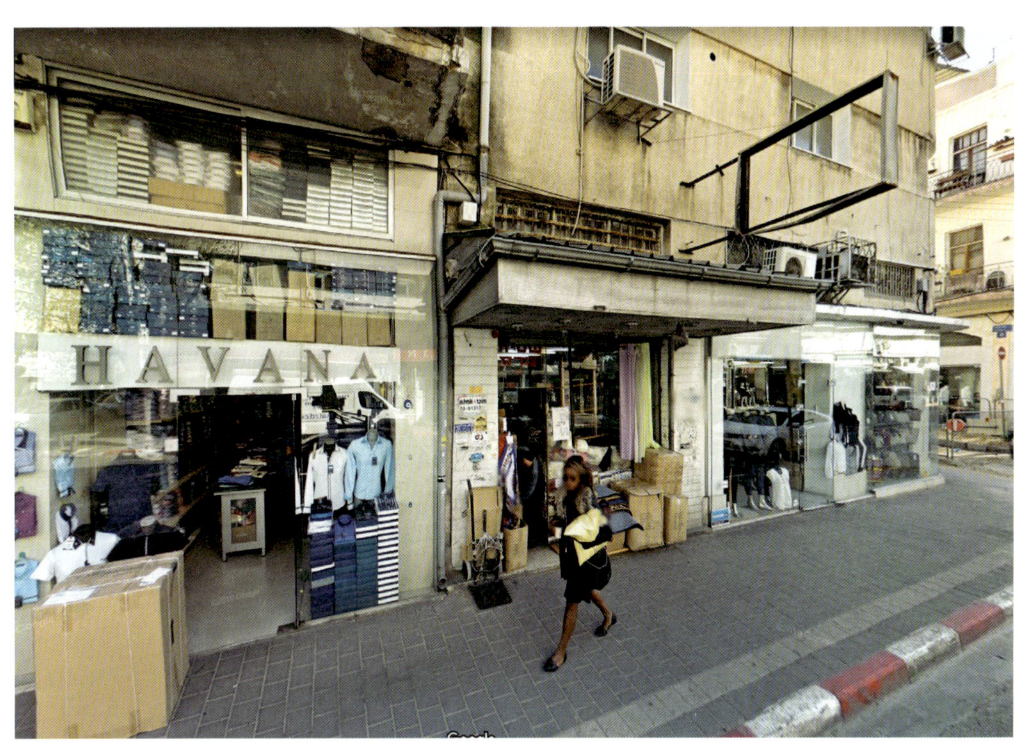
HAVANA

Google street views in Tel Aviv-Jaffa (research for Blue White High, 2013/2017), accessed May, 2021

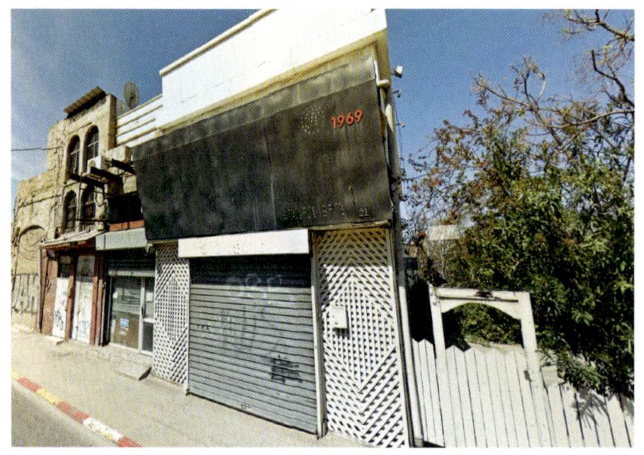

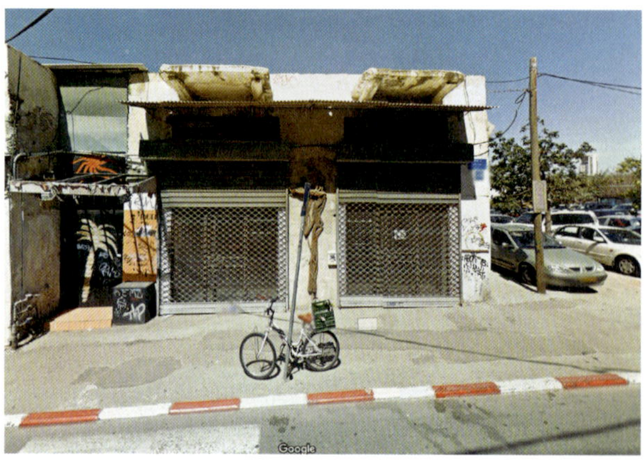

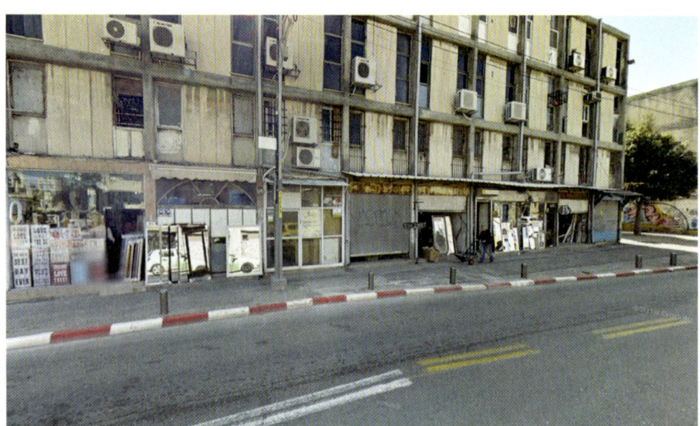

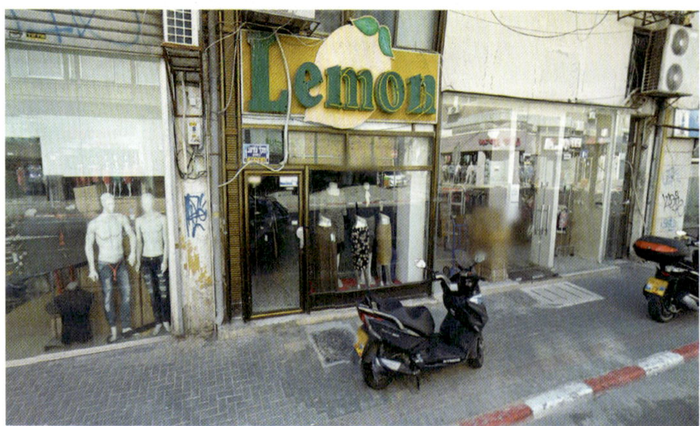

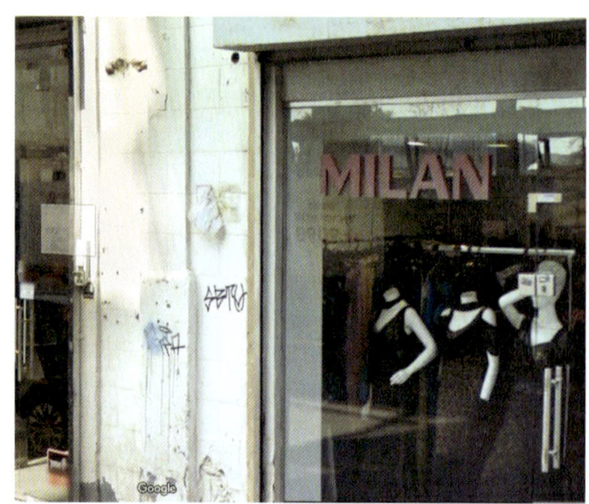

Google street views in Tel Aviv-Jaffa (research for Blue White High, 2013/2017), accessed May, 2021

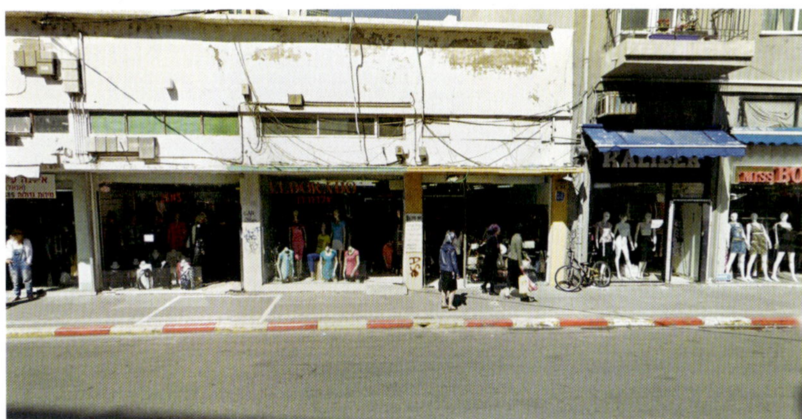

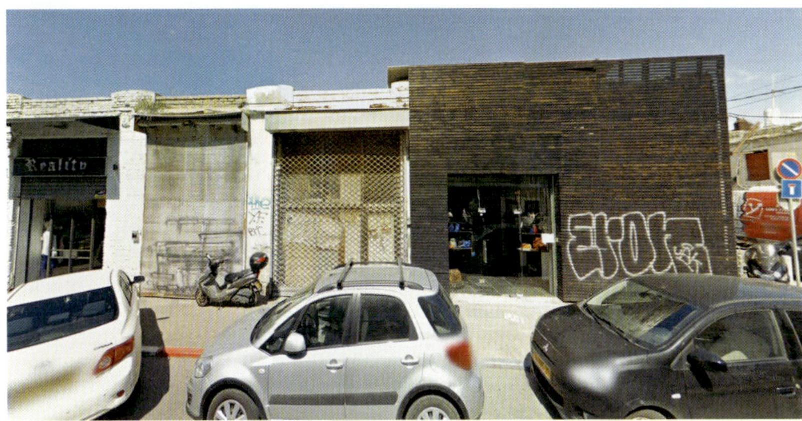

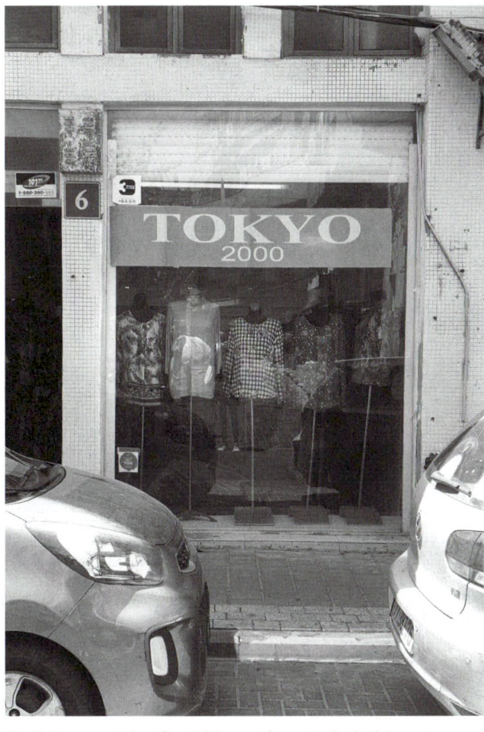

A picture sent by Omri Livne of a retail clothing store in Tel Aviv-Jaffa, 2021

Maghreb Trasporti Internazionali, view out of the studio, Basel, 2019

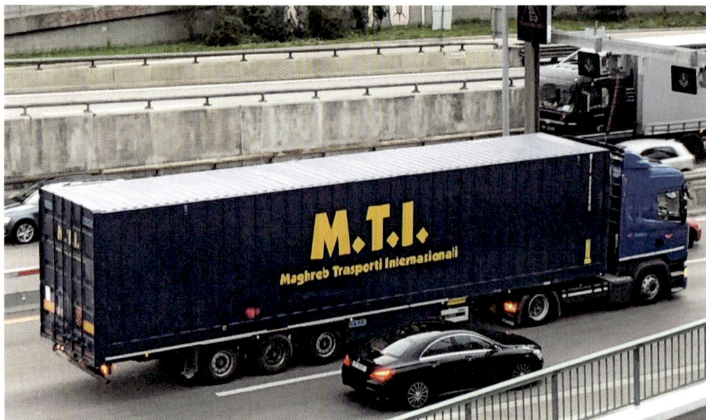

Reich Transport, view out of the apartment, Basel, 2019

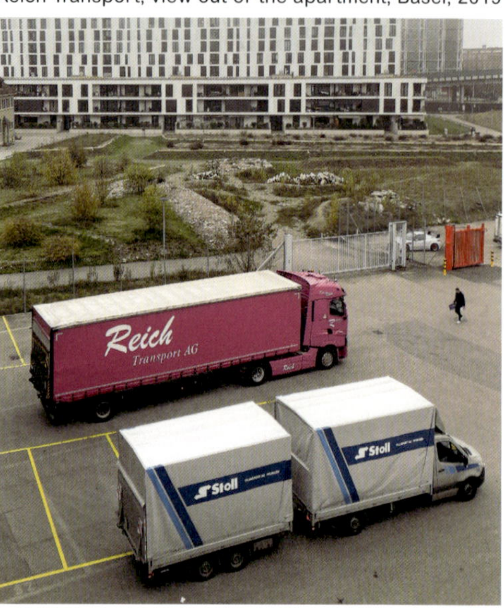

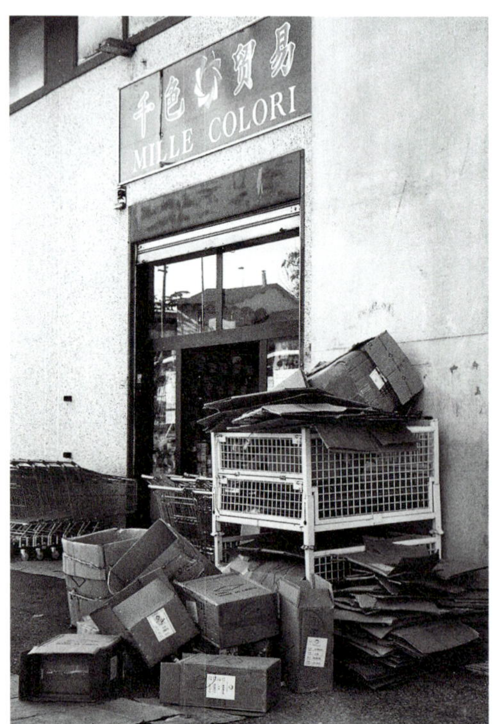

MILLE COLORI wholesale, Torre Angela, Rome, 2016

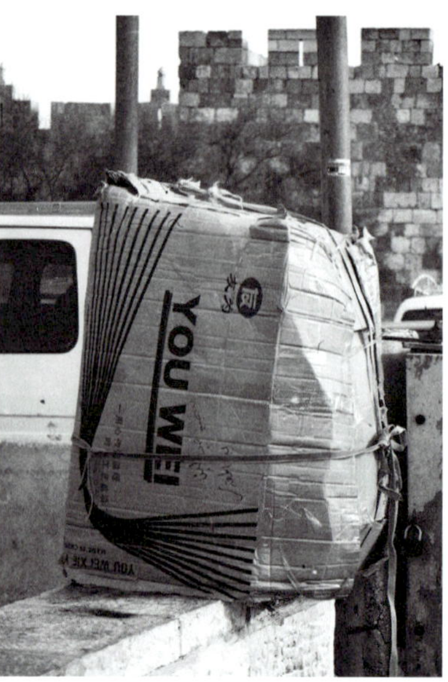

YOU WEI, burst cardboard box at
Damascus Gate, Jerusalem, 2012

Old El Paso delivery truck, Basel, 2020

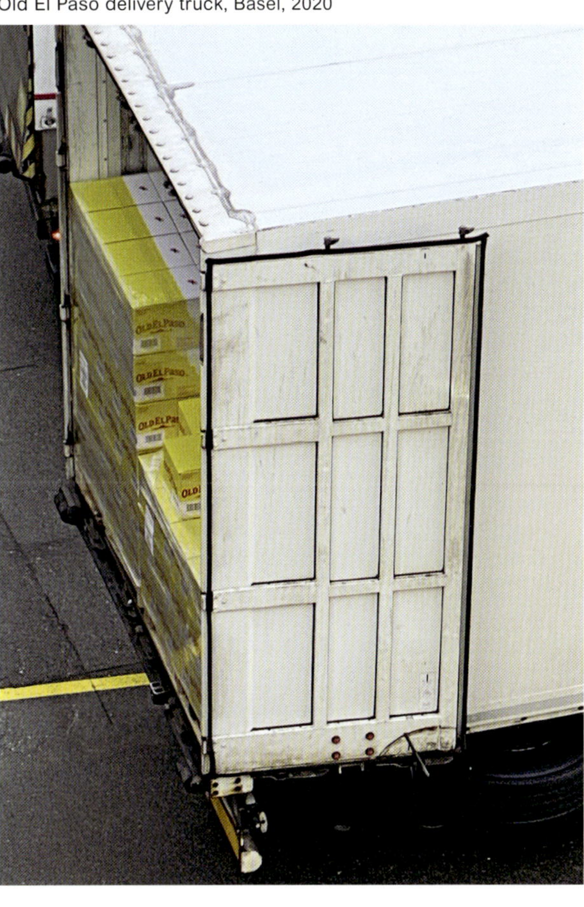

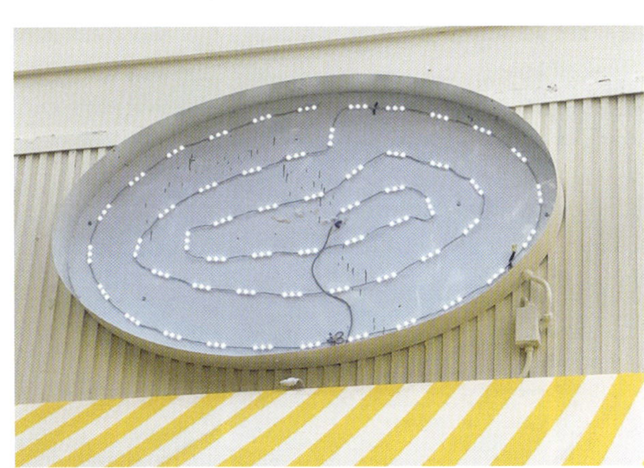

Blank restaurant light box, Manhattan, New York City, 2018

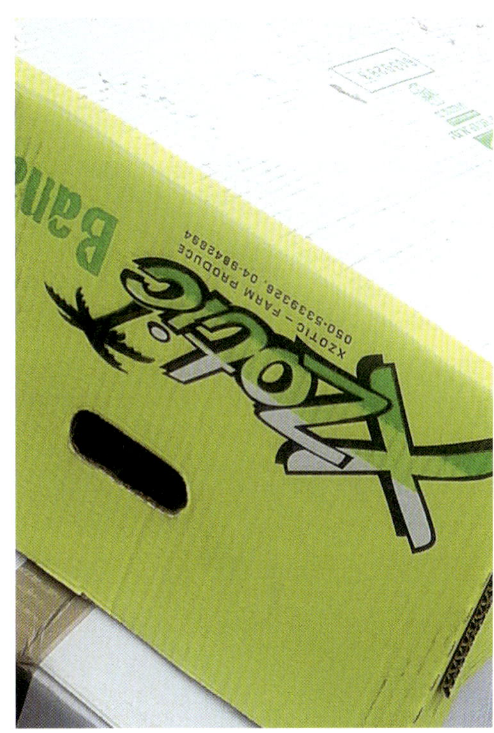

Xzotic, empty banana box, Tel Aviv-Jaffa, 2012

Still frames of *Blue White High*, 2013, updated in 2017, HD video, 23'29"

SX Sphinx

Sinai Model

SeXso

Purple

EXO.

Obsession

eXzotica

Siluet

Nine-T-Nine

Joya Me

Beautiful

Chic

What's App

Egoista

Hypnotic

Reality

Chicks

Troya

Cicily

Retro Chic

Run Way

King David

Blue White High	Eldorado	Pure	Madness
New Heaven	Animale	Lemon	Popcorn
Fly	Alice	Cactus	Panda
Dinamit	No Way	Menta	Punto
Bombes	Mademoiselle	Moti Top	Sorento
Bazooka	No Problem	Joy Tapuz	Trend
Sun Rise	Esposa	Toot	Lens
Starlight	O la la	Ksoot	Focus
Paradise	Kiss-me	Absolute	Forplay

Still frames of Blue White High, 2013, updated in 2017, HD video, 23'29"

Mix

Bravo

Elite Couture

Orent Express Classa de Paris

Matrix

Cantino

Eleven pure

Star-el Paris

Tami Twist

Monaco

Ice Cube

Big

Tiamo

Monopol

American

King

Pepino

Tabasco

Union

Stigma

Ella

Espresso

Havanna

Sigmen

Ayala

Alfredo

Dollar

Signon

Elite

Amor

Rich Line

Ultima

Deja-Vu

Elor

Classa

Sexta

Special	Samsara	Libre	Miss Lona
Celeb's	Salina	Azur	Loco No Secret
Miss NRG	Stretch	Como	Marco Polo
Miss Boss-it	Reverz	Jack's	Walla
Police	Trip	Shelly's	Oscar
Poker	Sun Jet	Leo	Three-Star
Trucker	Metro	Jones	Kaliber
Zap	BH Jeans Canada	Joe's	Sample
Zen	Canada	Miss Lola	Papa

Still frames of <u>Blue White High</u>, 2013, updated in 2017, HD video, 23’29”

Tata	S.M.L	CL	Blue
Pasha	H&L	B	Blue Best
Ke Pasa	RIM	Wish	Yonka
Fiesta	JMJ	Win	Favola
Jo	MGA	All in	Capital
Lai	MNO	All in one	Cinema
Moma	P.O	Lord	Milan
Moma Showroom	D.M	Booba	Loren
Studio 54	N.B	Pink	Lev

We-Well	Red Zed	Gallery-X	Simply you
CockTail	ZooZ	Vogue	PoXse
Terry Star	Gutti	Vitrina	Pogal
Tiago	Yucca	Miss Millennium	Pierro
Blanco	Tenzo	Titanium	Prato
Blue Dog	Gitane	Miss Mary	Milano
Besos	April	Angel	Vila
Ronson	Grass	Santie	Conso
Miss Red	Anti-Virus	Miss Sallie	Sioni

Still frames of <u>Blue White High</u>, 2013, updated in 2017, HD video, 23'29"

G-Spot
Bianco B Men
DJ Model
Dolce Vita
Gina
Italgo
Club Mode
Dulce Mia
Rotana
Parkingo
A 12
Zuchra
Togana
Segol
Lucky7
Camelea
Govana
Liraz
Tokyo 2000
Biba
Galliano
Agas
Payota
Lavanta
Antonio came
Agadu
Patent
Suzany
Ciao Bella
Optimi
Miss Lapis
Pishuni
Grosso Italia
Shirel. B. by Bagutti
Miss Kaza
Karina

Kasuf	Yupi Du	Stardust	All in Love (Herz)
Kashi	Dreamline	Rosabella	Golden Rose
Keshet	Headline	Pamella	
Coket	Spicy	Daniella	
Kokotek	Juicy	L.A.	
X-Tik	Tonic	From Lemons to Limonada	
Comix	Touch		
Chic Chic			
Canavaro			

The Role of Translation

by Simone Neuenschwander

A big book is not a "great evil"—even if the encyclopedist Callimachus is said to have thought otherwise[1]—but behaves more like a room that can be furnished. A volume that opens up its own laws in time and space as we turn its pages, pausing at, returning to, or skipping passages, as well as in its sensory characteristics as an object. With their free combinations of images and language unfolding on and between pages, artists' books can function like an exhibition—a micro-architecture in which the pages become gallery walls, and through which we can move through the unfolding of different connections.[2] Judith Kakon's book *Stolen Language* can also be understood as an exhibition in which her works and working materials are brought into relation and curated anew. Within its pages the artist develops non-hierarchical and non-linear settings for photographs of her works, production photographs, technical sketches, scans and reference images, which she has either found or produced herself. She assembles her visual research in the book in open indexes and inventories which examine select terms and observations about her work. Interactions and contiguities emerge between the disparate images in a way similar to what curator Lucy Lippard describes in regard to her editorial work: "The double spread is ground zero for the ... bookspace. One image speaks for itself, another criticizes it. One image can be powerful, another can disarm it, stoke it up, change its meaning entirely, begin a new sequence, say more."[3] With its rhythmic arrangement of images, *Stolen Language* is not a manual to Kakon's working method, but instead builds an individual archive—a collection of translation processes which become a work in its own right.

MIND MAPPING

In addition to views of her work ¤ (2020) on the back wall of Kunsthalle Basel, Judith Kakon has included a variety of visual materials in this book, presenting them on equal footing with her own artistic work (pp. 66–77). This includes historical images such as the frontispiece of Franciscus Aguilonius's *Six Books of Optics* (1613) by Peter Paul Rubens, announcing the book's title in classical capital letters on a stone monument (p. 67). Another illustration depicts early stone molds in which bronze, gold, and silver were used to cast weapons or jewelry (p. 67). If we compare the images with the hand-turned wrought iron letters of ¤, we begin to discover loose, unexpected connections—a mind map of formal and textual simultaneities. This also occurs with a photograph of cellophane-wrapped flower bouquets placed on commemorative plaques at the memorial to the fallen on Rue de Rivoli in Paris (p. 67). The same motif is echoed in the monumental bouquet in Basel's Restaurant Kunsthalle (p. 66), whose withered flowers were exchanged weekly between the letters of neoliberal terms such as "Real," "Estate," or "Prime" in Kakon's work ¤. The vanitas motif of flowers can be found on several levels in the book, from the citations at public memorials to the ephemeral luxury of the flowers in the Restaurant Kunsthalle (p. 66), an important business lunch location in Basel and therefore a hub for economic exchange.

In a time of rapid economic and technological development, mappings—as visual models or mental orientation aids—can be a means with which we can identify claims to knowledge and investigate power structures. According to cultural theorist Rosi Braidotti, the methodology of cartographies should avoid grand theories and remain grounded through embodied and embedded perspectives.[4] To resist universalist endeavors maps must retain their locally situated views and reflect non-hierarchical complexities, which help challenge taken-for-granted assumptions and practices.[5] Braidotti suggests that cartographic accounts should also help to understand the actual and simultaneously hypothesize the virtual.[6] In her book, Kakon carries out various temporal and spatial surveys without losing sight of the specific environment in which her work ideas are rooted. Her mind maps always remain connected to her subjective perception of certain situations and forms, which she also discovers and documents in other contexts during her working process—such as the photograph of a courtyard she visited in Marrakech (p. 68), whose wrought ironwork of railings and ceiling grilles recall the protective architectural elements of expensive real estate in downtown Basel. Eventually, the virtual aspect that emerges in the analogue medium of the book takes place in the productive free spaces and gaps between the images and their possible analogies.

TURN IT UPSIDE DOWN

Pattern recognition is one of the central activities of the human brain, as media theorist Marshall McLuhan pointed out in the late 1960s. McLuhan saw the ability to increase our pattern recognition as a kind of "survival technique" in the face of information overload, so as not to lose track of things.[7] He considered artists as being particularly able to study patterns in order to make them usable in modified form.[8] Kakon also examines mass media and institutional patterns in her work. Closely observing situations in her immediate surroundings, she directs her gaze to circulation in commerce, the production of goods and the associated exercises of power in public space. She is particularly interested in the linguistic codes of marketing and its product names, when the human rationale behind them becomes apparent. In her series *Untitled (Alibaba)* (2016–2020), for example, she documented her email correspondence with sellers on the Chinese online sales platform Alibaba. The answers to her purchase requests were partly generated by chatbots, but also included communication with real sellers. In the correspondence, these sellers take every opportunity to build a personalized relationship with their messages, often expressed in a somewhat cryptic, broken English. The messages' direct personal tone, intended to increase the buyer's incentive, reveals the ambition of the self-employed sellers to participate in the profit opportunities offered by the online platform. At the same time, they also point to the strong economic dependencies and the fear of failure they entail. Kakon has transferred sentences from her email exchanges with sellers into different formats, such as an artist's book, picture panels, and stickers, which are introduced into the public space as decontextualized advertising without losing their intention as emotional triggers (pp. 42–50). Reflecting on the mechanisms of profit maximization by means of extraction and isolation, Kakon highlights and exposes the deeper messages. Similarly, in her video *Blue White High* (2013/2017), she investigates the sometimes flawed yet imaginative marketing language used in an area close to her former home in Tel Aviv, collecting the names of small family-run retail clothing shops along the main roads to Jaffa. Concentrating on these as titles, the work presents over 200 names, including "Joya Me," "Loco No Secret" and "Orient Express Classa de Paris," which appear in succession in white letters on a black background (pp. 16–23). Through this deliberate reduction, the interwoven messages of wealth, extravagance and internationality become transparent and make the viewers aware of their own ability to recognize patterns. In her book, both of these works are featured along with visual and textual references that accompanied their production process. They reveal the circulation of thoughts that take place as the artist develops her works and how she elaborates the communicative structures of repetition from social, economic and linguistic fields.

TRANS/POSITION

As the title of Judith Kakon's book, *Stolen Language* formulates an assertion and an irony at the same time. Can a language be stolen? What art accomplishes is to translate meaning into a different set of signs than that of language. Art pursues an alternative economy of meaning than language by shifting, exchanging and valuing concepts, logic and ideals in a different way. Conversely, a translation of art into language is confronted with multiple uncertainties. According to Ian Burn and Mel Ramsden of the artist group *Art & Language*, the language we use determines what (and how) we see: "... our language screens the object, it's the grid which structures our perceiving."[9] The linguistic translation of visual experience thus influences what is perceived and further interprets it through the cultural codes inscribed in the language used.

In her book, Kakon translates her observations into an artistic system of signs, offering various visual translations in and about her work. This is not a "translation" of realities, but instead reflects how the artist works at the intersection of different contexts, their cultural attributions and value chains, and how modes of expression influence the readability of the artworks. This is particularly evident in *Date Series* (2017), which continually activates linguistic interpretations while simultaneously evading them (pp. 113–115). The glass objects fuse the forms of dried dates with those of glass flacons that preserve precious liquids. Depending on where they are seen and shown, the objects can foreground topics such as nutrition, water scarcity, conservation or luxury. The issue of fabrication also comes into play, as it does in much of Kakon's work, as she made the vessels with graphite and plaster molds she produced herself, using an ancient glassblowing technique used by the Romans over 2,000 years ago. This original handicraft contrasts with the serial nature of the works and their respective subtitles, named after various date varieties such as "Medjool," "Deglet Nour" and "Barhi," which are available to us through global supply chains. Like an oxymoron, the glass objects reveal contradictory resonances and, as "empty" containers, they demand to be filled with linguistic meaning by viewers.

With the interpretive shifts that Kakon initiates through and in her works, we each have to perform our own translation in order to recognize the patterns, twisting and turning through our experiences and knowledge of the world, flipping book page after book page, in search of linguistic attributions. *Stolen Language* can be understood as a withdrawal from the signifying power of language and conveys the self-awareness required to read the signs of our world autonomously and independently, allowing them to be freely re-contextualized time and again.

1 Callimachus was a Hellenic poet, linguist and Alexandrian librarian in the 4th/3rd century BCE. "'Big book, big evil' (μέγα βιβλίον μέγα κακόν, mega biblion, mega kakón) is another saying attributed to him, often thought to be attacking long, old-fashioned poetry." https://alchetron.com/Callimachus, accessed June 13, 2021.

2 Anna-Sophie Springer, "Volumes: The Book as Exhibition," *C Magazine* 116 (Winter 2012), 36–44; "Moreover, when speaking of 'site' and 'space', it becomes important to think about the 'architecture' of a publication—by understanding, for instance, the pages of a book as equivalent to the walls of a gallery, or by seeing the book primarily as a kind of 'place' through which one can move in different ways and which produces all kinds of relationships, but also by pondering a publication's relation to objecthood." 37.

3 Lucy Lippard, "Double Spread," in *Put About: A Critical Anthology on Independent Publishing*, eds. Maria Fusco with Ian Hunt (London: Book Works, 2004), 83.

4 Rosi Braidotti, *Posthuman Knowledge* (Cambridge, UK: Polity Press, 2019), 136.

5 Marguerite Koole, "Review of Rosi Braidotti (2019). Posthuman Knowledge," *Postdigital Science and Education* 2 (2020), published online on June 3, 2020, 1052–1056: 1055, https://link.springer.com/content/pdf/10.1007/s42438-020-00139-y.pdf, accessed June 15, 2021.

6 Rosi Braidotti, *Posthuman Knowledge* (2019), 137.

7 Marshall McLuhan, *Counterblast* (Toronto: McClelland and Stewart, 1969), 132: "Faced with information overload, we have no alternative but pattern-recognition."

8 Marshall McLuhan, "Man and Media," 1979, in *Marshall McLuhan. Understanding Me: Lectures and Interviews*, eds. Stephanie McLuhan, David Staines (Cambridge, MA: MIT Press, 2003), 285: "The artist's insights or perceptions seem to have been given to mankind as a providential means of bridging the gap between evolution and technology. The artist is able to program, or reprogram, the sensory life in a manner which gives us a navigational chart to get out of the maelstrom created by our own ingenuity."

9 Ian Burn, Mel Ramsden, "The Role of Language," 1969 (first published 1968), in *Art in Theory 1900–1990: An Anthology of Changing Ideas*, eds. Charles Harrison, Paul Wood (Oxford, UK and Cambridge, MA, USA: Blackwell Publishers, 1992), 880; also "Thus whatever attitude we have to seeing may depend very much on the kinds of distinctions we typically use in language, and in fact on the way in general that we set out to describe our visual experiences." 881.

Construction site on Safra Square, Jerusalem, 2014

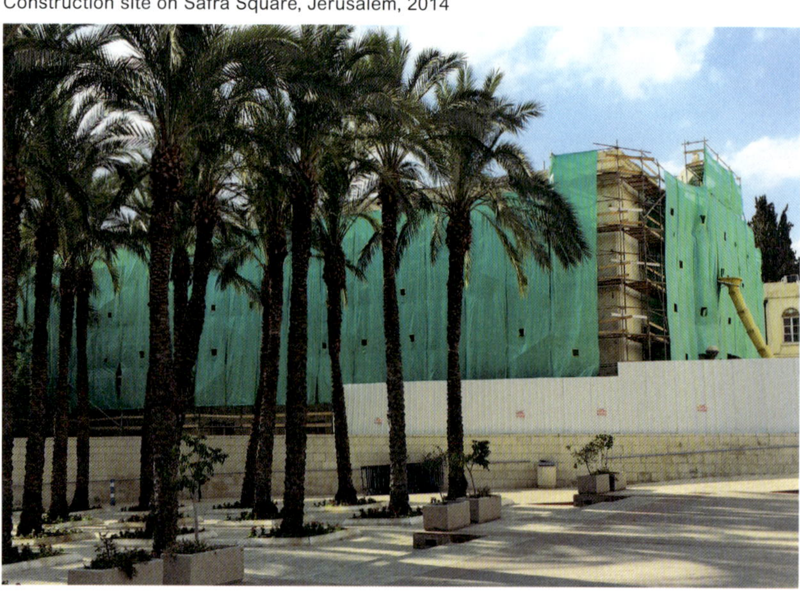

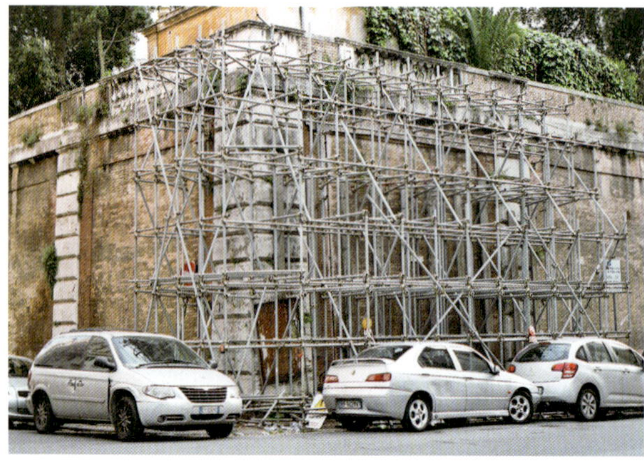

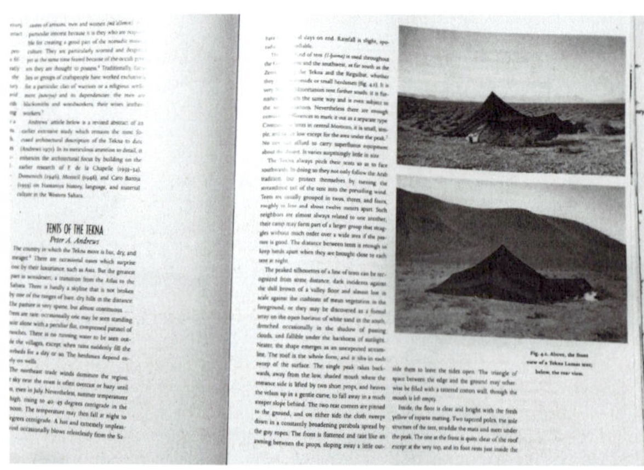

TENTS OF THE TEKNA

Peter A. Andrews

Construction site on Via Lombardi, Rome, 2016, offset print, framed, 12 × 18 cm, edition 1/50

From African Nomadic Architecture: Space, Place and Gender by Labelle Prussin (Washington, D.C.: Smithsonian Institution Press, 1995), 66–67 (Tekna Kansas tents)

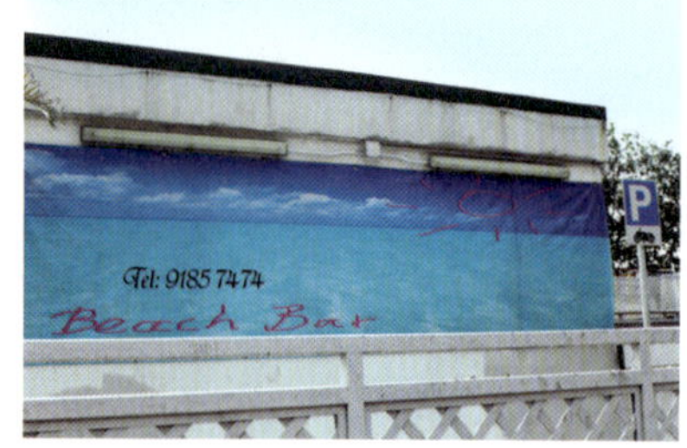

Beach Bar on Hong Kong Island, seen from a cab, 2015

Permanent construction on Basel Street, Petah Tikva, 2009

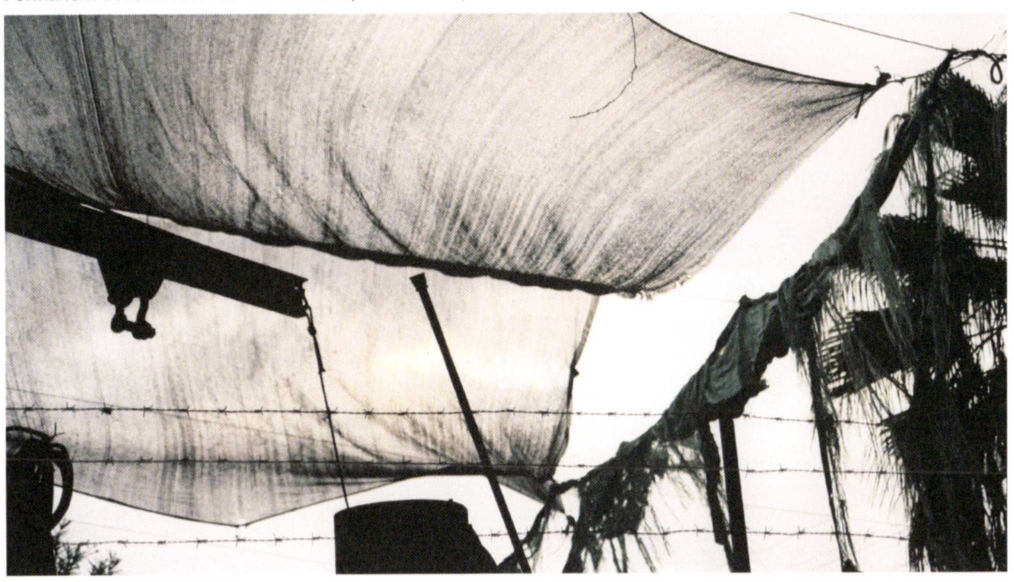

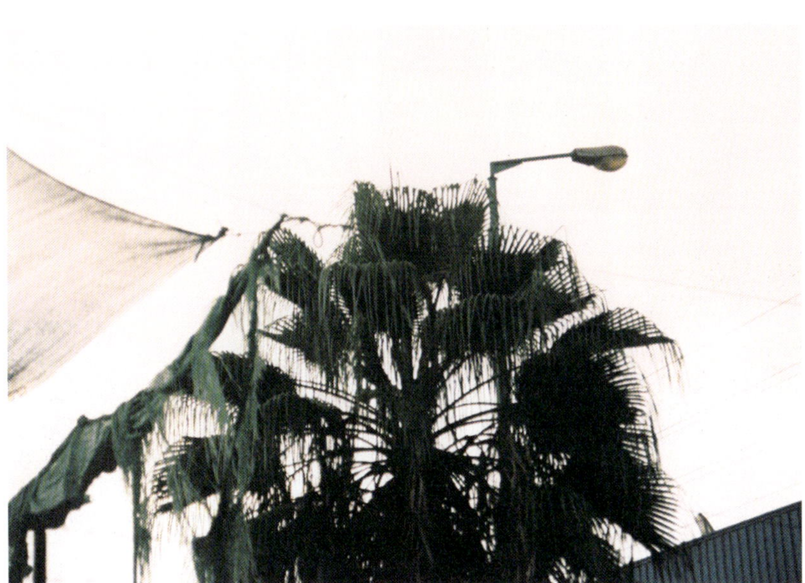

Permanent construction on Basel Street, Petah Tikva, 2009

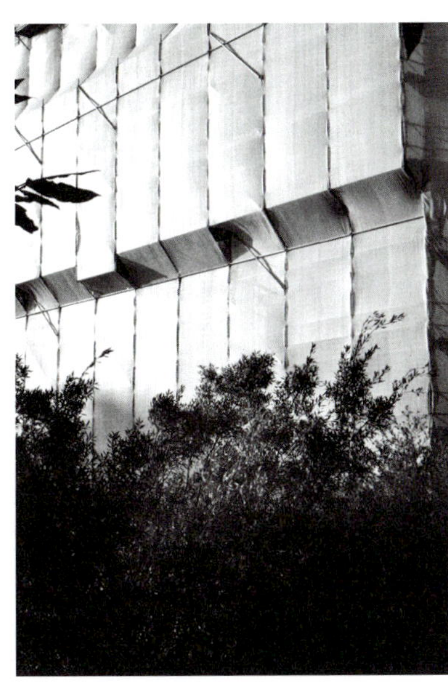

Construction site opposite Villa Maraini, Rome, 2016, offset print, framed, 18 × 12 cm, edition 1/50

Shade roof on Via della Missione,
Rome, 2016

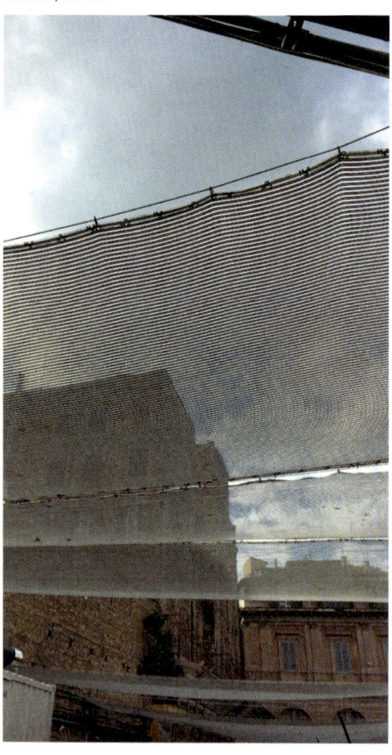

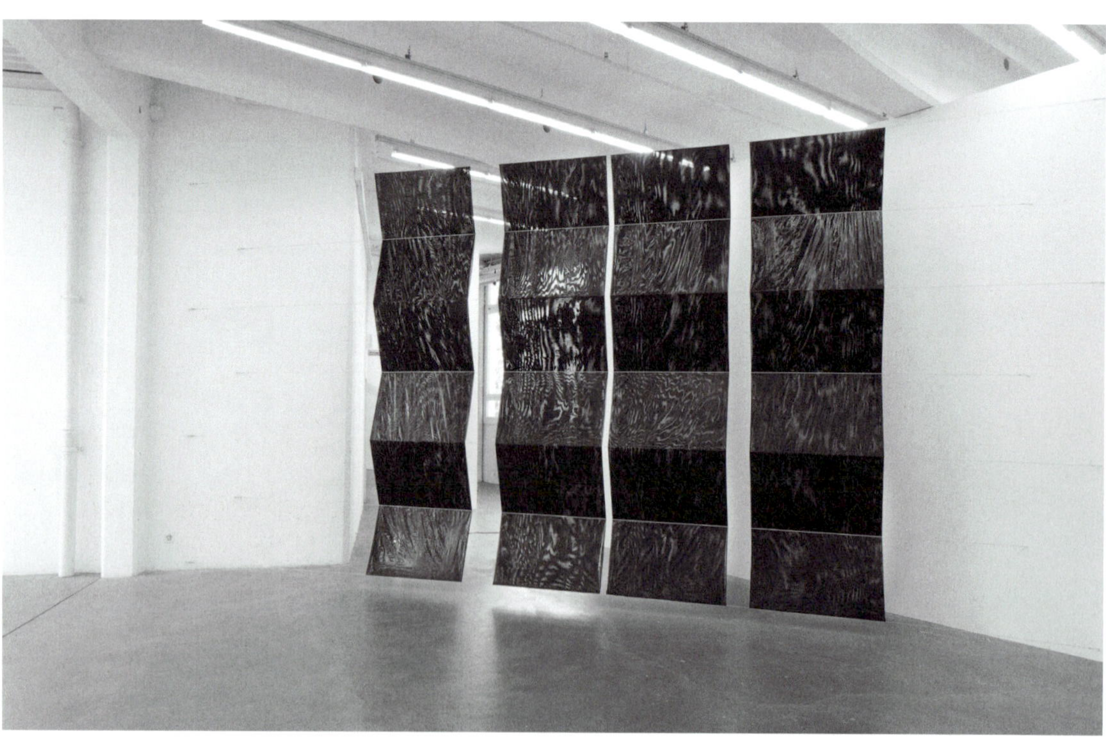

Untitled (Weedblock), 2014, PVC (weed block), steel ropes, variable dimensions,
Kunsthaus Baselland, Muttenz, 2014. Exhibition view: Sylvain Baumann

From <u>African Nomadic Architecture: Space, Place and Gender</u> by Labelle Prussin (Washington, D.C.: Smithsonian Institution Press, 1995), 69 (drawings after E. Rackow and W. Caskel, 1938)

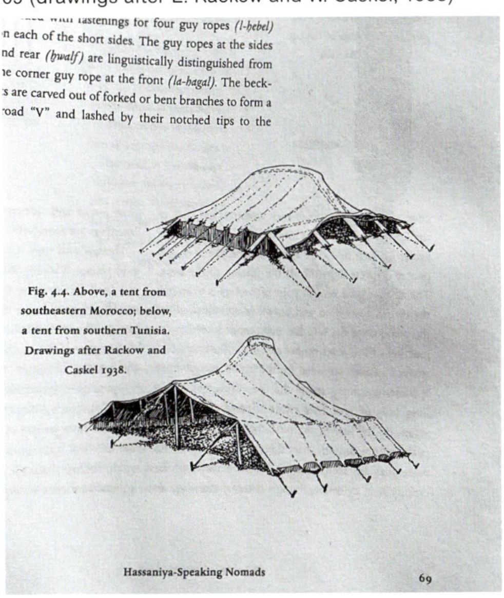

...with fastenings for four guy ropes *(l-ḥebel)* ...n each of the short sides. The guy ropes at the sides ...nd rear *(ḫwalf)* are linguistically distinguished from ...e corner guy rope at the front *(la-ḥagal)*. The beck...s are carved out of forked or bent branches to form a ...road "V" and lashed by their notched tips to the

Fig. 4.4. Above, a tent from southeastern Morocco; below, a tent from southern Tunisia. Drawings after Rackow and Caskel 1938.

Hassaniya-Speaking Nomads 69

Construction site at Theater Basel, opposite Kunsthalle Basel's back wall, 2021

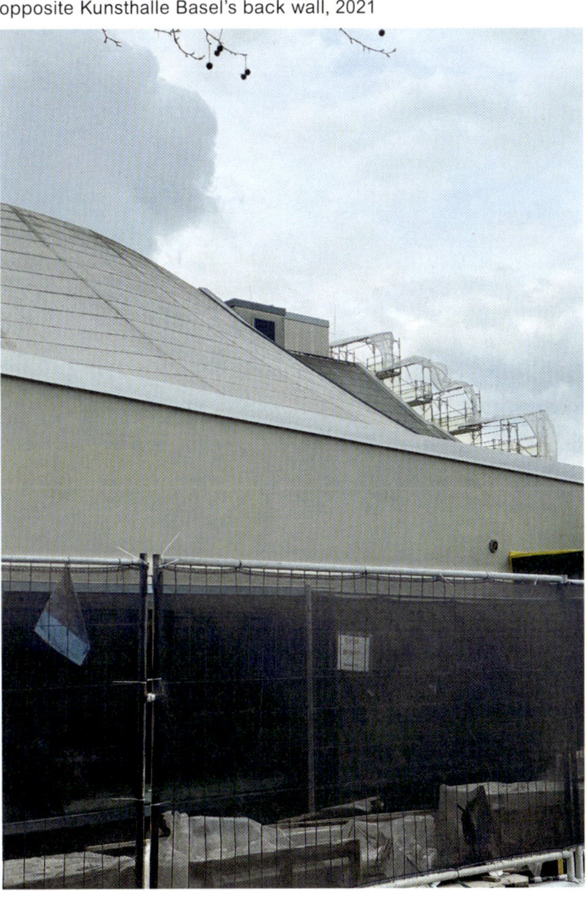

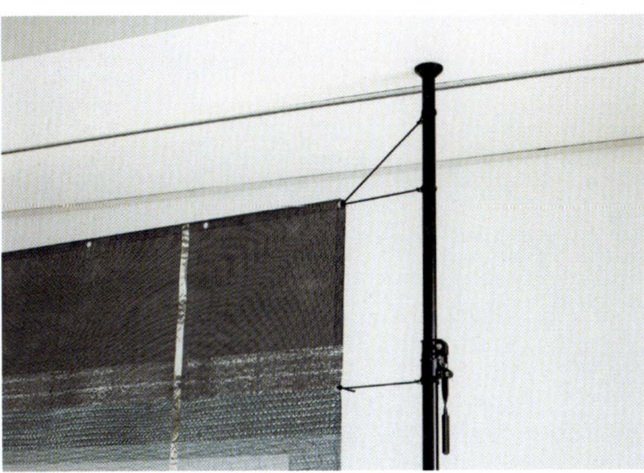

Detail of <u>(sic) 2</u>, 2013, mesh tarpaulin, digital print, autopoles, 202 × 380 cm, Herzliya Museum of Contemporary Art, Herzliya, 2014

Detail of Untitled (Weedblock), 2014, PVC (weed block), steel ropes, variable dimensions,
Kunsthaus Baselland, Muttenz, 2014

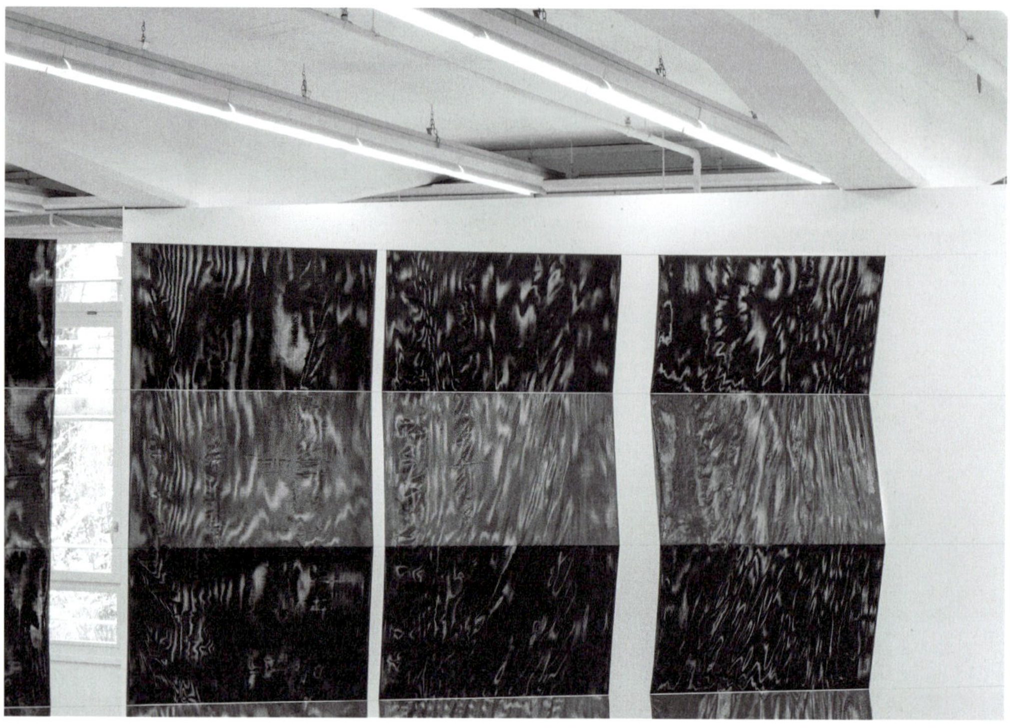

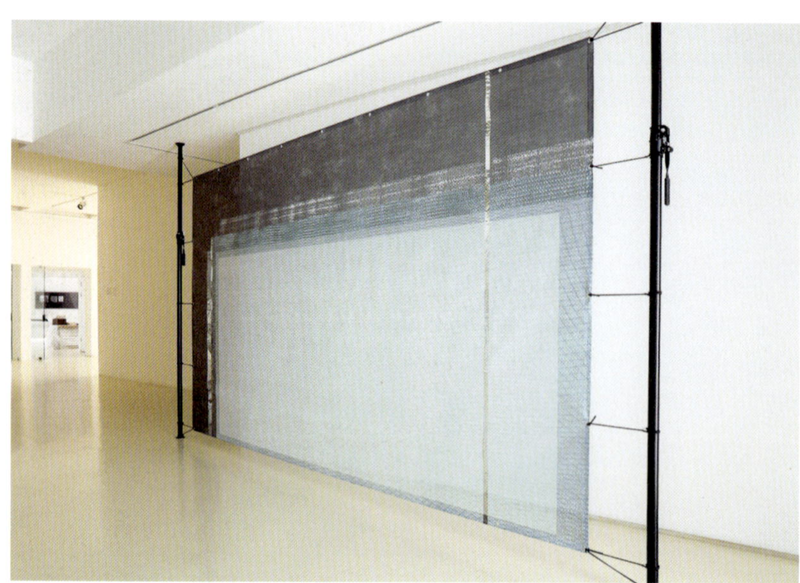

(sic) 2, 2013, mesh tarpaulin, digital print, autopoles, 202 × 380 cm,
Herzliya Museum of Contemporary Art, Herzliya, 2014

(sic), 2013, mesh tarpaulin, digital print, 300 × 1200 cm, Kunsthaus Baselland, Muttenz, 2014

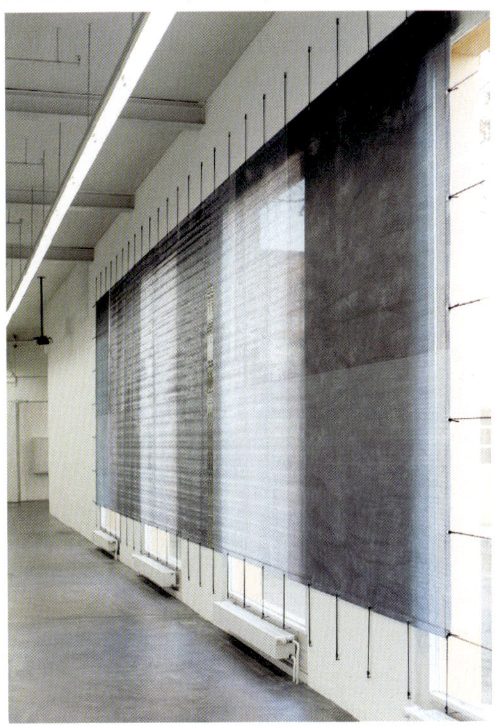

Detail of a shade roof on Via della Missione, Rome, 2016

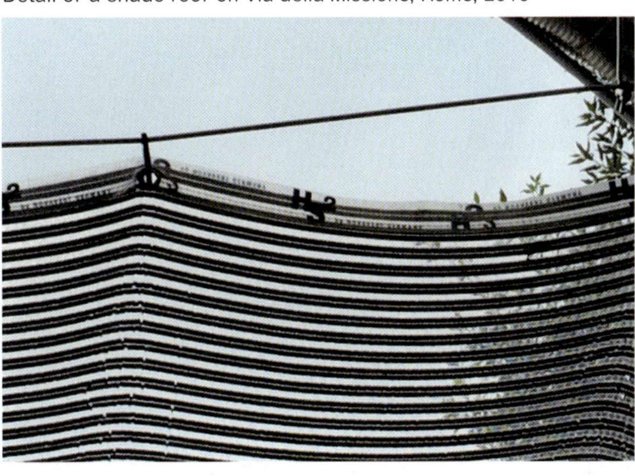

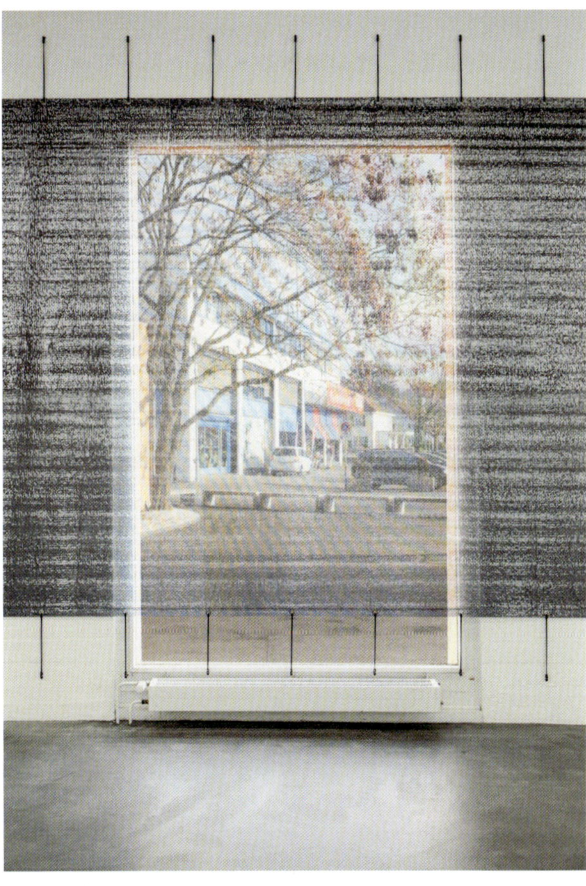

Detail of (sic), 2013, mesh tarpaulin, digital print, 300 × 1200 cm, Kunsthaus Baselland, Muttenz, 2014

Mural paintings in a hallway of Castel Sant'Angelo, Rome, 2016

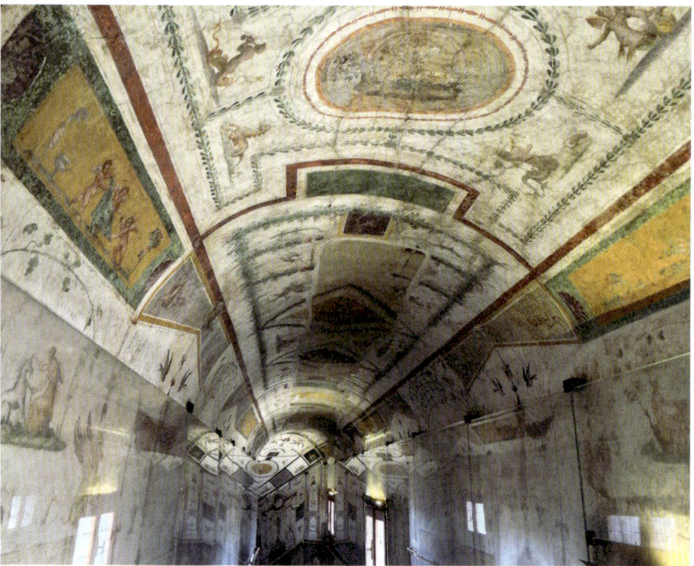

Empty show cabinet with hooks, Trevi, Rome, 2016, offset print, framed, 18 × 12 cm, edition 1/50

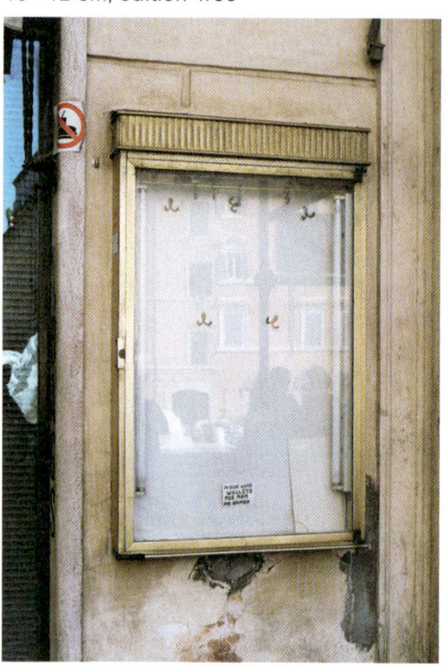

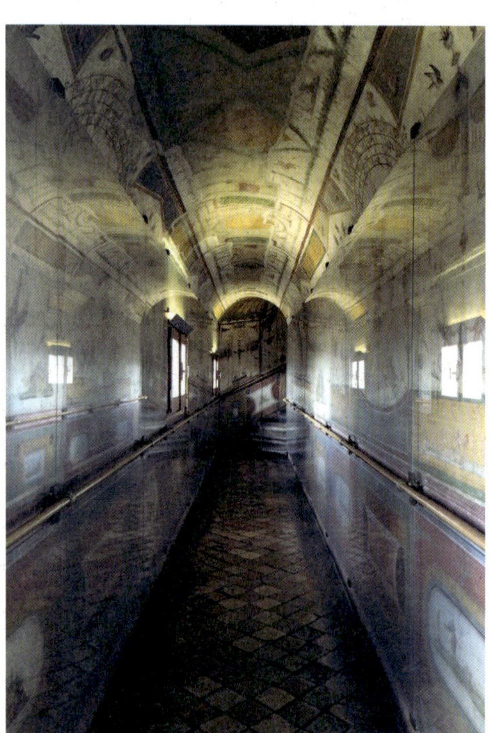

Mural paintings covered with glass in a hallway of Castel Sant'Angelo, Rome, 2016

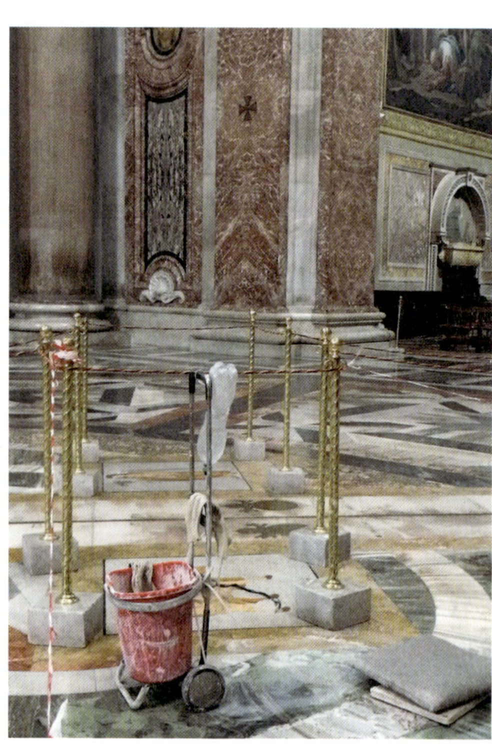

Renovation works in the church of Santa Maria degli Angeli e dei Martiri, Rome, 2016

Empty show cabinet lined with velvet, Trevi, Rome, 2016, offset print, framed, 18 × 12 cm, edition 1/50

Advertising in Castel Sant'Angelo, Rome, 2016

In the Gallery of Paintings and Mosaics, Palazzo Massimo, Rome, 2016, offset print, framed, 12 × 18 cm, edition 1/50

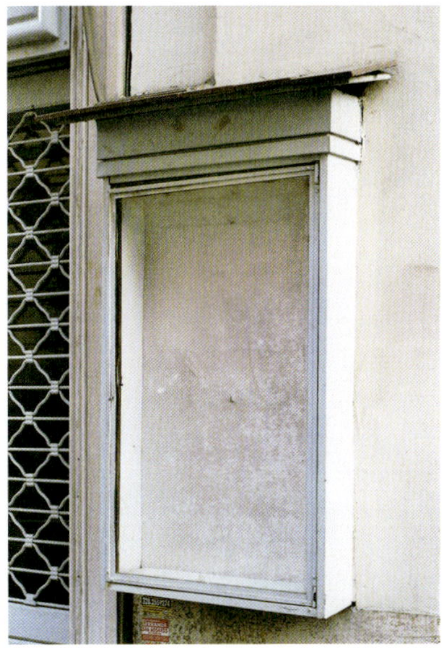

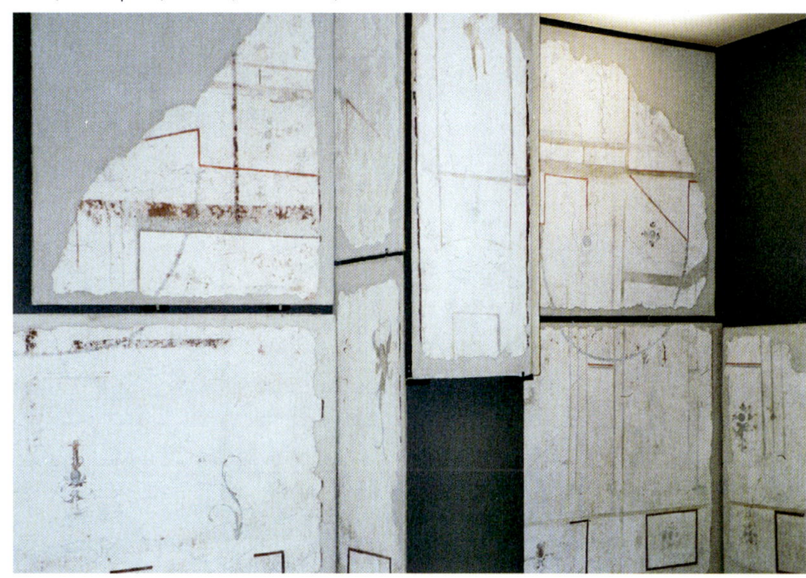

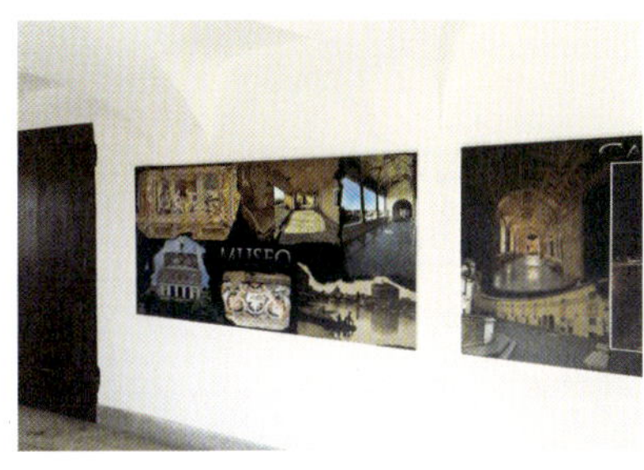

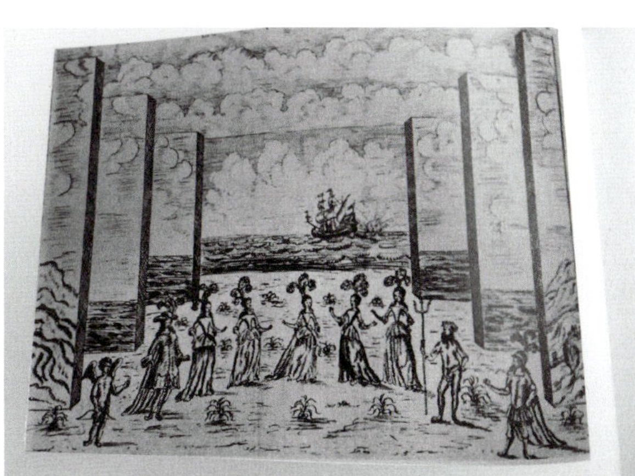

From Surface: Matters of Aesthetics, Materiality, and Media by Giuliana Bruno (Chicago: University of Chicago Press, 2014), 150 (6.5. Precinematic screens in a set designed in 1690 for a staging of the play "La fiera, el rayo y la piedra" by Pedro Calderón de la Barca, 1652)

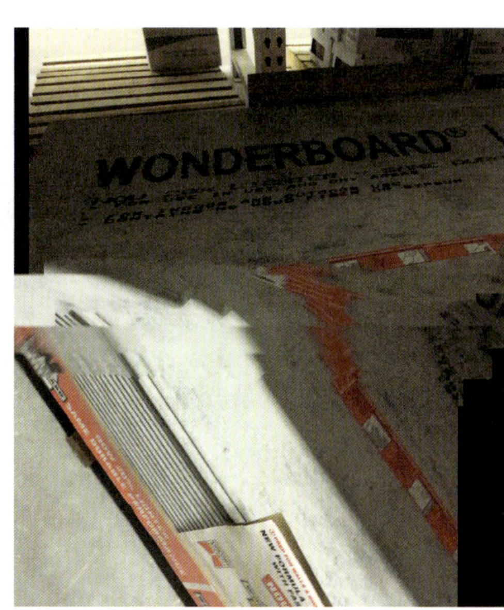

WONDERBOARD, backer boards at The Home Depot store in Kingston, New York, 2016

Mural painting at Chillon Castle, Veytaux near Montreux, 2018

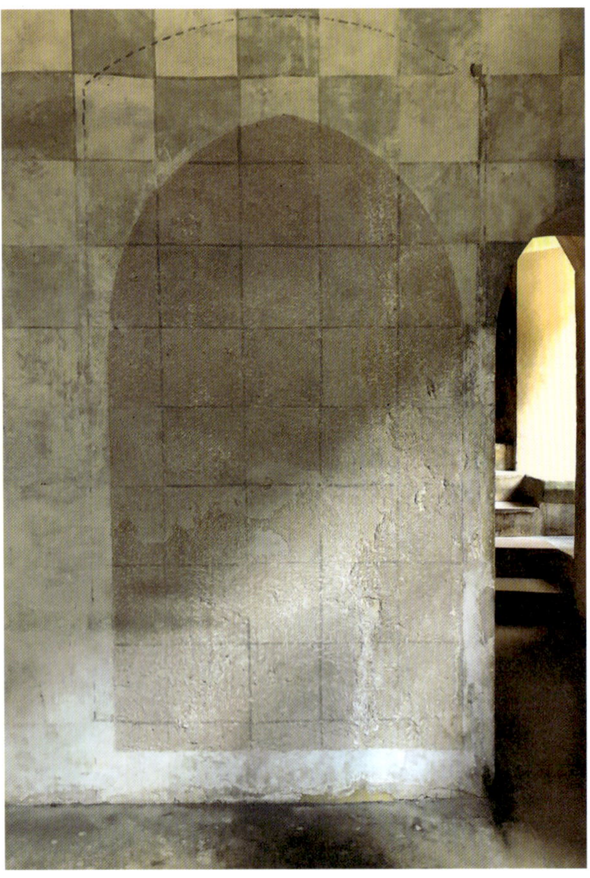

The Hour of Subjective Refuge, empty built-in poster site of a former cinema at Via Lombardia, Rome, 2016, offset print, framed, 18 × 12 cm, edition 1/50

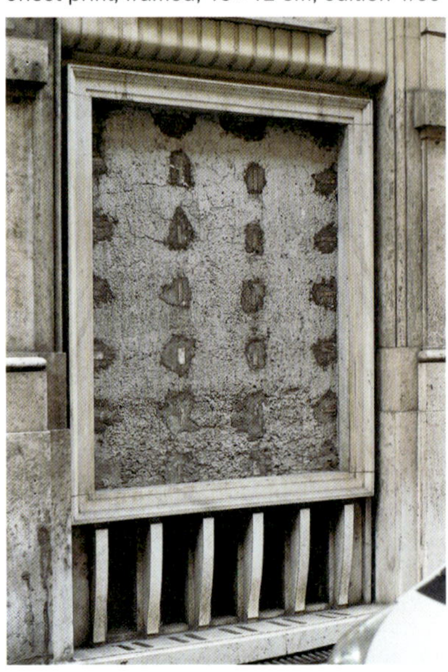

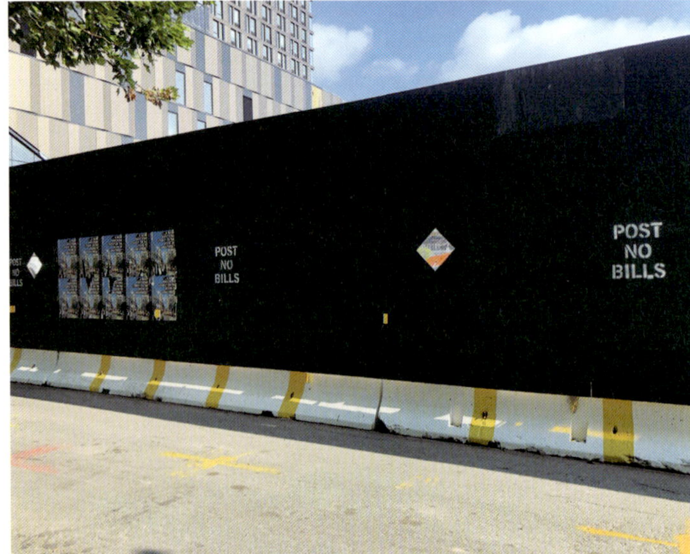

Construction site on the Lower East Side, New York City, 2018

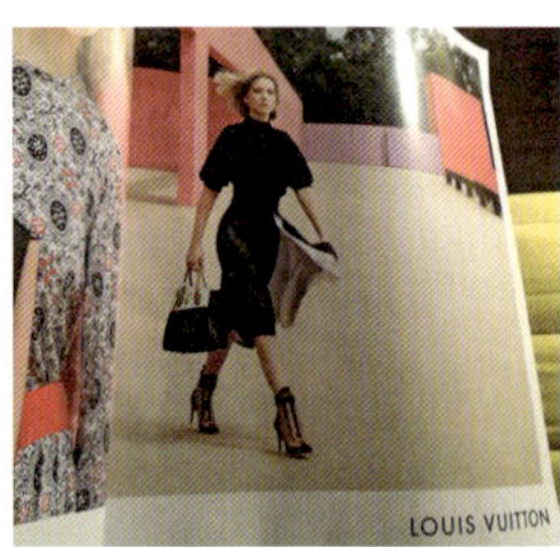

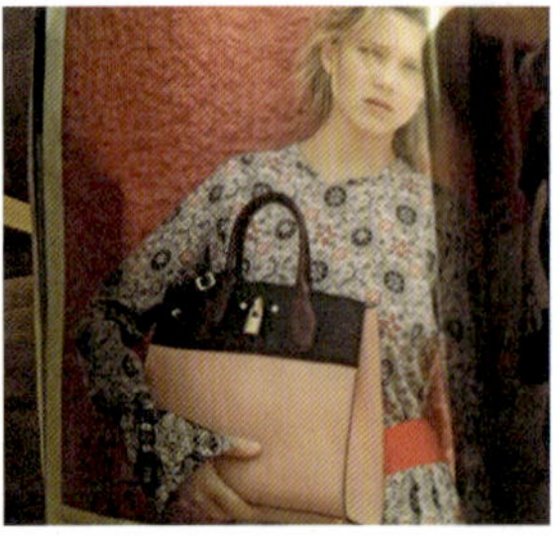

From a Louis Vuitton campaign featuring Léa Seydoux at Cuadra San Cristóbal in Mexico, designed by Luis Barragán, 2016

Antipodes, Via Lombardia, Rome, 2016,
offset print, framed, 12 × 18 cm, edition 1/50

Guilty Containers, Via Lombardia, Rome, 2016,
offset print, framed, 18 × 12 cm, edition 1/50

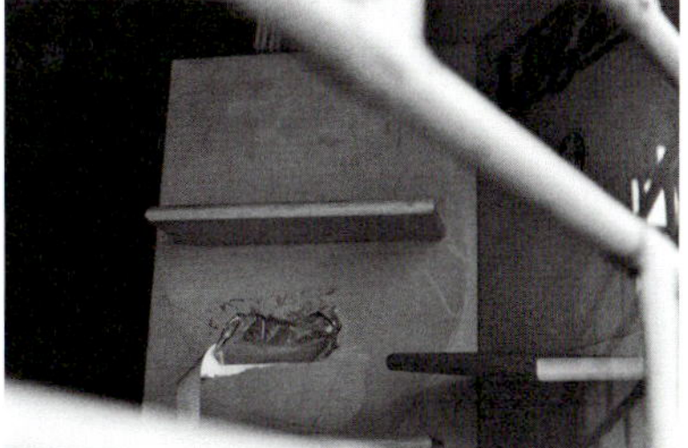

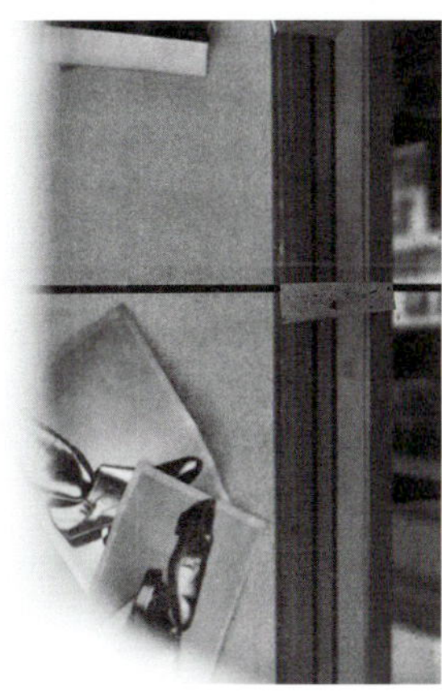

Tracing the cracks on the ceiling of Paul Cézanne's studio in Aix-en-Provence, 2018

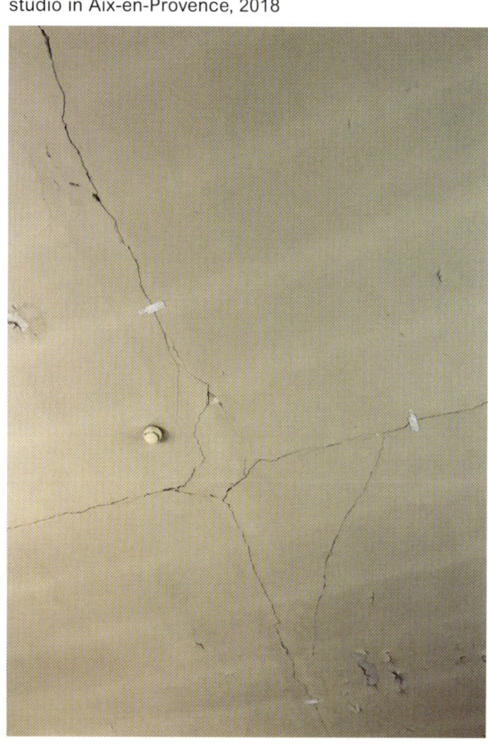

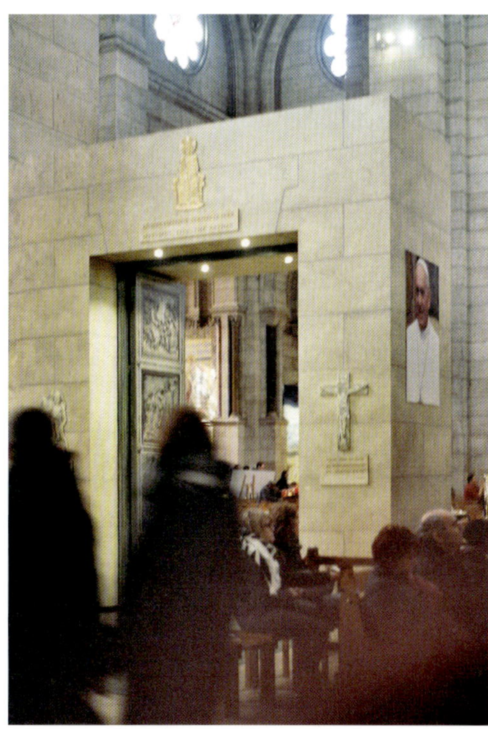

The Holy Door, Paris, 2016, offset print, framed, 18 × 12 cm, edition 1/50 (the Holy Door of Saint Peter's Basilica was rebuilt at Sacré-Cœur de Montmartre for the Extraordinary Jubilee Year of Mercy, 2015/2016)

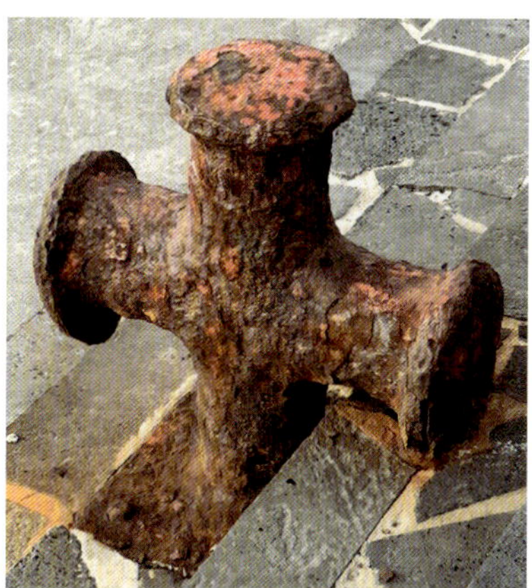

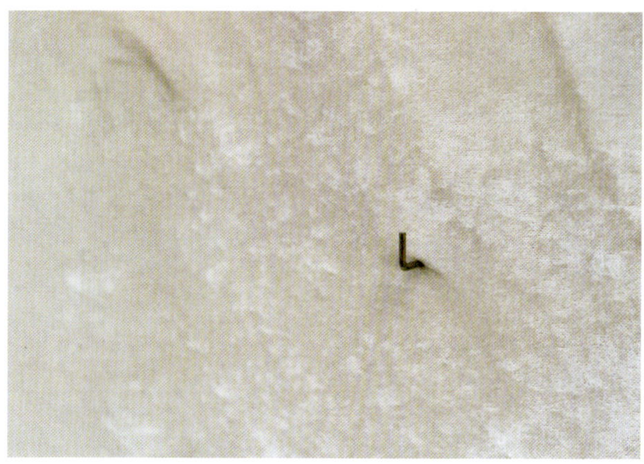

Oxidizing mooring bollards (cross) in El Hierro, Canary Islands, 2017

Velvet lined cabinet with hook, Trevi, Rome, 2016

Detail of Learn to lay brick I-VIII, 2015, drywall, concrete, iron-oxide, hematite, each 250 × 125 cm. Image: Gina Folly

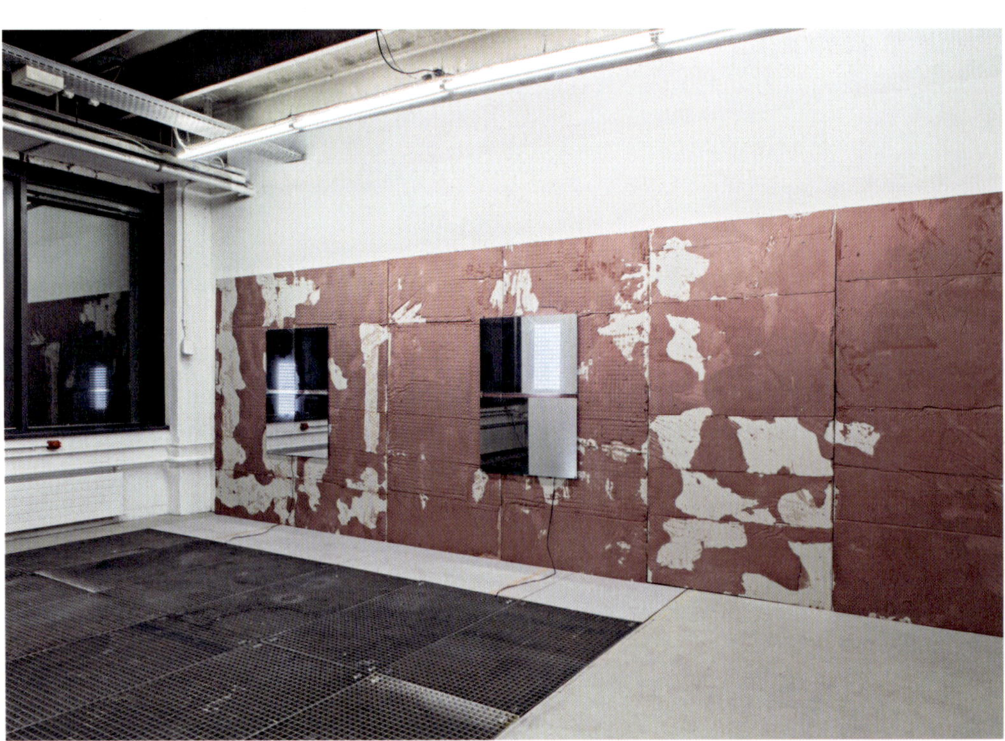

A stream with bright fish, Taylor Macklin, Zurich, 2015. Exhibition view: Gina Folly

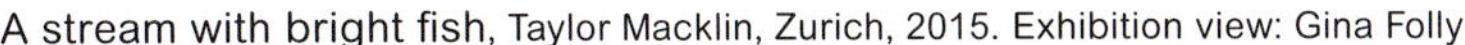
A stream with bright fish, Taylor Macklin, Zurich, 2015. Exhibition view: Gina Folly

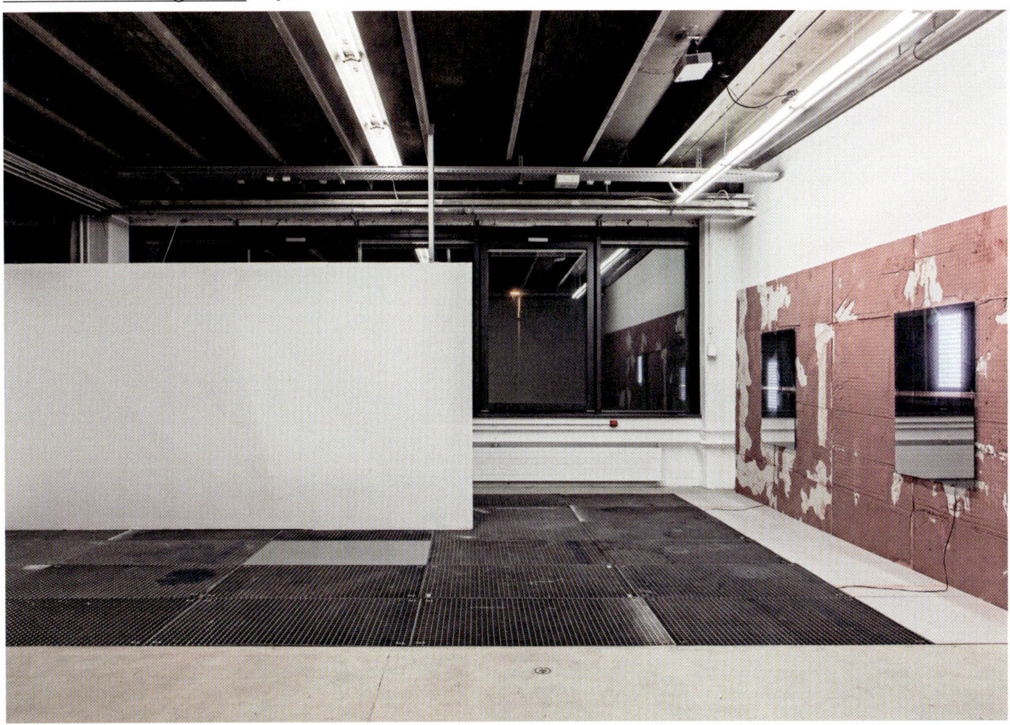

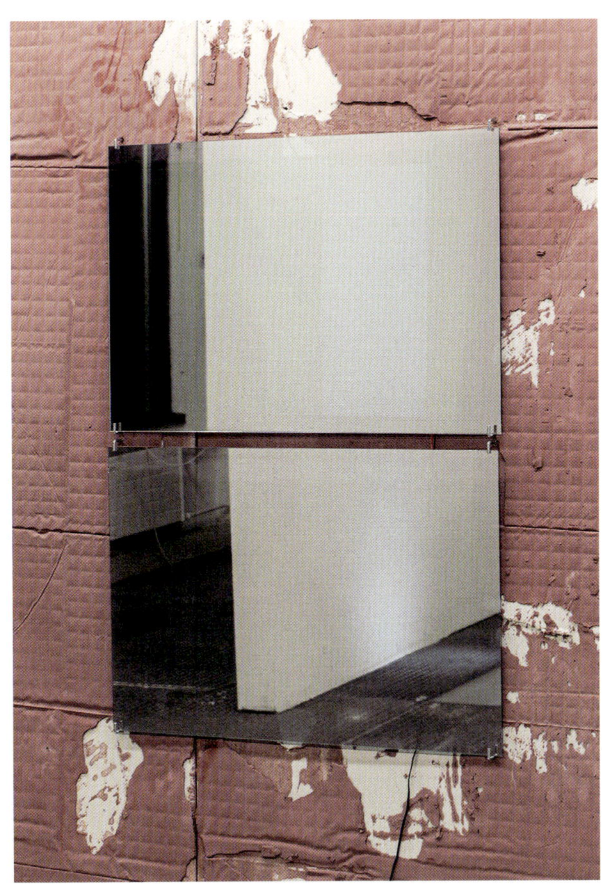
Wellcome I, 2015, glass, Silver 20 Interior film, LED light sheets, Arduino boards, 90 × 60 cm. Image: Gina Folly

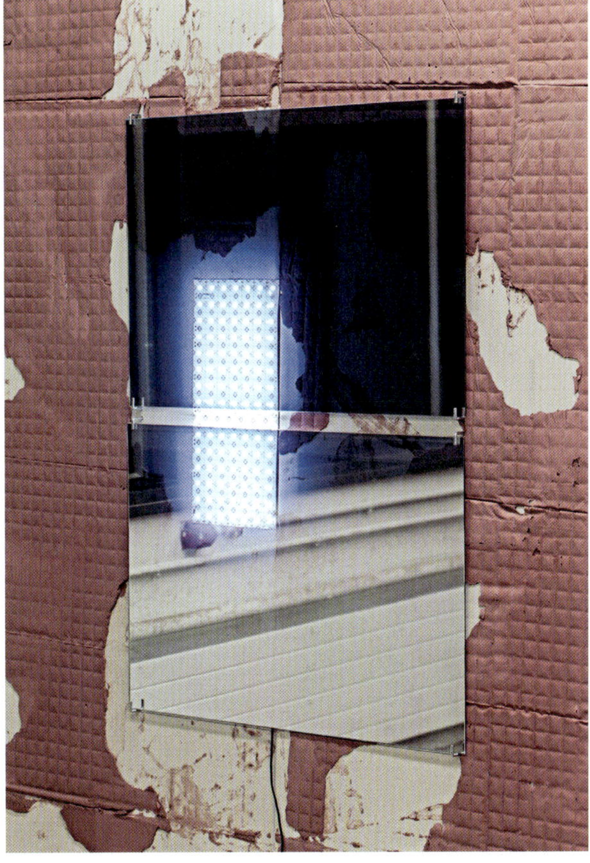
Wellcome II, 2015, glass, Silver 20 Interior film, LED light sheets, Arduino boards, 90 × 60 cm. Image: Gina Folly

Detail of Limi-tropical, 2015, glass, Silver 20 Interior film, LED light sheets, Arduino board, UV print on silk, 146.5 × 86.3 × 0.2 cm. Image: Gina Folly

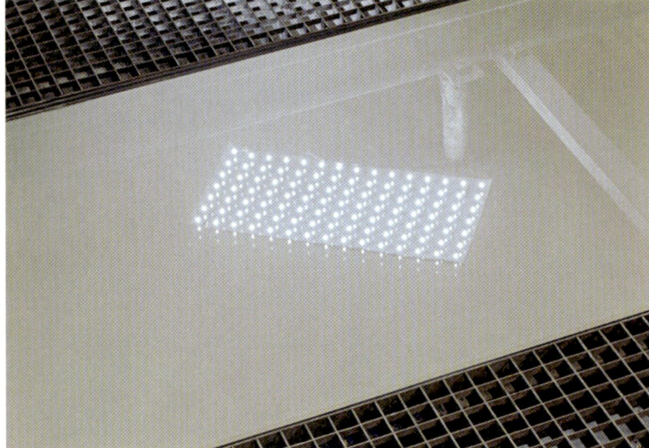

A stream with bright fish, Taylor Macklin, Zurich, 2015. Exhibition view: Gina Folly

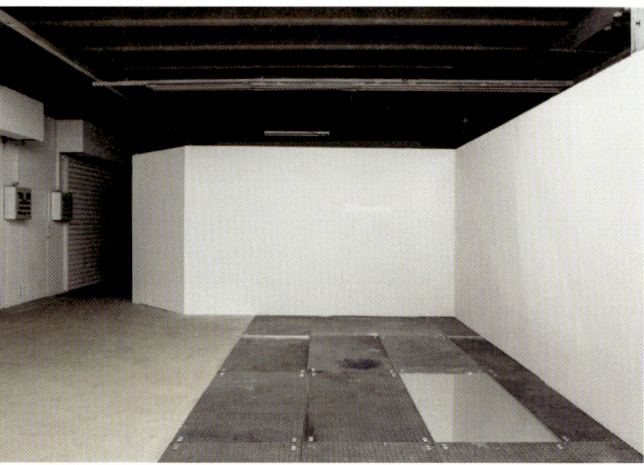

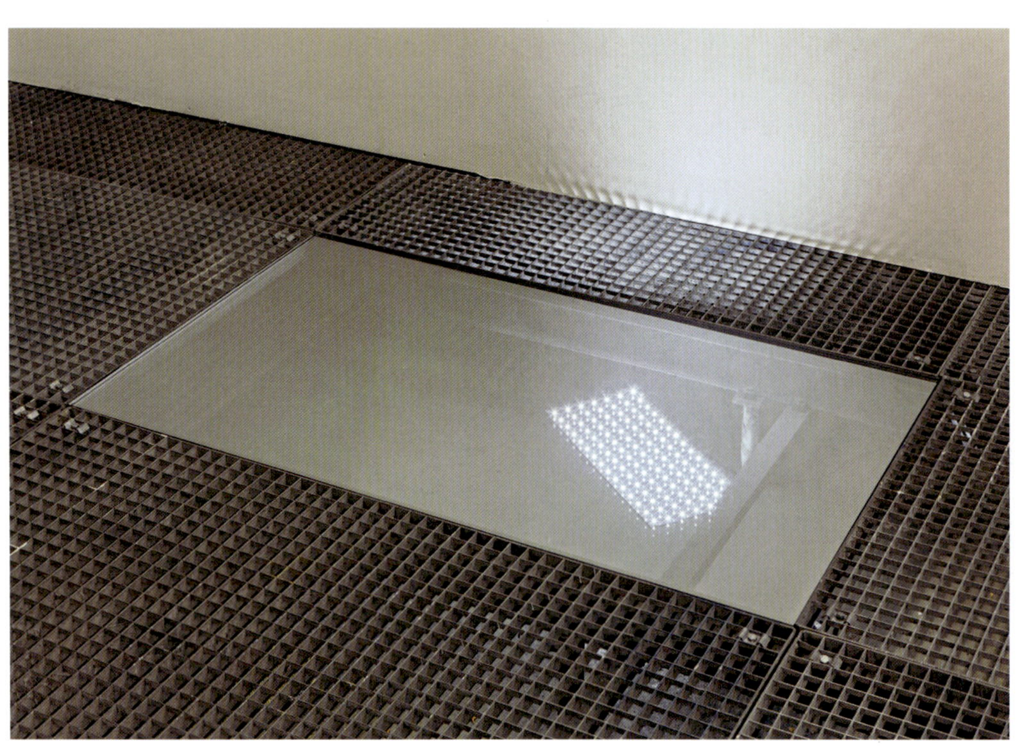

Limi-tropical, 2015, glass, Silver 20 Interior film, LED light sheets, Arduino board, UV print on silk, 146.5 × 86.3 × 0.2 cm. Image: Gina Folly

Mermaid Wang, 2015, glass pane, Silver 20 Interior film, LED light sheets, Arduino board, Xerox print, 3D print (ABS), 90 × 60 cm, Kunsthaus Glarus, Glarus, 2015. Image: David Aebi

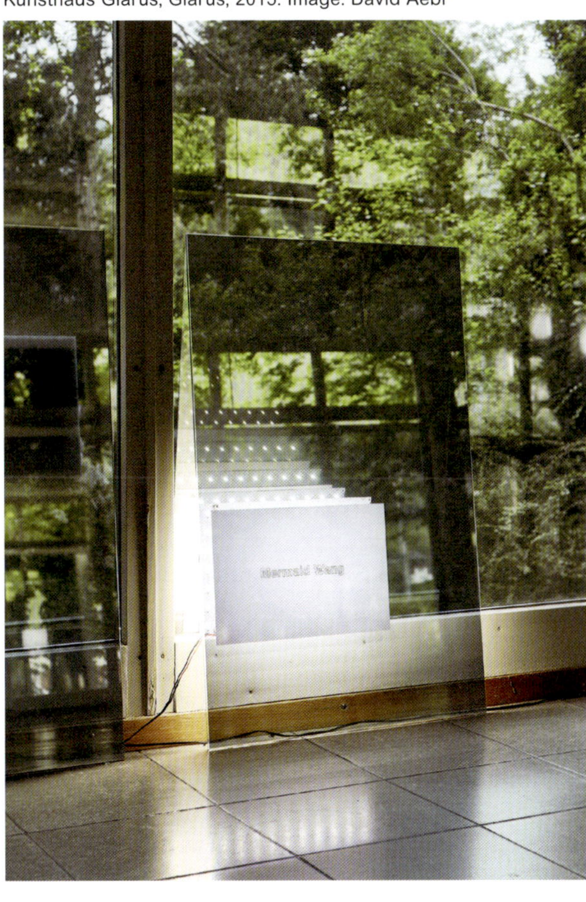

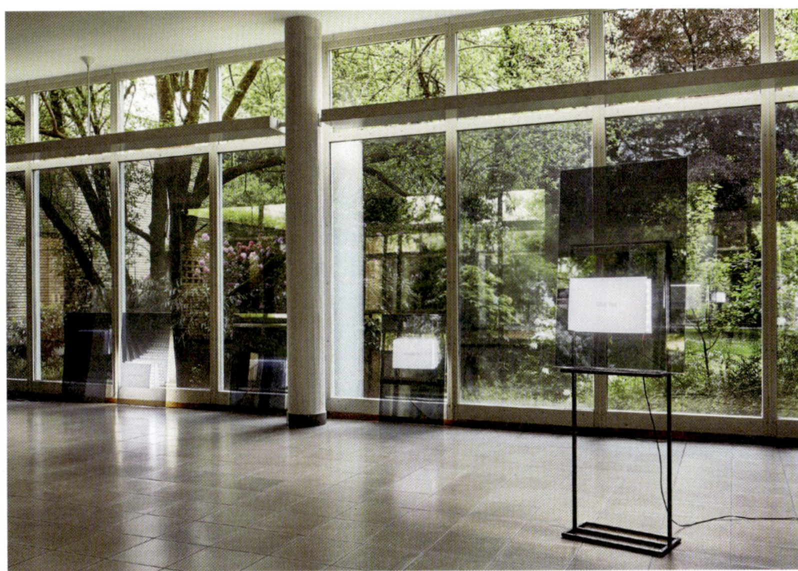

Fiona Zhu, Christy Deng, Rainey Lee, Mermaid Wang, Summer Pine, Luna Sun, Tina Tan, Ruby Cheng, Summer Zuo, Summer Xia, 2015, glass panes, Silver 20 Interior film, LED light sheets, Arduino boards, Xerox prints, 3D prints (ABS), each 90 × 60 cm, Kunsthaus Glarus, Glarus, 2015. Exhibition view: David Aebi

Slides from Fiona Zhu, Christy Deng, Rainey Lee, Mermaid Wang, Summer Pine, Luna Sun, Tina Tan, Ruby Cheng, Summer Zuo, Summer Xia, 2015

Fiona Zhu	Christy Deng	Rainey Lee
Mermaid Wang	Summer Pine	Luna Sun
Tina Tan	Ruby Cheng	Summer Zuo
Summer Xia		

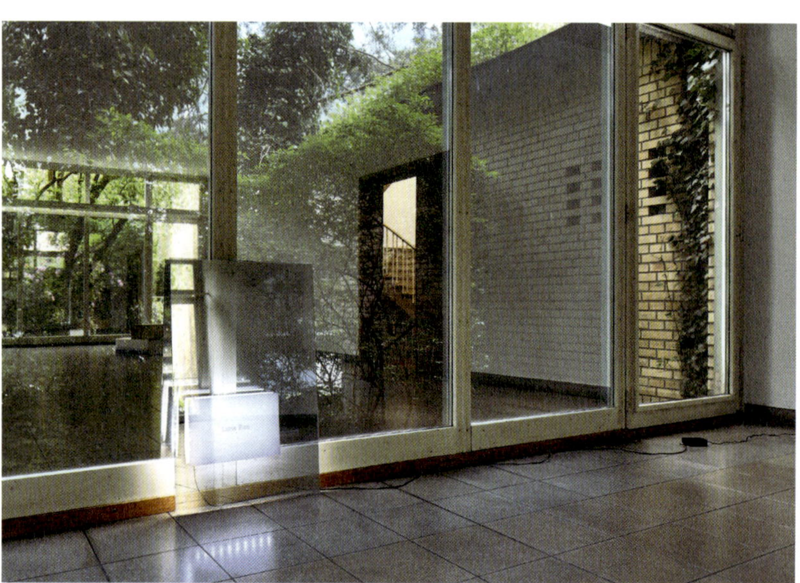

Mermaid Wang, 2015, glass pane, Silver 20 Interior film, LED light sheets, Arduino board, Xerox print, 3D print (ABS), 90 × 60 cm, Kunsthaus Glarus, Glarus, 2015. Exhibition view: David Aebi

Fiona Zhu, Christy Deng, Rainey Lee, Mermaid Wang, Summer Pine, Luna Sun, Tina Tan, Ruby Cheng, Summer Zuo, Summer Xia, 2015, glass panes, Silver 20 Interior film, LED light sheets, Arduino boards, Xerox prints, 3D prints (ABS), each 90 × 60 cm, Kunsthaus Glarus, Glarus, 2015. Exhibition views: David Aebi

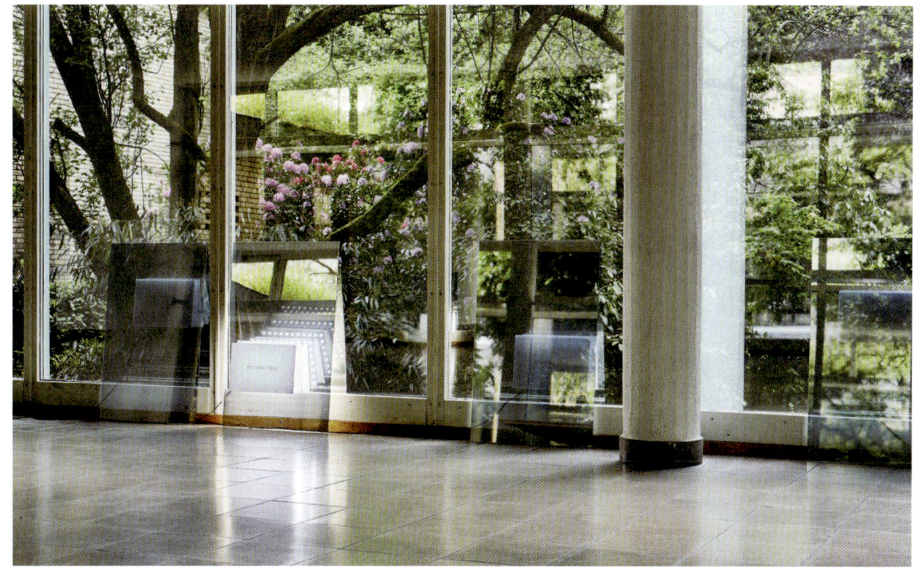

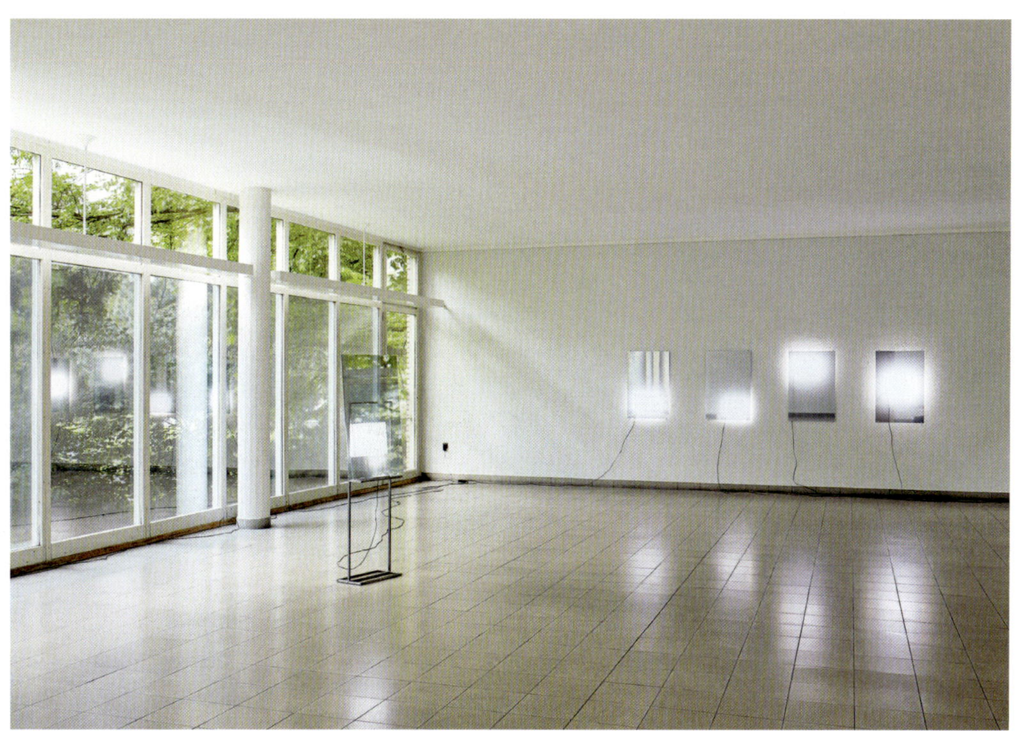

Untitled (Alibaba) I, 2017,
C-print, framed, 90 × 60 cm

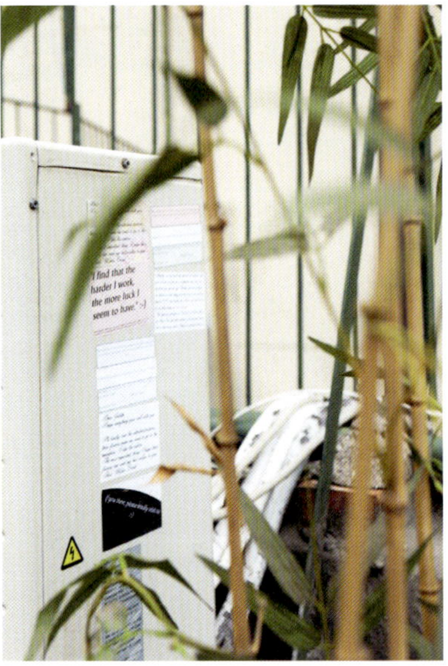

Untitled (Alibaba) II, 2017,
C-print, framed, 90 × 60 cm

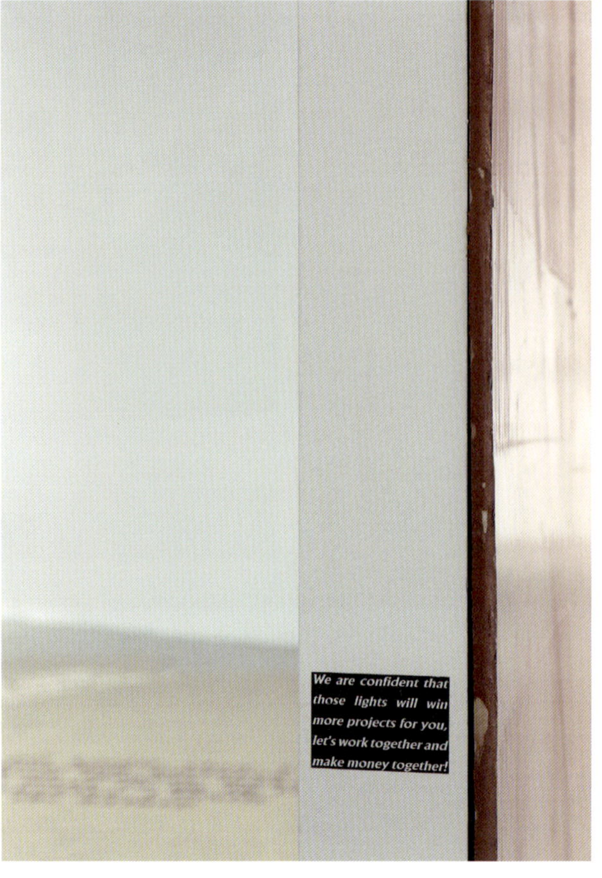

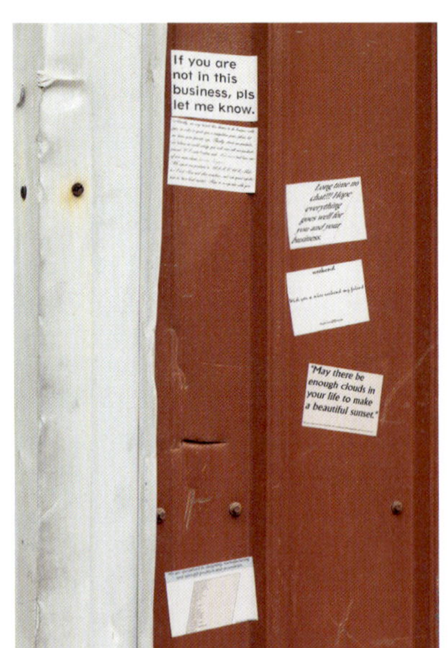

Untitled (Alibaba) III, 2017,
C-print, framed, 90 × 60 cm

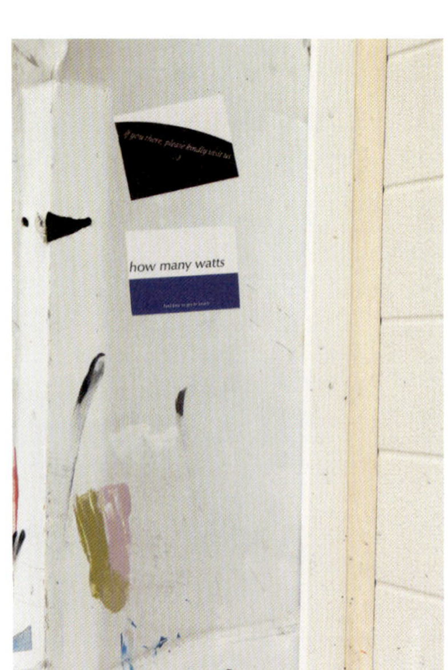

Untitled (Alibaba) IV, 2017,
C-print, framed, 90 × 60 cm

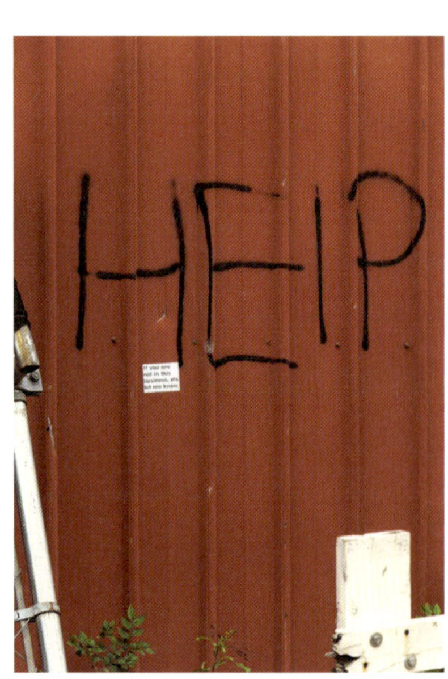

Untitled (Alibaba) V, 2017,
C-print, framed, 90 × 60 cm

Untitled (Alibaba) VII, 2017,
C-print, framed, 60 × 90 cm

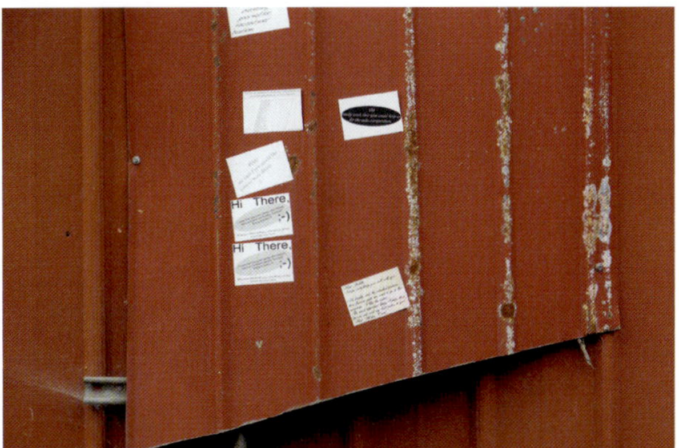

Untitled (Alibaba) VIII, 2017,
C-print, framed, 90 × 60 cm

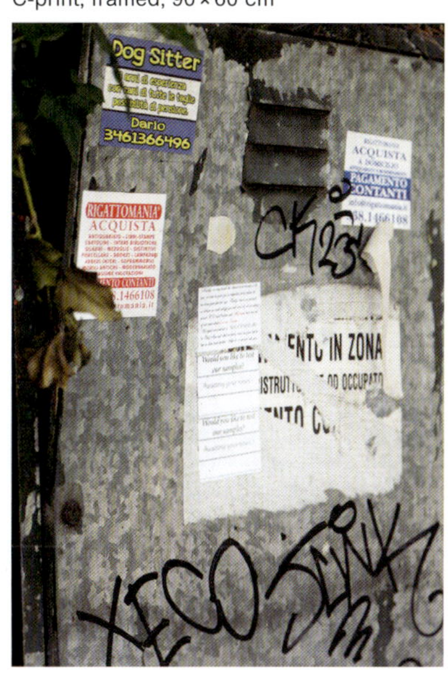

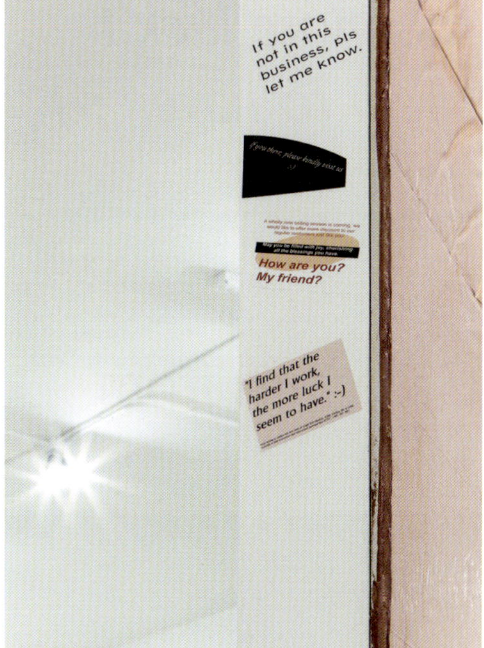

Untitled (Alibaba) VI, 2017,
C-print, framed, 90 × 60 cm

Untitled (Alibaba, Stickers), 2016/2017,
inkjet print on stickers, 36-parts, each 8 × 10 cm

We just shipped 40pcs 200W LED High Bay Light/ Flood Light with driver cover and slip fitter to USA market for the parking lot project:

Wish you and your family have a nice day.

Should anything we can help, please feel free let us know. Best Regards, Amy, Sales 30

"May there be enough clouds in your life to make a beautiful sunset."

For your reference, here the photo of a waterproof 160 degree lens LED Lattice light bar.

"I find that the harder I work, the more luck I seem to have." :-)

*Here writing to update the new item of single LED Module, 2.5W, 220Lm, DC 6~24V, available in non-waterproof and waterproof, optional lens 8*75°, 140°, 30°, 90°.*

Greetings from Miya.

We have new price list.

Merry Christmas and happy New Year!
The Christmas and New Year holiday is coming near once again. We would like to extend our warm wishes for the upcoming holiday season and would like to wish you and your family a Merry Christmas and a prosperous New Year. May your world be filled with warmth and good cheer this Holy season, and throughout the year! Wish your Christmas be filled with peace and love. Merry Xmas. It's my honor to contact you before, and my duty is to give you our best products and excellent service. Hope the next year is a prosperous and harvest year for both of us!
Last but not least, once you have any inquiry about our products in the following days, hope you could feel free to contact us, which is much appreciated.
MERRY CHRISTMAS :)

Hi,

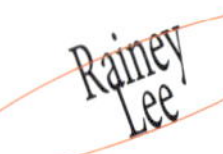

For your reference, we already returned to normal work from the wonderful spring holiday.

*Now I am refreshed and full of enthusiasm for my work and life. Wish we both can make a break-through and welcome a bumper harvest this year! ^_^*
Is there anything I can do for you this moment?

Appreciate your kind response.

Hope my email did not bother you, my friend.

The good business starts here!

Are you interested in saving some money?
are you interested in good quality with good prices?
And are you interested in small orders with fast delievery?
So it is our pleasure to tell you we can offer all of it to you.

Please feel free to let me know if you have any similar project need our products. Our engineer will recommend the best solution for you.

Thanks for your cooperation and support on my job in the past year.

My Skype; wellinled8 and Whatsapp: +86 15750816462 for easy and urgent contact

24hrs/7days.

Best regards, Amy

Is there any update about the exhibition project in Switzerland? Please let us know if you would need further information about our products, please contact me via email.

If you are not in this business, pls let me know.

Would you like to test our samples?

Awaiting your news:)

Thanks for your cooperation and support on my job in the past year

We are specialized in designing, manufacturing and sales gift products and accessories.

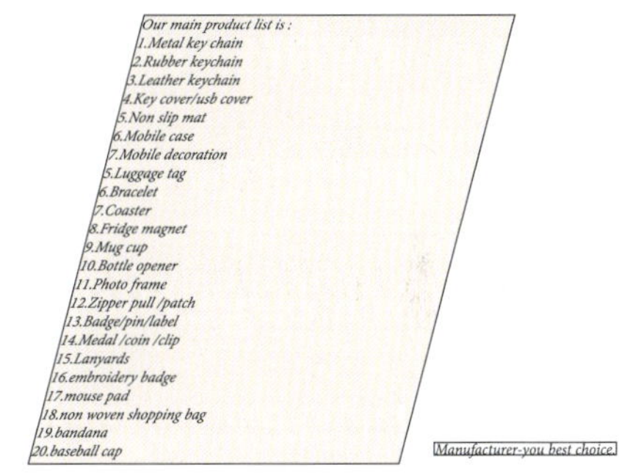

Merry Chirstams and happy New Year! This is Helen, our colleague Tina has left our company.

From now on, I am coming to serve you.

Here comes another client's project picture of our „iT" series light with C style bracket on the top of building in TX, USA for you to check:

Please add my Skype:wellinled8 and WhatsApp: +8615750816462 for easy contact.

Untitled (Alibaba, Stickers), 2016/2017,
inkjet print on stickers, 36-parts, each 8 × 10 cm

Write
me back if you would like
to know more details
;-)

We are confident that those lights will win more projects for you, let's work together and make money together!

Dear Judith,
I hope everything goes well with you .

Pls kindly view the attached pictures , these flowers make me want to go to the mountain. I like the nature .
The most important thing, I hope these flowers can send my best wishes to you.
Best Wishes, Coral

Dear Judith,
I hope everything goes well with you .

Pls kindly view the attached pictures , these flowers make me want to go to the mountain. I like the nature .
The most important thing, I hope these flowers can send my best wishes to you.
Best Wishes, Coral

Wish
everything goes well with your business.
As a reward to our customer, this season we
would like to offer a favorable price
to you:

how many watts do you want?

Feel free to get in touch

„it is so much brighter"!

For more details, pls feel free to contact me, thanks!

2015, let's go green!

Aw:Need your assistance in „sales competition“

Good day !
Did you receive and check my email below ?
Honestly, this is a very big competition with hundreds of enterprises and more than 500 sales people. We very much hope to receive your kind support to win the competition !!!!
(All of us under big stress, everyday 7:30 we go to the office and 22:00 back home, but it's very important and a great breakthrough for us)
As promised, we are providing a lot of preferential policy. And I'm sure will apply for the most preferential price for you if you could help.
Thank you in advance.
Rainey

Good day to you.

This is Summer working in a factory

We really hope our lights can help you win more projects and explode your business.

Please feel free to let me know if you have any interests in this,whatever interior project or exterior project, we will provide the best solution for you.

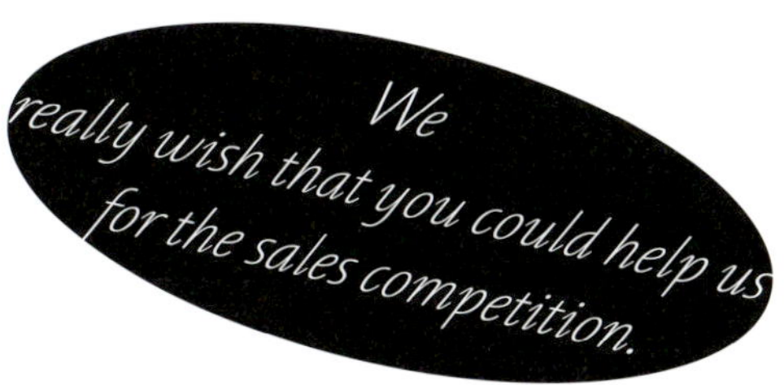

How was your weekend ?

Please kindly visit us :-)

Nice to contact you here

This is Amy.

skype:junlon15
mobile:0086-13318272029
Tel:0086-760-88622218 Fax:0086-760-88554970

Hi There,

I hope that you,your family and friends have a wonderful Easter Sunday! Enjoy holiday !!! ;-)

May your filled with joy, cherishing all the blessings you have.

A wholly new selling season is coming, we would like to offer more discount to our regular customers just like you:

May you be filled with joy, cherishing all the blessings you have.

How are you? My friend?

Untitled (Alibaba, Stickers), 2016/2017,
inkjet print on stickers, 36-parts, each 8 × 10 cm

Actually, we very herish this chance to do business with you, in order to quote you a competitive price, please let me know your favorite size. Finally, about our products, we believe we could satisfy you well since all our products passed CE certi×cation and Wal-mart had been one of our main clients for over 5 years.
We export our products to USA, EUR, Midle- East, Aisa and other countries, and win great reputation in their local market. Hope to co-operate with you.

Long time no chat!!! Hope everything goes well for you and your business.

How are you? My friend?

A wholly new selling season is coming

We would like to offer more discount to our regular customers, just like you.

weekend

Wish you a nice weekend my friend

skype:craftforyou

<u>Untitled (Alibaba, Corona)</u>, 2020,
inkjet print on canvas, 4-parts, each 105 × 75 cm

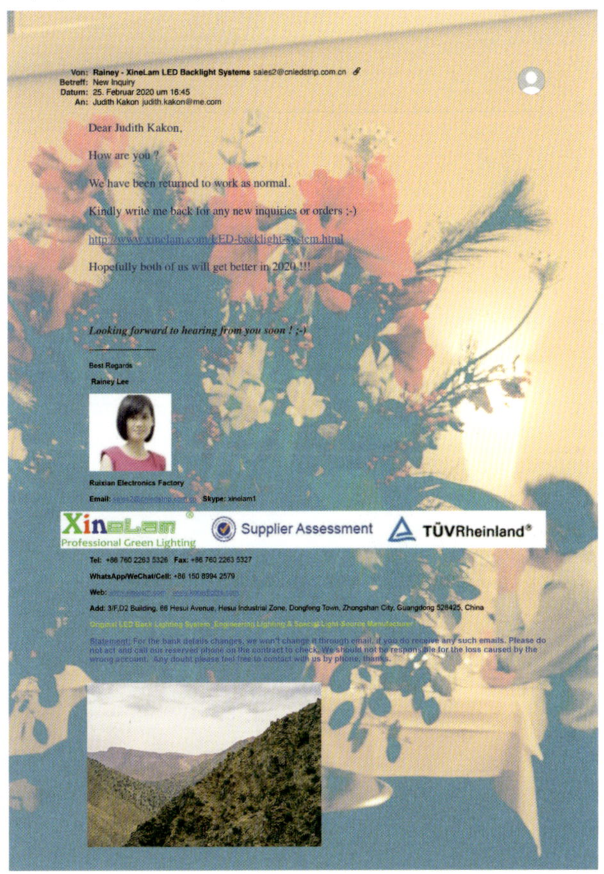

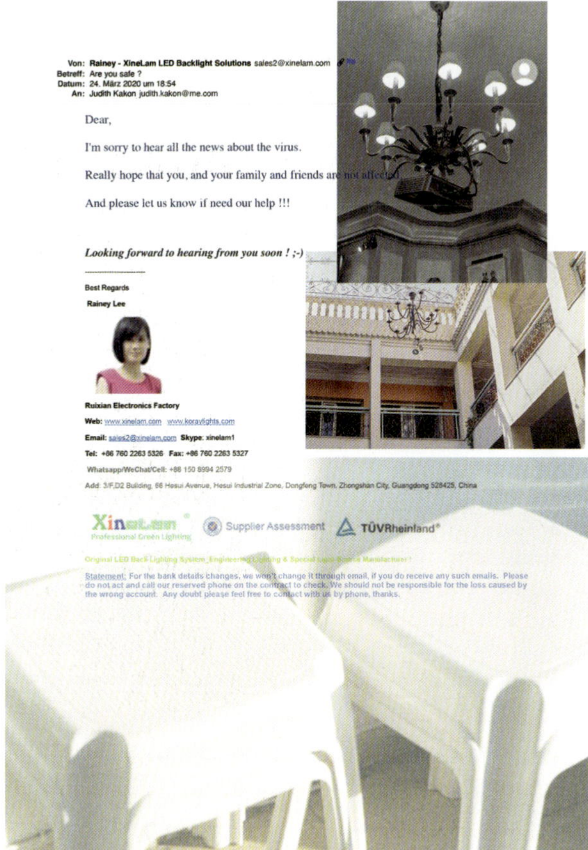

Untitled (Alibaba, Corona), 2020,
inkjet print on canvas, 4-parts, each 105 × 75 cm

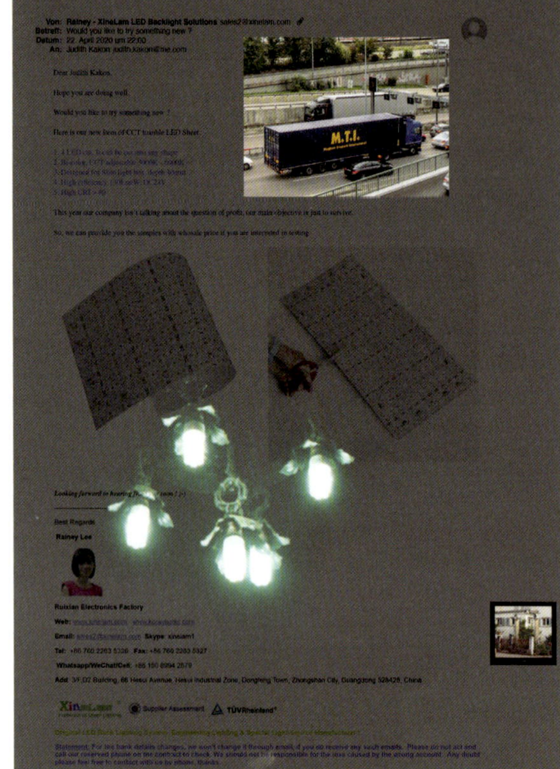

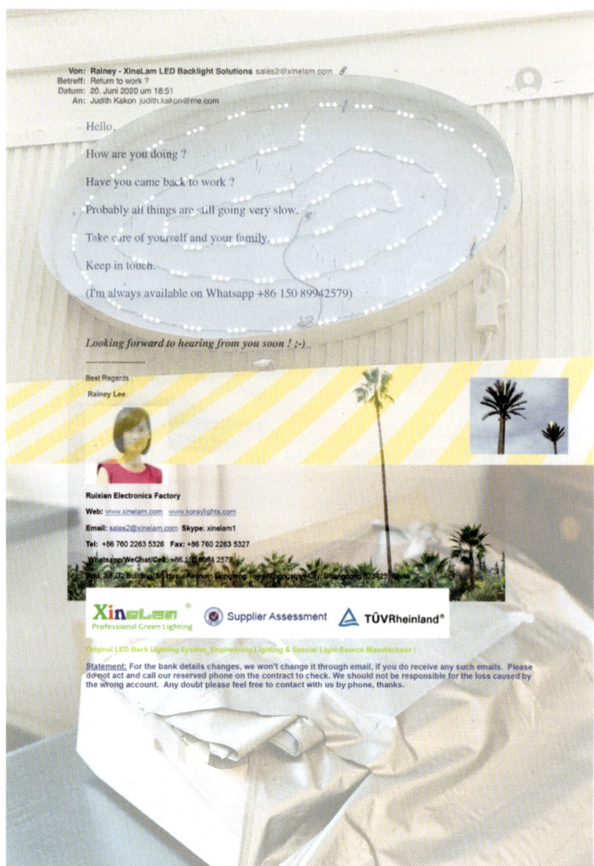

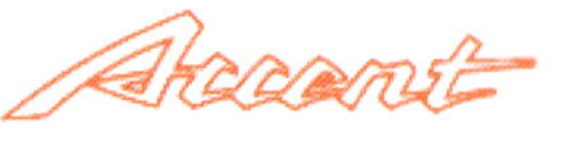

Hyundai Accent
(LC, 2000–2005)

Hyundai Accent
(X3, 1994–2000)

accent

Accent			
Acclaim	Aegea	Airstream	
Accord	Agila	Alhambra	Alphard
Adam	Airflow	Alliance	Alpine

Tone of Voice (Version I), 2015, PowerPoint presentation, car model names from 1860 to 2015, listed alphabetically

Tone of Voice (Version I), 2015, PowerPoint presentation,
car model names from 1860 to 2015, listed alphabetically

Altea

Amazon

Ambassador

America

Ami

Antique

Apache

Apollo

Arcadia

Arena

Arosa

Astra

Atlantic

Augusta

Aura

Aurora

Avalanche

Avenger

Aviator

Aztek

Bagheera

Barracuda

Beat

Beetle

Belair

Bermuda

Boxer

Bravo

Bravo Brava

Cadenza

Caliber

Calibra

Cambridge

Capri

Caravan

Carnival

Carol

Carribean

Cascada

Cayenne

Celebrity

Celeste

Cent

Centurion

Century

Challenger

Champion

Charger

Charmant

Chimaera

Cirrus

City

Civic

Classic

Clubman

Cobalt

Colibri

Colony Park

Colorado

Colt

Comet

Compass

Concorde

Confederate

Conquest

Consort

Consul

Continental

Cordoba

Corsica

Cosmopolitan

Countryman

Tone of Voice (Version I), 2015, PowerPoint presentation,
car model names from 1860 to 2015, listed alphabetically

Crew	Defender	Duett	Electric
Crossfire	Delta	Dynasty	Element
Cube	Deluxe	Eagle	Elise
Custom	Demon	Eclat	Elysée
Cygnet	Dignity	Eclipse	Elysion
Daffodil	Dino	Edge	Enclave
Dakota	Diplomat	Egoista	Endeavor
Dart	Discovery	Elan	Envision
Dauphine	Dolomite	Eldorado	Envoy

Eon

Eos

Epsilon

Equator

Equinox

Escalade

Escort

Espace

Estate

Europa

Evolution

Excel

Excelle

Excursion

Executive

Expedition

Explorer

Express

Falcon

Felicia

Fetish

Fiesta

Firedome

Fireflite

Firesweep

Fit

Flex

Florida

Fluence

Flying Spur

Focus

Forester

Fortuner

Fox

Freelander

Frégate

Tone of Voice (Version I), 2015, PowerPoint presentation, car model names from 1860 to 2015, listed alphabetically

Fulvia

Fury

Fusion

Futura

Galant

Galaxy

Gazelle

Gemini

Genesis

Ghibli

Ghost

Giulia

Giulietta

Gladiator

Globus

Gloria

Go

Golf

Grandeur

Hatch

Hawk

Horizon

Hurricane

Ibiza

Idea

Imp

Imperial

Indica

Indigo

Innova

Insight

Inspire

Integra

Interceptor

Intrigue

Invictus

Ion

Isar

Isis

Jet

Jetta

Joice

Journey

Kangoo

Karif

Karma

Khamsin

Kingsway

La Femme

Laguna

Lambda

Laser

Latitude

Leaf

Legacy

Legend

Levante

Liberty

Life

Lima

Linea

Lucerne

Lumina

Maestro

Majestic

Malaga

Malibu

Marathon

Marbella

Marquis

Master

Matador

Tone of Voice (Version I), 2015, PowerPoint presentation,
car model names from 1860 to 2015, listed alphabetically

Matrix
Maxi
Mayflower
Mebius
Medallion
Merak
Metro
Mexico
Millenia

Minor
Mirage
Mistral
Modus
Mokka
Monaco
Mondeo
Mondial
Mont Clair

Montana
Montreal
Mountaineer
Move
Multipla
Mustang
Nano
Neon
New Yorker

Nitro
Noble
Nomad
Nova
Oasis
Octavia
Olympia
Omega
One

Optima

Origin

Orion

Orthia

Outlook

Paceman

Pacifica

Palm Beach

Panther

Park Avenue

Passat

Pathfinder

Patriot

Perla

Persona

Phaeton

Phantom

Phoenix

Picasso

Pilot

Pixel

Polara

Pony

Popular

Prairie

Prefect

Prelude

President

Prima

Priora

Prizm

Publica

Puma

Punto

Quest

Rally

Tone of Voice (Version I), 2015, PowerPoint presentation,
car model names from 1860 to 2015, listed alphabetically

Rapide

Reach

Rebel

Relay

Rendezvous

Renegade

Renown

Rio

Riva

Roundup

Royal

Safari

Safrane

Saga

Sail

Samara

Samba

Santa Fe

Saratoga

Satellite

Savoy

Scénic

Sceptre

Scirocco

Scorpio

Senator

Seville

Shadow

Siena

Silhouette

Silver Cloud

Silver Ghost

Silver Seraph

Silver Wraith

Silverado

Silvia

Simba

Solo

Solstice

Sonata

Soul

Sovereign

Space Star

Special

Spider

Spin

Spirit

Spitfire

Squire

Starfire

Starlet

Stellar

Stilo

Storm

Strada

Stratus

Suburban

Sumo

Sunbeam

Sunbird

Super Bee

Super Snipe

Super

Superb

Supreme

Suprima

Symbol

Tacoma

Tahoe

Taigan

Talisman

Taurus

Tone of Voice (Version I), 2015, PowerPoint presentation,
car model names from 1860 to 2015, listed alphabetically

Tempest
Tempo
Terrain
Terraza
Thesis
Thunderbird
Tigra
Toledo
Torino

Tornado
Touareg
Town & Country
Town Box
Trailblazer
Travelall
Traverse
Trend
Trevi

Tribute
Tucson
Tundra
Universal
Vantage
Vectra
Vendome
Ventura
Venture

Viktoria
Villager
Violet
Vision
Vista
Vitesse
Viva
Vogue
Volt

Voyager

Wasp

Wildcat

Wind

Windstar

X-Trail

Xenon

Xterra

Ypsilon

Zephyr

Zero

Shop imitations (Bond Avenue, Cosmos, Headquarters, Nail Arts, Secret Garden)
at Bâleo Erlenmatt, Basel, 2020

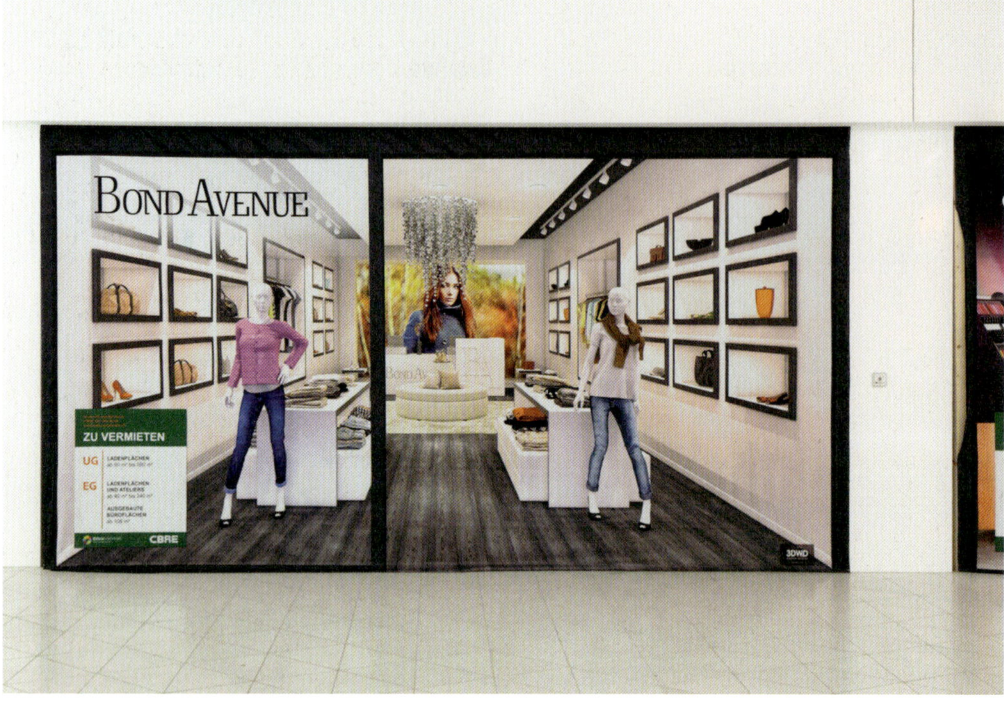

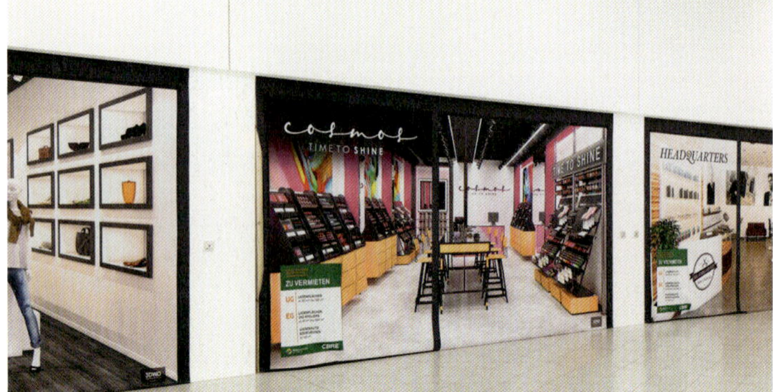

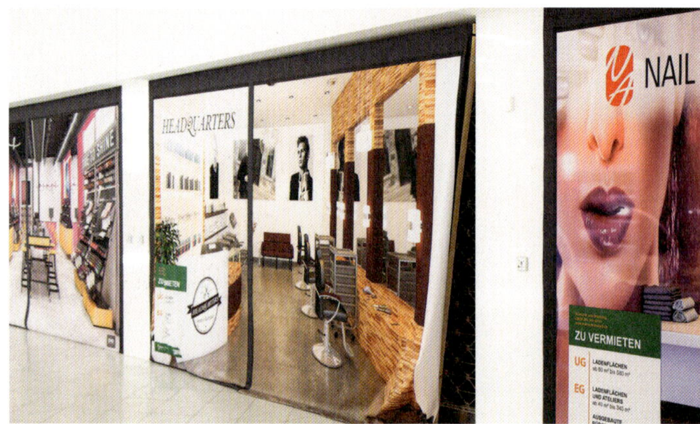

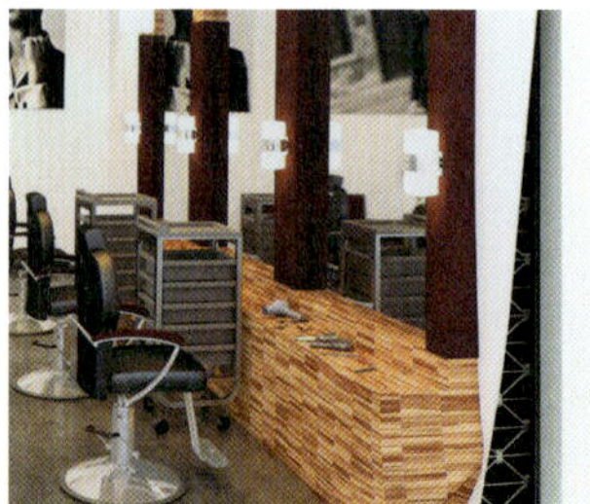

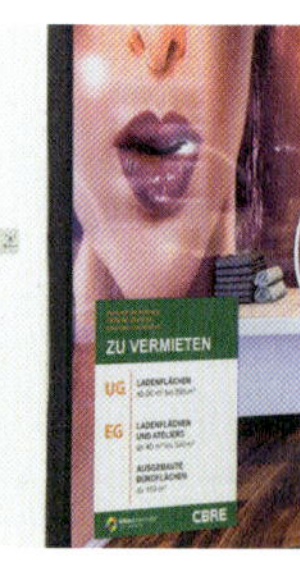

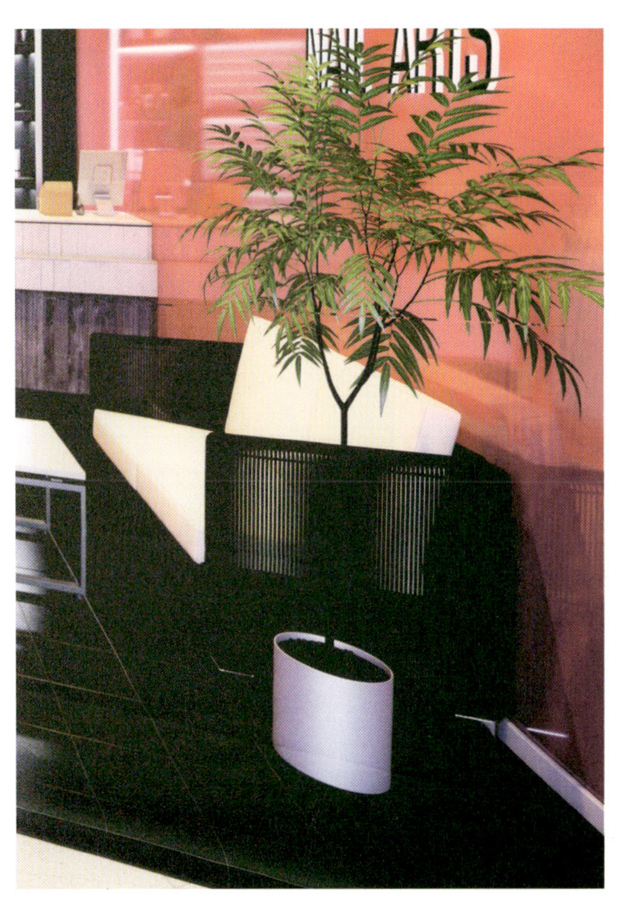

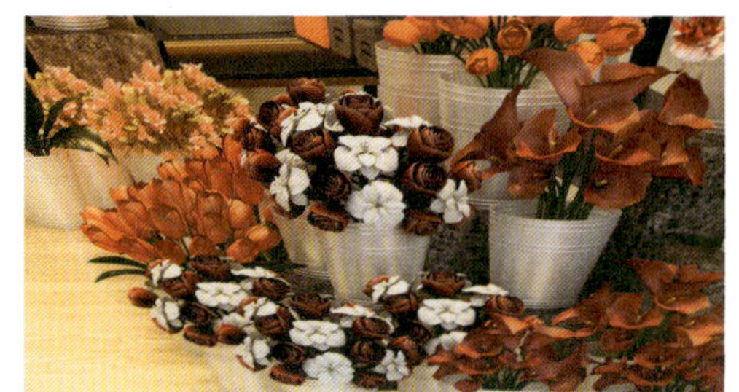

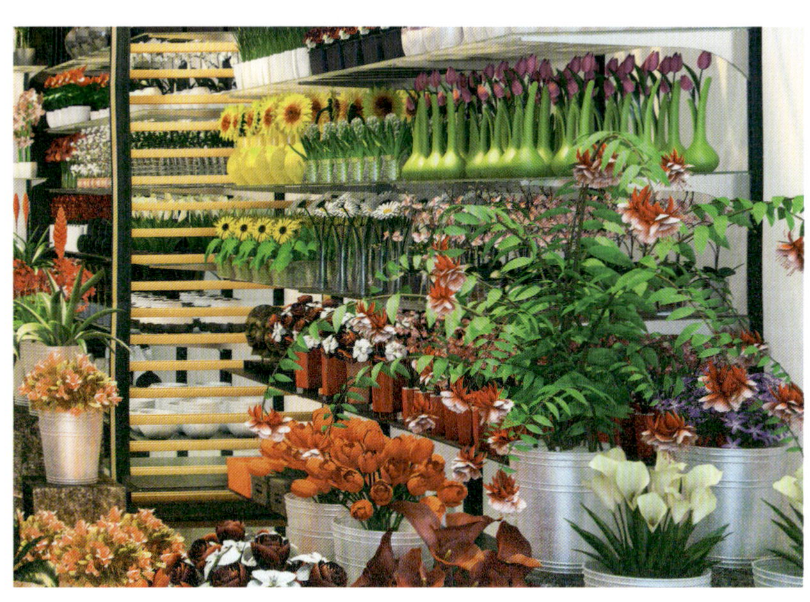

Floral bouquet in Restaurant Kunsthalle, Basel, 2020

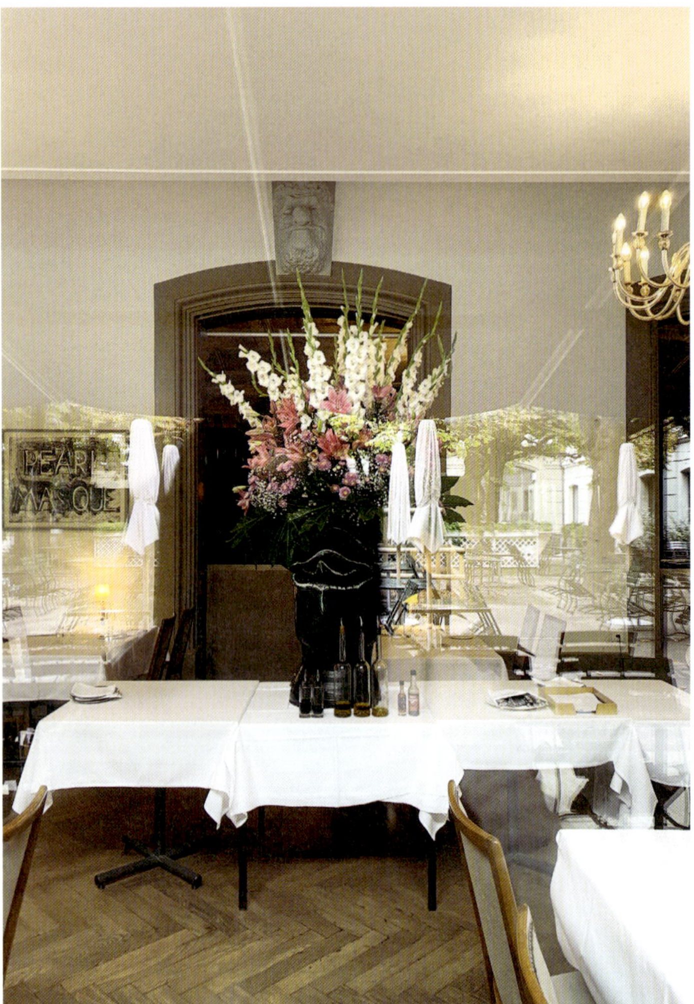

Flower logo of the Swiss construction company Implenia outside Kunstmuseum Basel, 2020

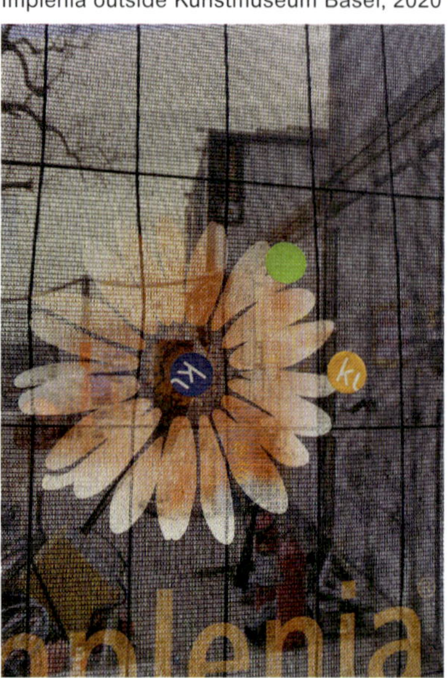

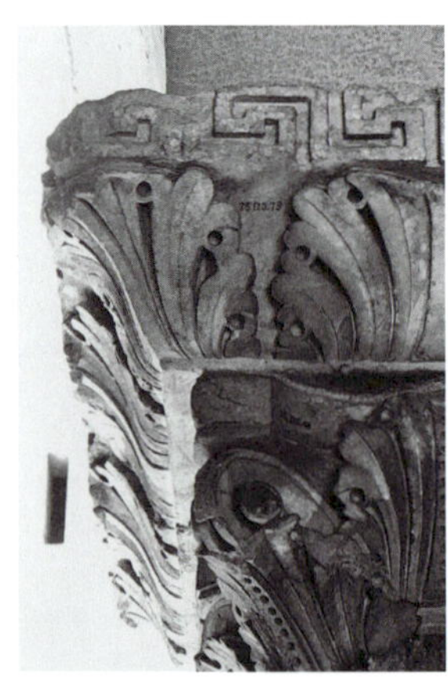

Reconstructed 20th century European or American column shaft at The Met Cloisters, Fort Tryon Park, New York City, 2018

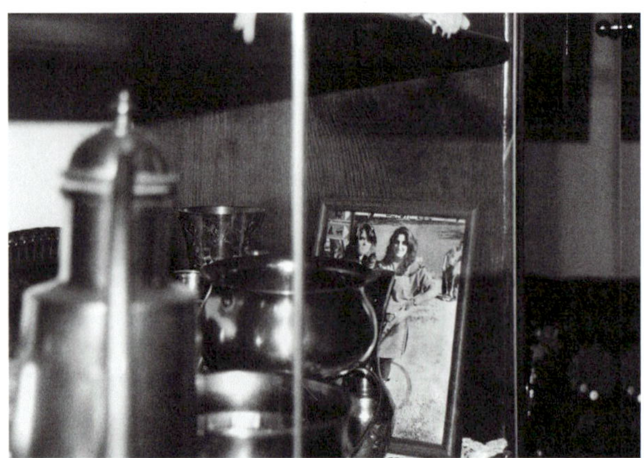

Living room cabinet with pewter mugs and photographs of the artist's aunts when they were younger, Petah Tikva, 2011

Frontispiece of Franciscus Aguilonius's Six Books of Optics (1613) by Peter Paul Rubens, from Florence and Baghdad: Renaissance Art and Arab Science by Hans Belting (Cambridge, MA: Harvard University Press/Belknap, 2011), 238

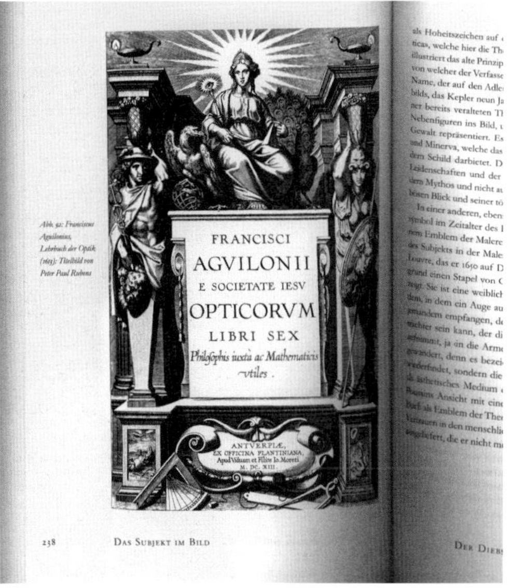

Cellophane wrapped flower bouquets, placed on commemorative plaques at the memorial to the soldiers and civilians killed in the liberation of Paris on the Place de la Concorde in August 1944, Rue de Rivoli, Paris, 2019

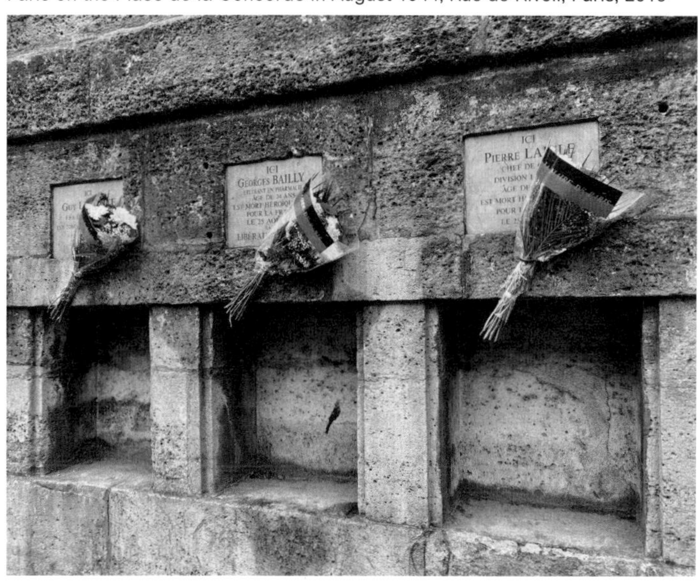

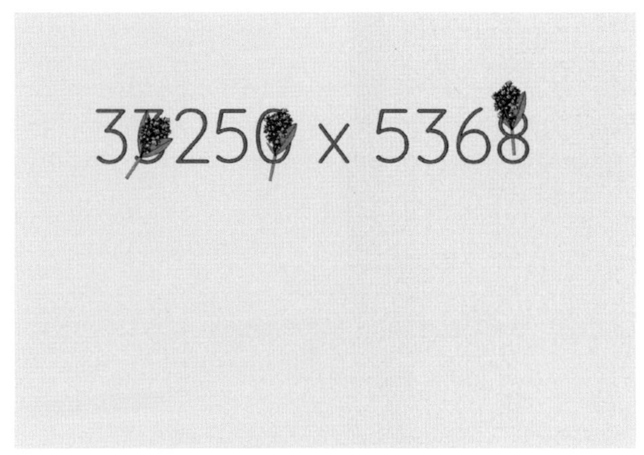

Rendering of the dimensions of the Kunsthalle Basel back wall in meters, equipped with flower bouquets, 2020

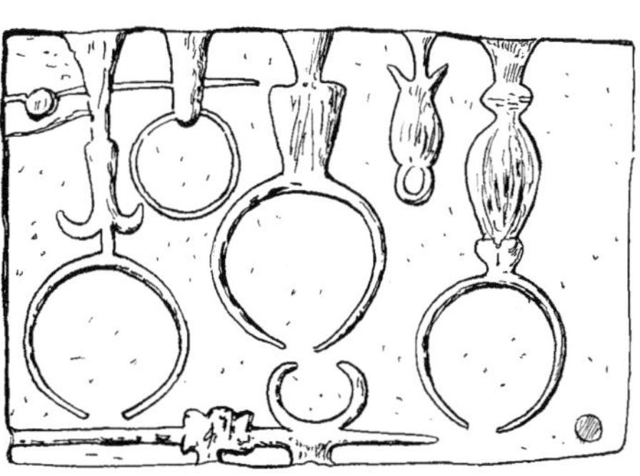

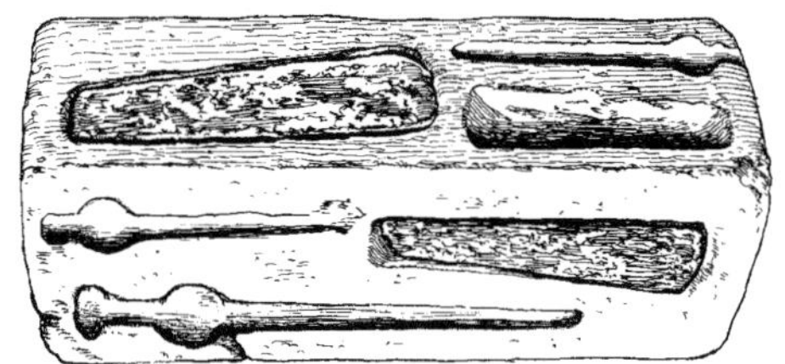

Examples of early stone molds, used for the production of weapons or jewelry cast in gold, silver or bronze, web screenshot, accessed October, 2020

Riad transformed to a residential and office building (chandelier, roof), Marrakech, 2020

Riad transformed to a residential and office building (hairdresser), Marrakech, 2020

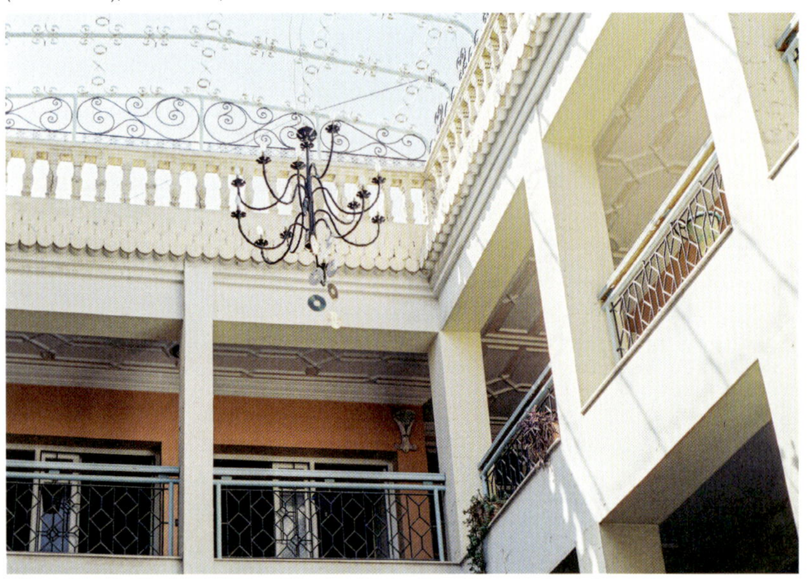

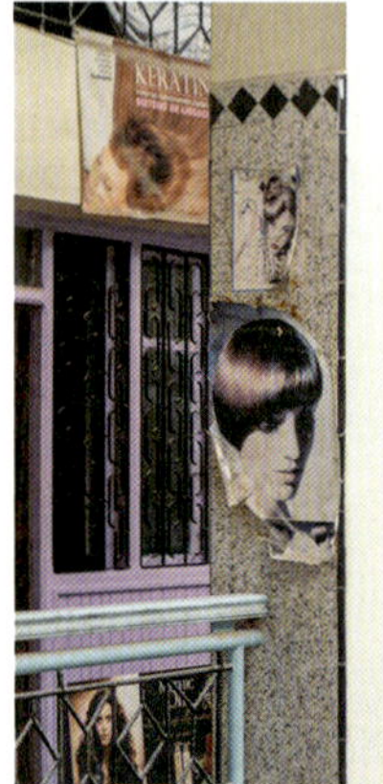

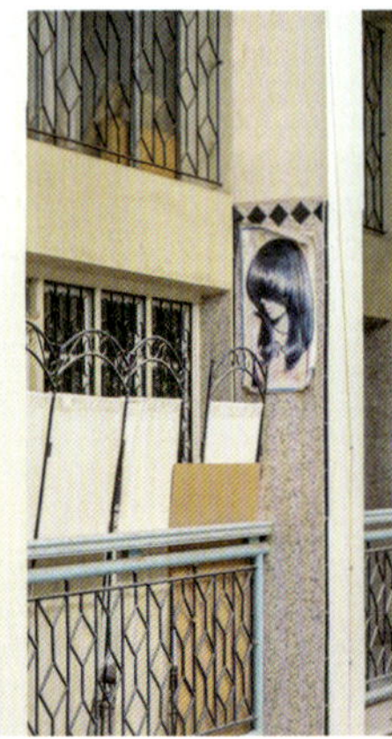

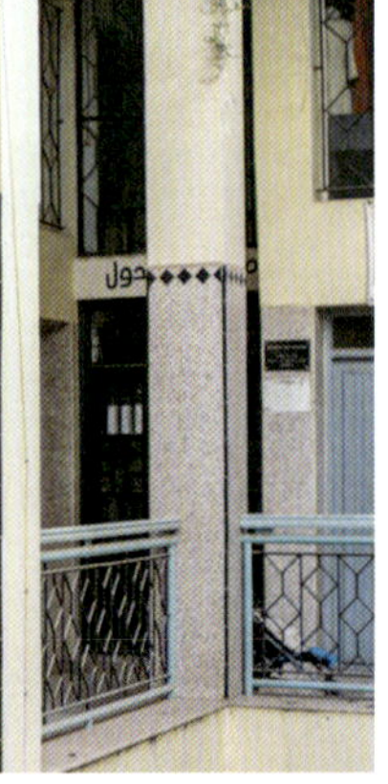

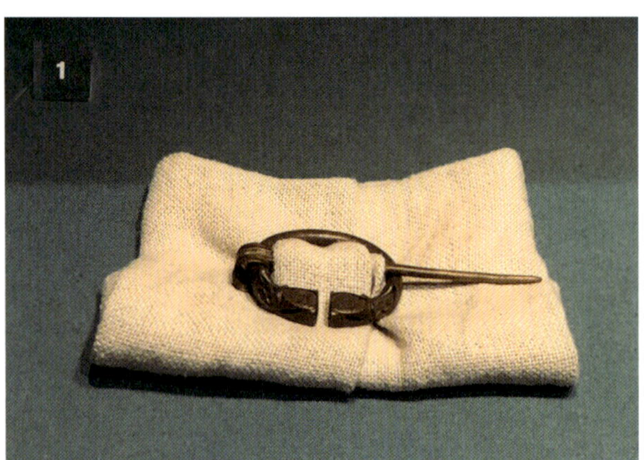

Ring brooch, mock-up with modern fabric, showing how the brooches were used, Tate Britain, London, 2019

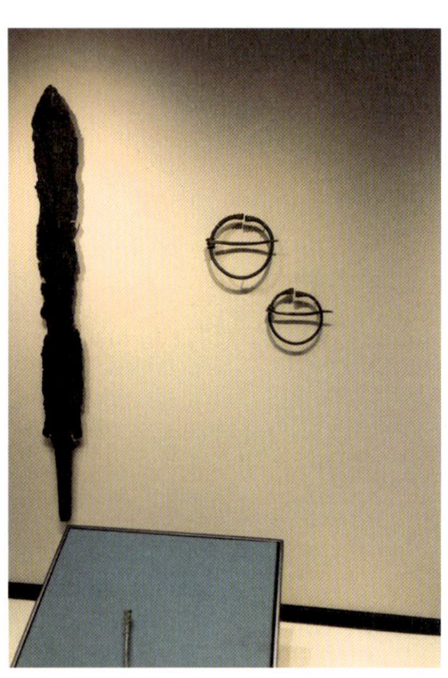

Ring brooches, traditionally made of copper alloy, Tate Britain, London, 2019

¤

by Sadie Plant

¤ was introduced as an ASCII placeholder for all and any currencies in the early 1970s. This was also the era in which what is now known as speculative or financial capitalism really seemed to take off: the gold standard was abandoned and the world's major currencies lost their relation to the precious and ill-gotten metals which had provided modernity with its start-up capital. The symbol, a circle with outside spikes placed at intervals of 90 degrees, came to function as a placeholder for currencies which had already become placeholders for nothing but themselves, fiat currencies with no content, spinning as though on axes of their own: no base metal, no bottom line, nowhere for the buck to stop. Capital became increasingly wrapped up in itself, its circulations chasing their own tails, feeding on themselves, making money and the world go round.

It could be a headless turtle, or an X with its axis concealed by an O, or something to be turned, a tap or steering wheel. But this symbol is a scarab, and a scarab is the beetle which was revered by the ancient Egyptians and has figured in Middle Eastern and then European art for thousands of years. There were scarabs on Wedgewood pottery in the mid-eighteenth century, when European designers scoured the world for exotic imagery, and they were worked into the pendants and brooches designed in the 1920s, when the discovery of Tutankhamun's tomb inspired an art deco fondness for Egyptian imagery. Recent examples are Estée Lauder's perfume compact, which takes the shape of a blue scarab, and Gucci's scarab jewelry range.

For the Egyptians, the scarab symbolized birth and rebirth, becoming and life, the passage of time: just as the sacred beetles, scarabaeidae, push their balls of dung over the ground, so Khepri, or Kheper, portrayed as a figure with a scarab for his head, was said to roll the sun across the sky each day and accompany it through the night before ensuring its rebirth at dawn, at which point the god was portrayed with open wings. The scarabs' connection with renewal was sealed by the fact that beetles seemed to multiply in these balls, from which they do indeed emerge: the balls work as mobile nests which serve to protect the eggs which are secreted and carried inside them. The name of the god and the beetle translates as "to come into being."

In ancient Egypt, and in many later cultures too, scarab figures were produced from clay and stone, sometimes also gold and semi-precious stones. They were not used as any kind of currency, but they had high value and magical properties and were worn as jewelry, used as seals, and carried as amulets, even in death: Hatnefer, whose tomb was found in the 1930s, was buried with a scarab of green feldspar and gold engraved with a passage from the Book of the Dead which concerns the way in which the heart is judged in order to gain access to the afterlife.

It is not difficult to see why the Egyptians held the scarab in such high esteem. It is extremely striking in appearance—many scarabs have metallic shells, and shine in purples and blues and greens, and by forming excrement into balls which it then collects and buries underground, the scarab not only ensures its own life and reproduction, but also enriches the soil in its role as a highly efficient processor and distributer of nutrients. It also seems to be the only known animal to navigate by the stars: the African dung beetle uses the sun to orient itself by day, and climbs onto its ball to survey the Milky Way before setting out with its dung by night.

And here it is, a metal beetle climbing on a Basel wall, after the fashion of the wrought iron that was the other great metal of modernity: steam-powered blast furnaces allowed iron to become one of the great drivers of industrialization, and while cast iron is brittle and liable to crack, the low carbon iron that has been warmed and worked—or wrought—is durable, but soft and malleable too. Wrought iron was laid as railway tracks, worked and wrung into the frameworks of Eiffel Tower and the Statue of Liberty, forged into shackles and chains, rivetted into bridges and ships, and twisted and looped to embellish the bourgeois world with ornate gates and railings, grills and screens. Later it too was supplanted: mild steel is now almost exclusively deployed in the construction industry, and the nineteenth century development of new metal-processing techniques encouraged the use of a wide range of lighter alloys and non-ferrous metals which had long been crucial for finer metalwork. Even in the fifteenth century, when the typeface in which the Basel scarab has been set was first designed, it was a mixture of lead, tin, and antimony that was poured into the matrices that formed the characters of early moveable type.

Judith Kakon's steel scarab resembles iron, stands for gold, and is attached to a grey wall which makes reference not only to the frames and housings of programs and screens and also the many shades of metals to which they in turn refer. Kakon throws a digital character back into solidity, allowing its history to be explored, rendering visible its materiality, reminding the digital frameworks and platforms, the new wrought infrastructure of financial capital, that they too are playing in a real live world of materials and goods, energies, desires, living bodies and communities. She gives the placeholder a position, plucking it out of the thin airs of pure speculation and insisting on its place in the here and now. This gives it an air of permanent display. But it too will fade: the scarab will rust and the wall will fall away, and look: already there are flowers, like those left at the scene of an accident, or crime.

Kheper, the scarab, der Käfer: an amulet, a pilot, a composter. Maybe even a bug in the machine?

Renderings of twisted mounting rings, 2020

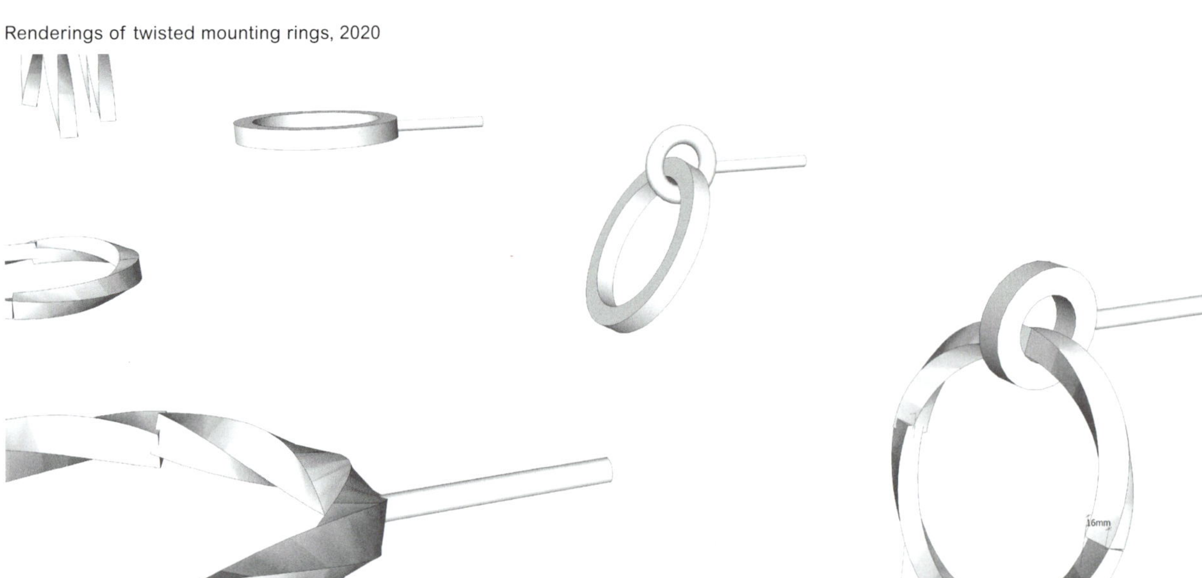

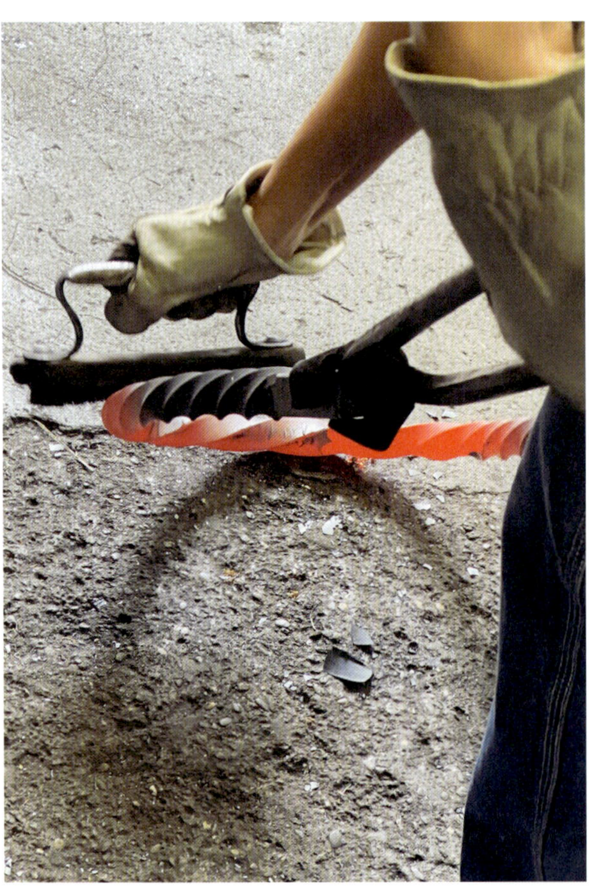

Julia Pfisterer working on the bending of a twisted iron letter, Binningen near Basel, 2020

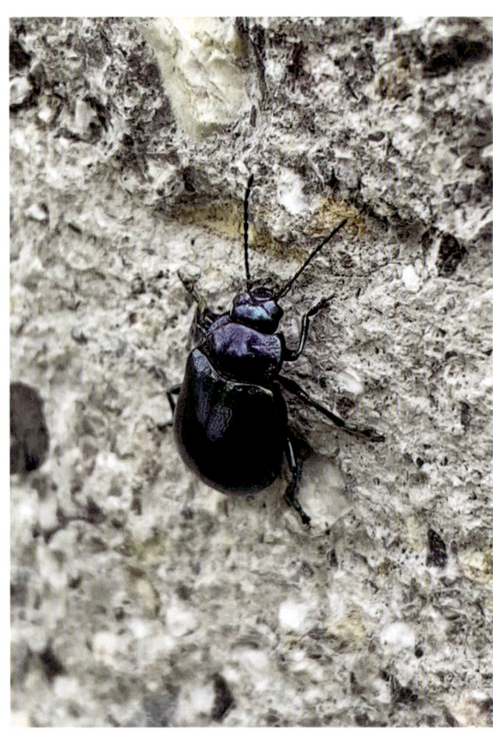

Earth boring dung beetle at Richisau, Glarus, 2021

Typeface Damianus Moyllus Sans 36,
developed by Ronnie Fueglister, 2020

ESTATE	%
EMPIRE	REAL
2020	
GAME	
PRIME	
TRUST	¤

Detail of ¤, 2020, Kunsthalle Basel back wall, Basel, 2020.
Installation view: Gina Folly

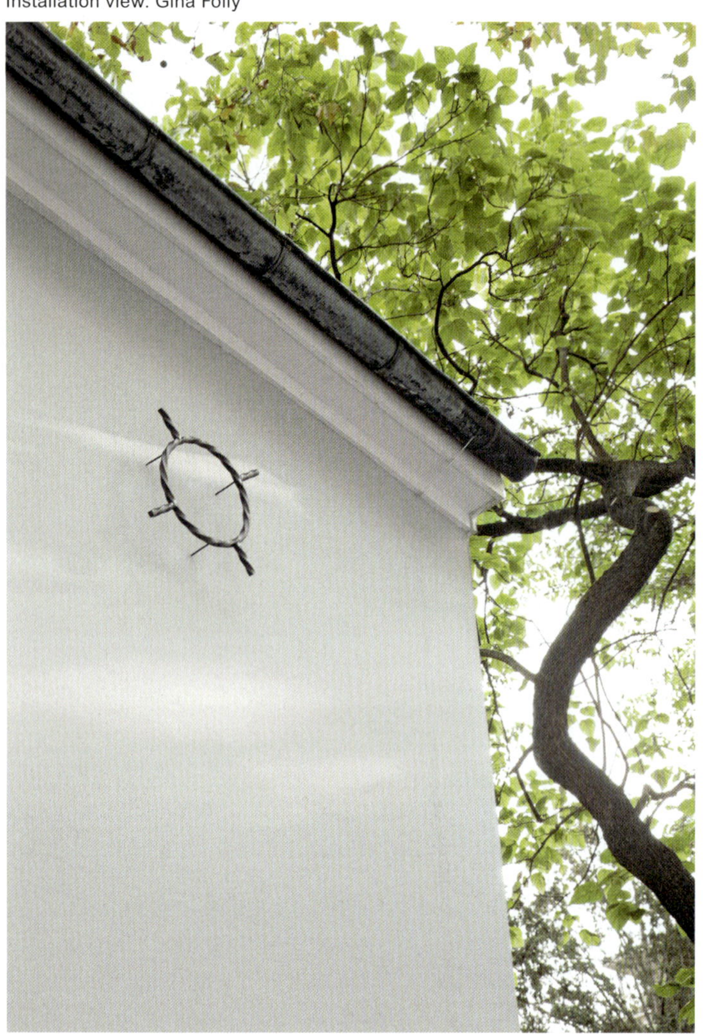

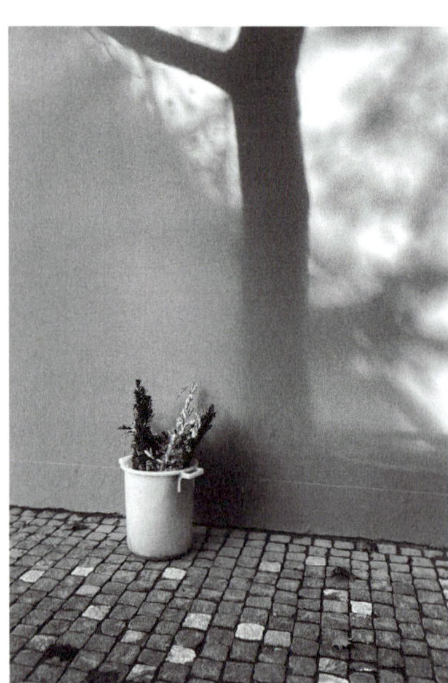

Exchanging the flowers, Kunsthalle Basel back wall, Basel, 2020

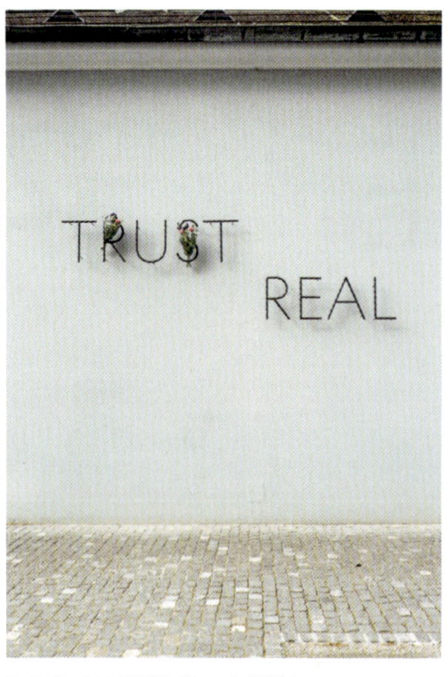

Detail of ¤, 2020, Basel, 2021.
Installation view: Kunsthalle Basel

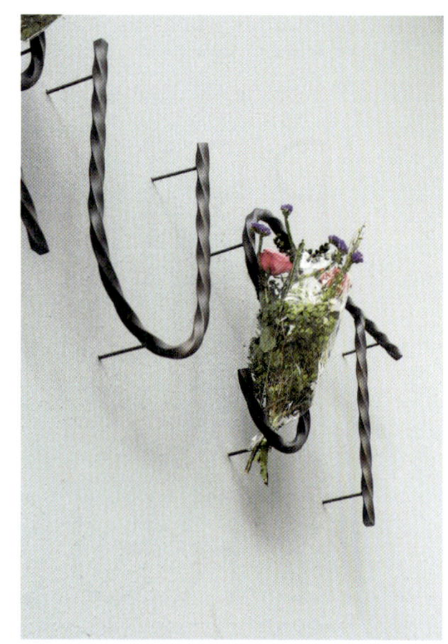

Detail of ¤, 2020, Basel, 2021.
Installation view: Kunsthalle Basel

Suddenly a newly opened café appears in front of ¤, 2020, Basel, summer 2021

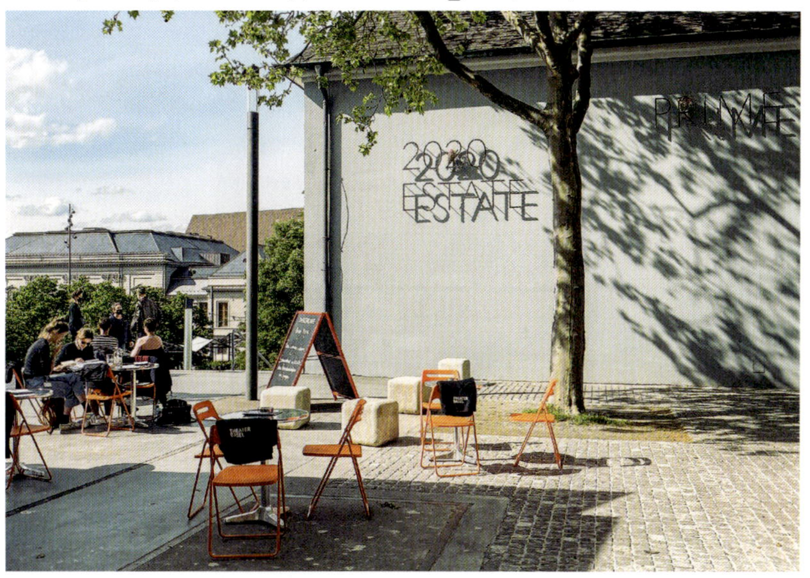

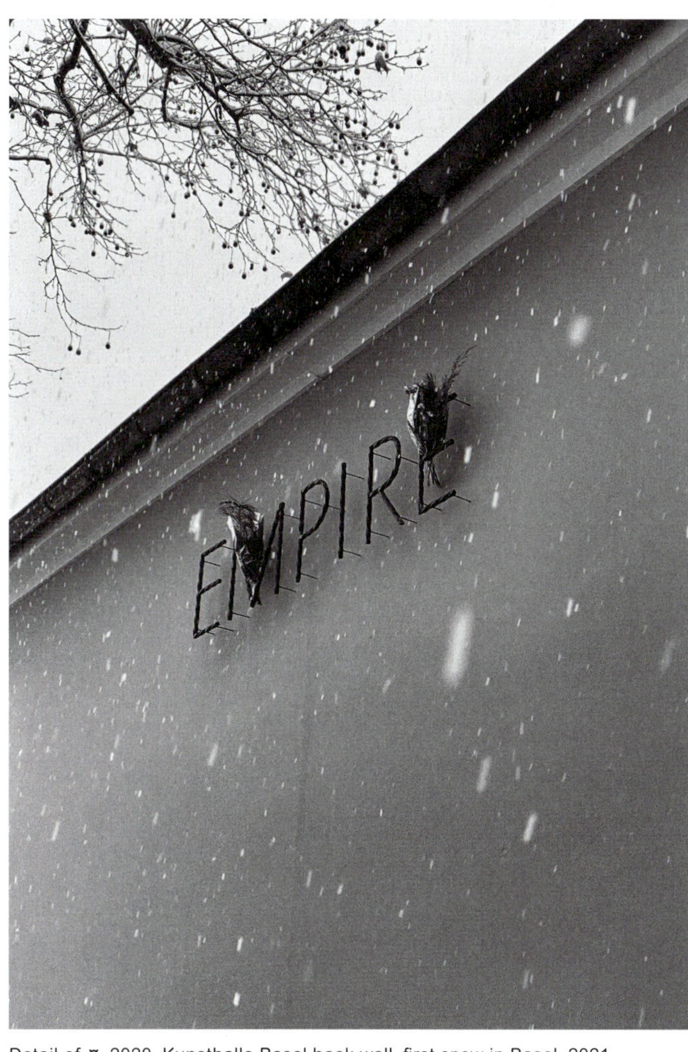

Detail of ¤, 2020, Kunsthalle Basel back wall, first snow in Basel, 2021

A woman laces her shoes in front of ¤, 2020,
another woman approaches from behind, Basel, 2021

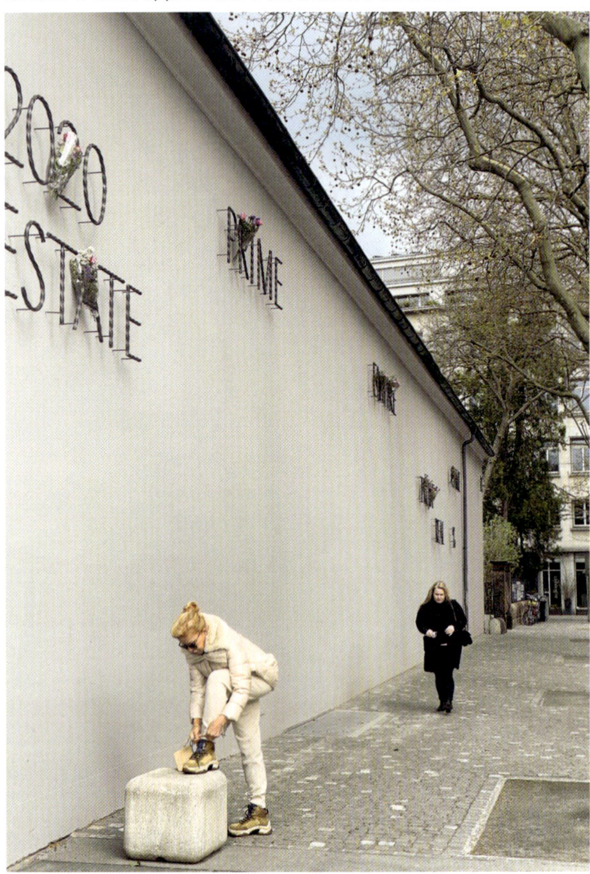

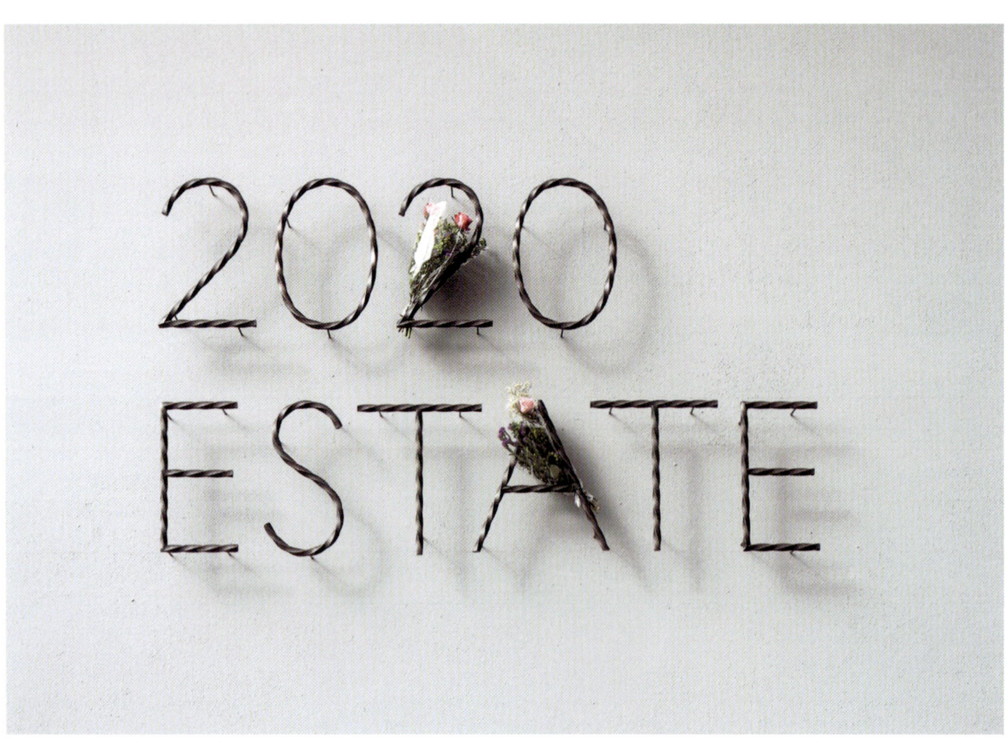

Detail of ¤, 2020, Kunsthalle Basel back wall, Basel, 2020. Installation view: Kunsthalle Basel

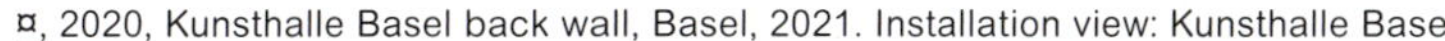

¤, 2020, Kunsthalle Basel back wall, Basel, 2021. Installation view: Kunsthalle Basel

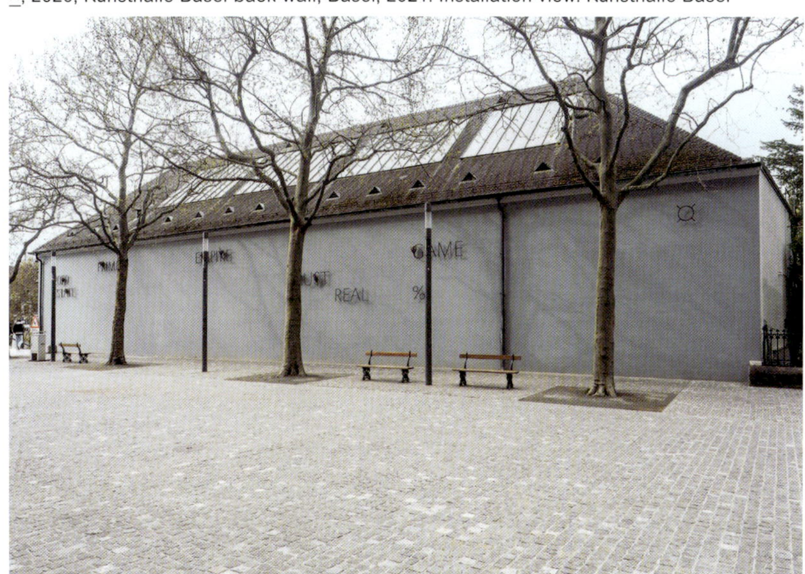

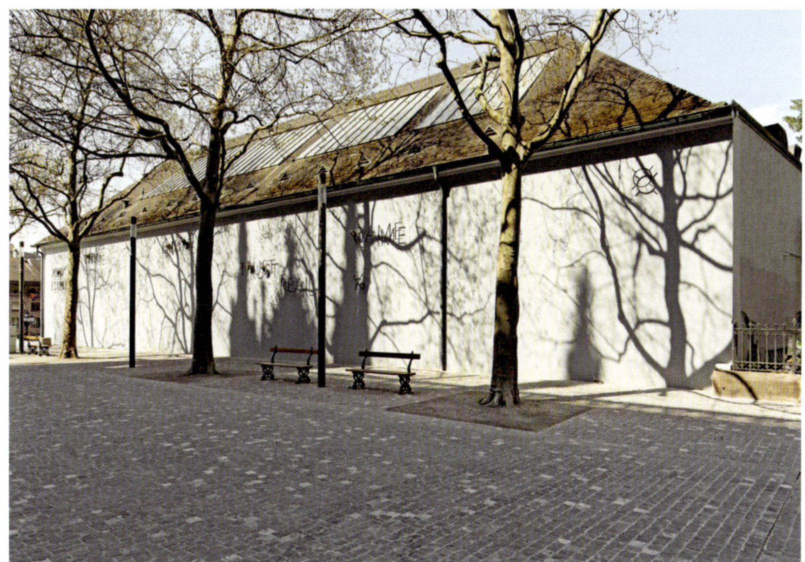

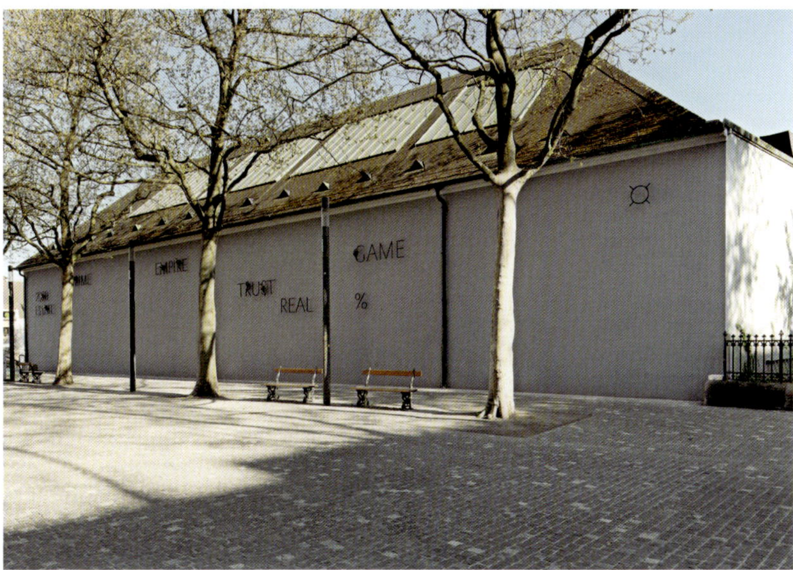

¤, 2020, Kunsthalle Basel back wall, Basel, 2021. Installation view: Gina Folly
¤, 2020, Kunsthalle Basel back wall, Basel, 2021. Installation view: Gina Folly

¤, 2020, Kunsthalle Basel back wall, Basel, 2020. Installation view: Gina Folly

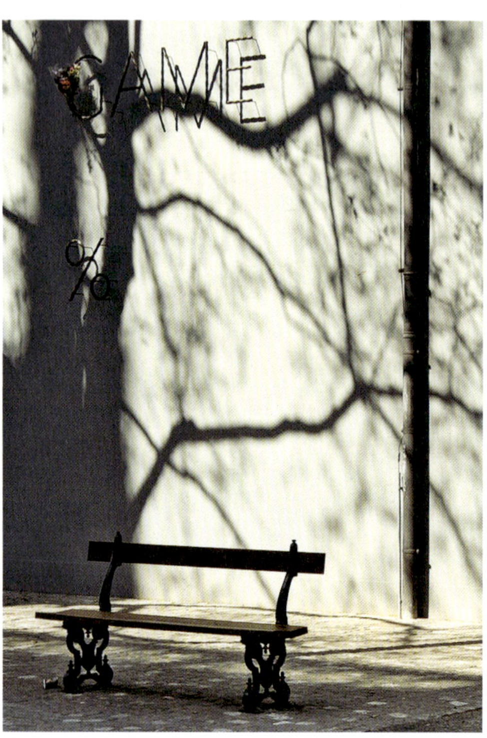

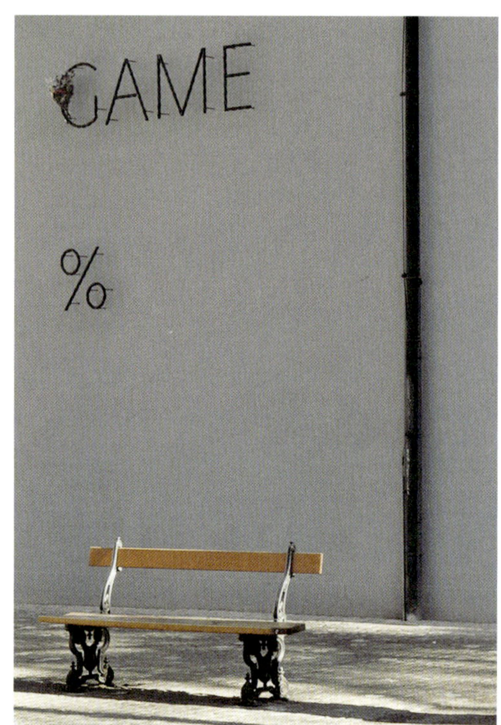

Details of ¤, 2020, Kunsthalle Basel back wall,
Basel, 2021

A woman takes a photograph of the shadow play on ¤, 2020, Basel, 2021

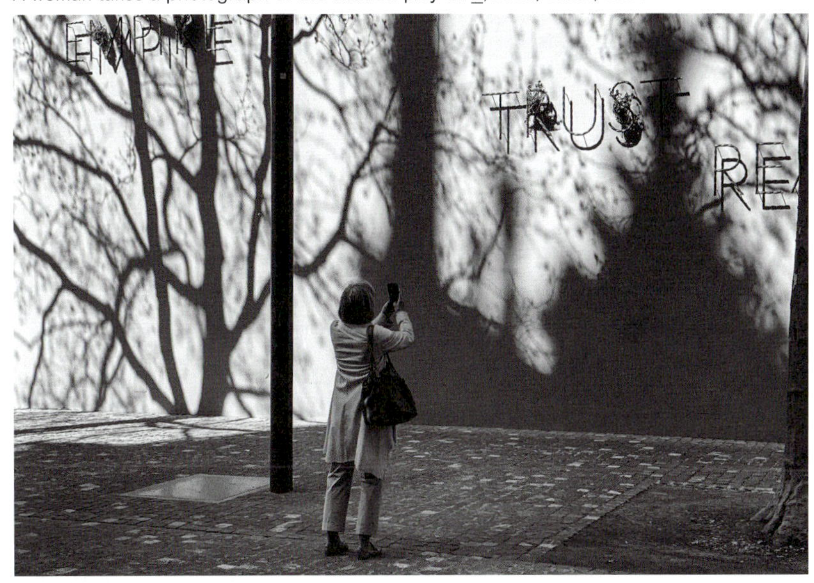

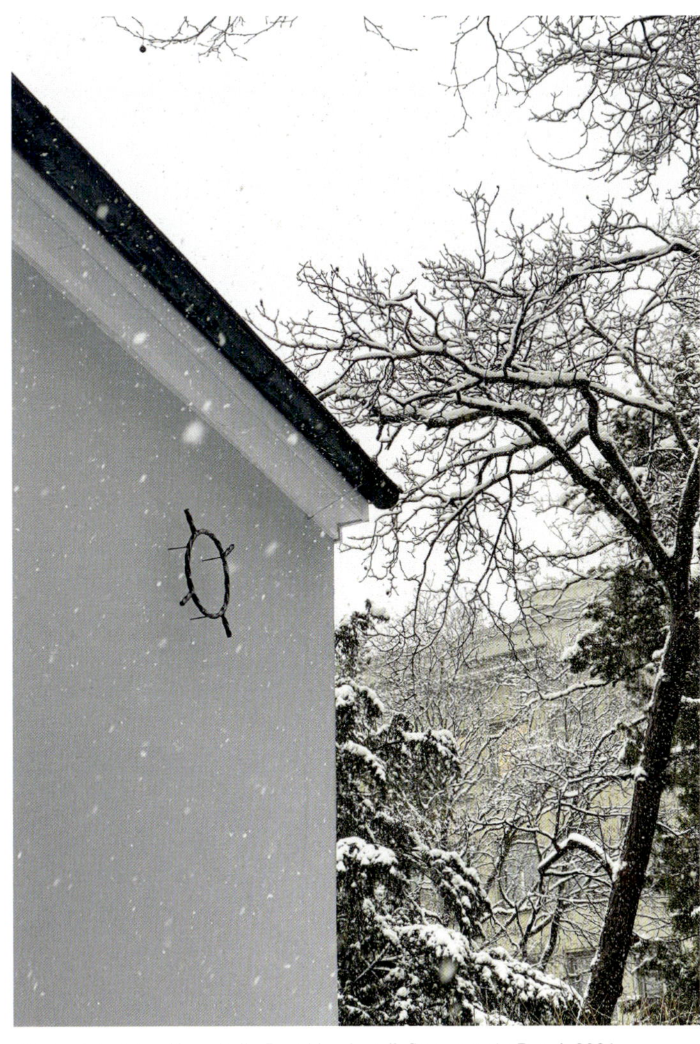

Detail of ¤, 2020, Kunsthalle Basel back wall, first snow in Basel, 2021

Brother, 2015, inkjet prints, each 14.8 × 10.5 cm, edition of 50 cuttings of a self-test page of a Brother printer

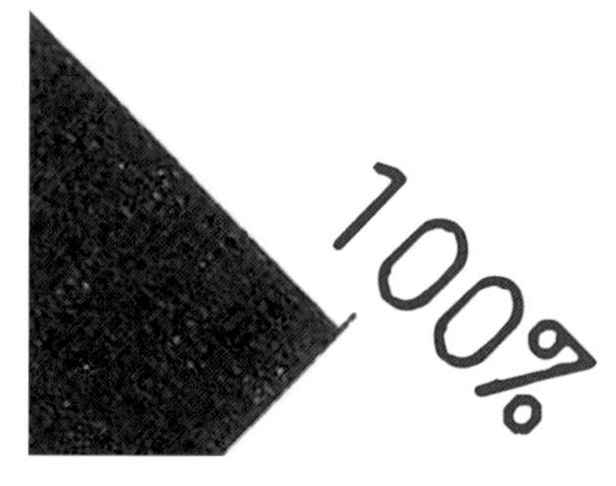

GGGGG

50%

EEEEEEE F

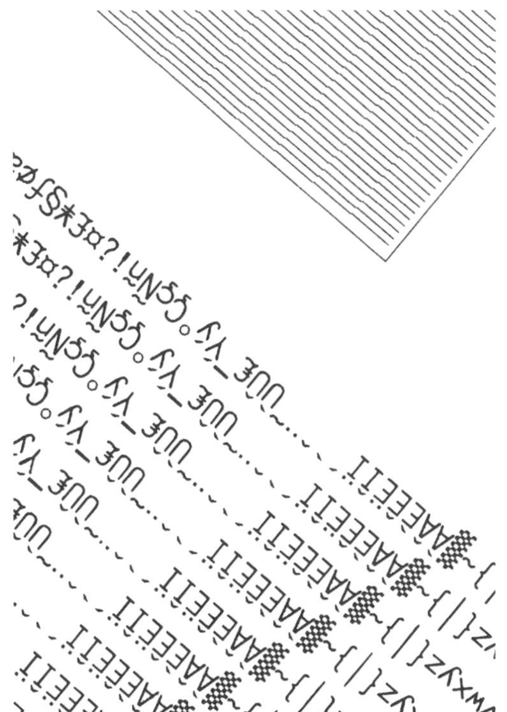

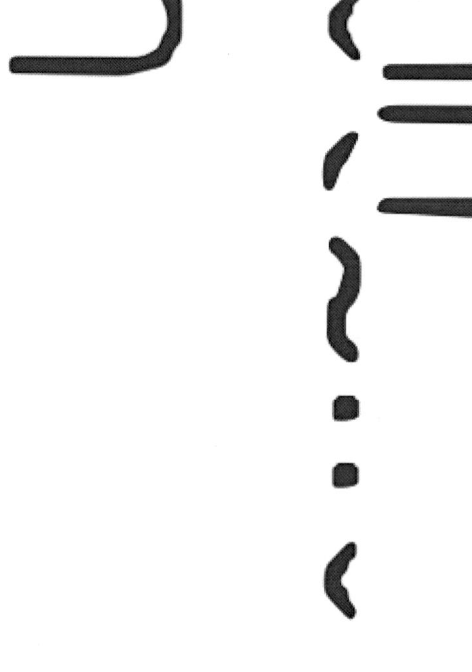

Brother, 2015, inkjet prints, each 14.8 × 10.5 cm,
edition of 50 cuttings of a self-test page of a Brother printer

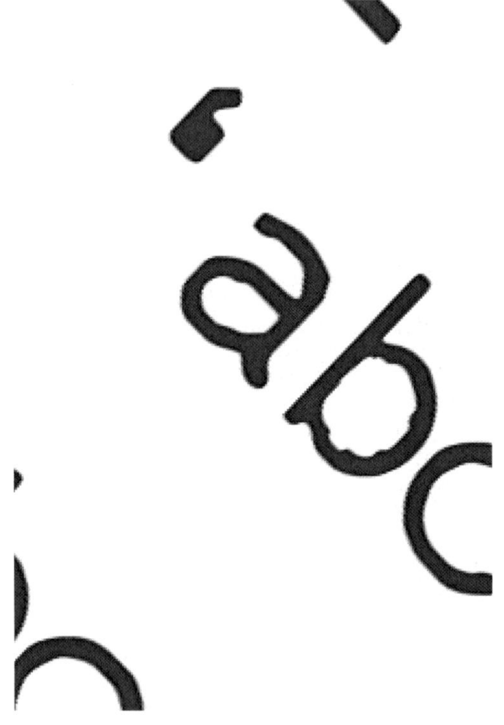

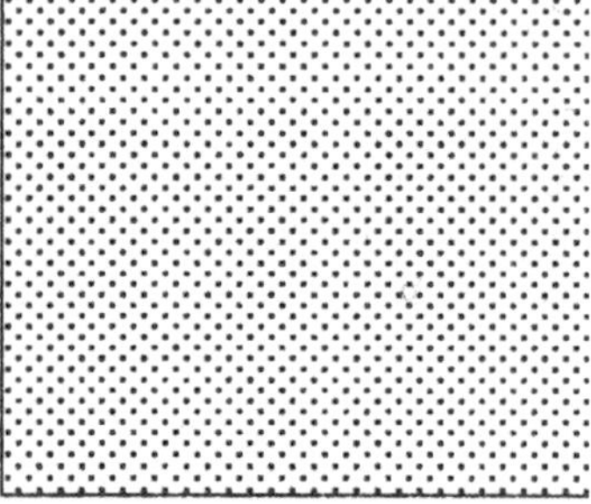

/01234

01234

012345

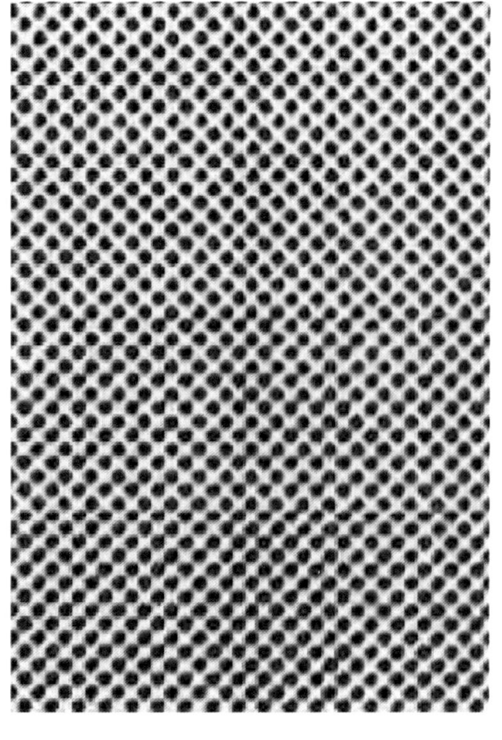

Brother, 2015, inkjet prints, each 14.8 × 10.5 cm, edition of 50 cuttings of a self-test page of a Brother printer

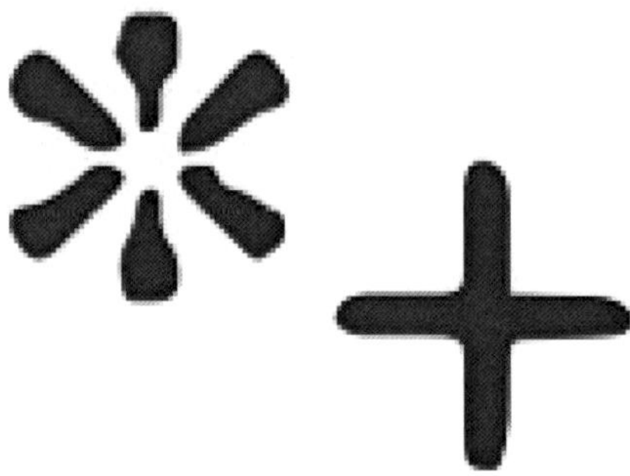

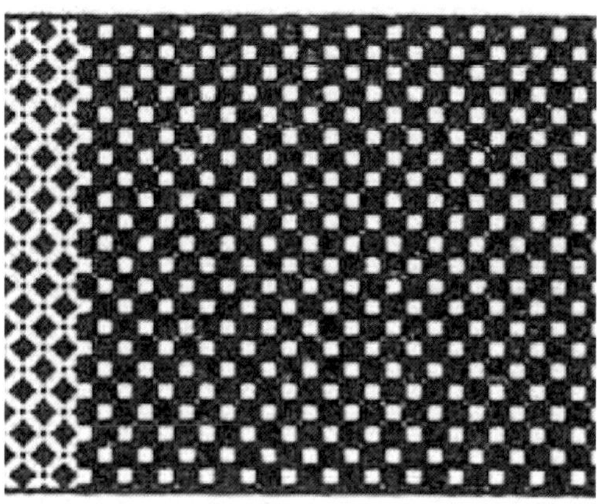

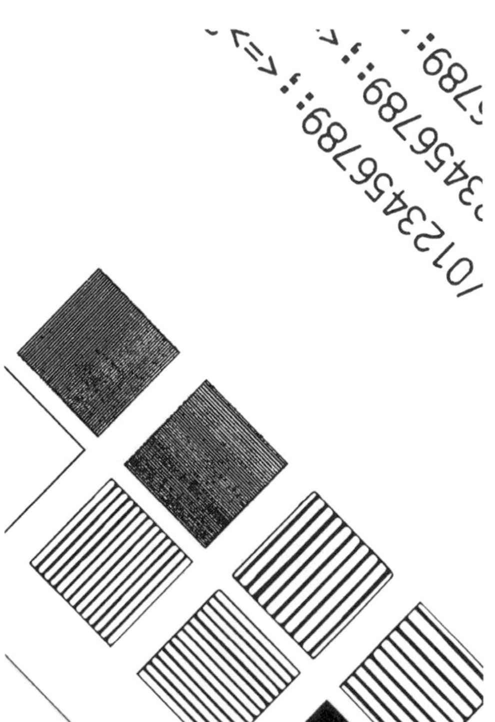

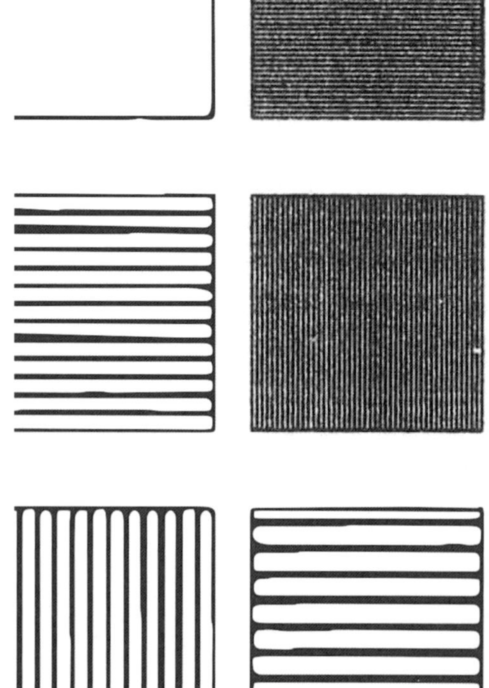

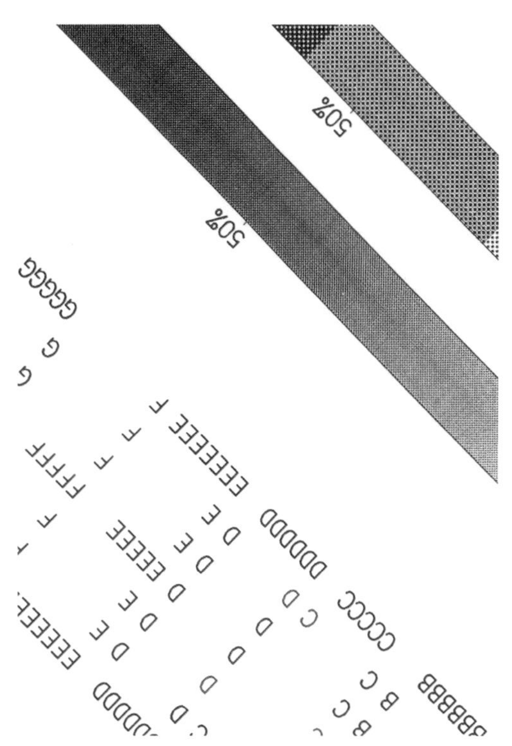
50%
50%

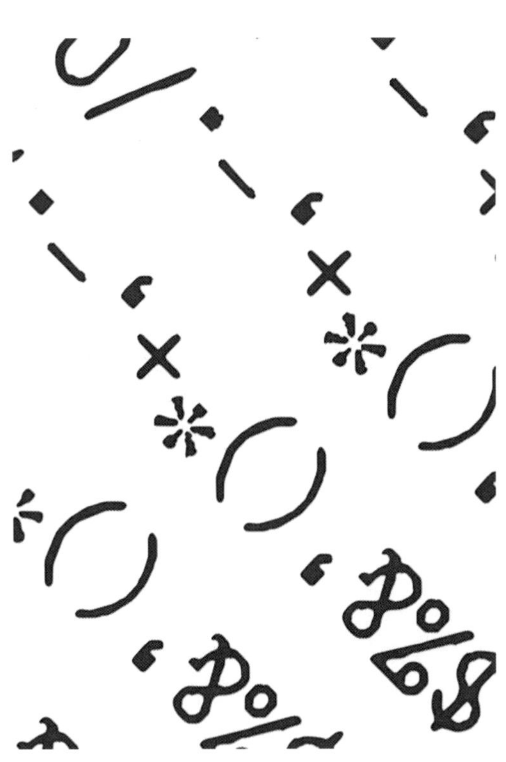

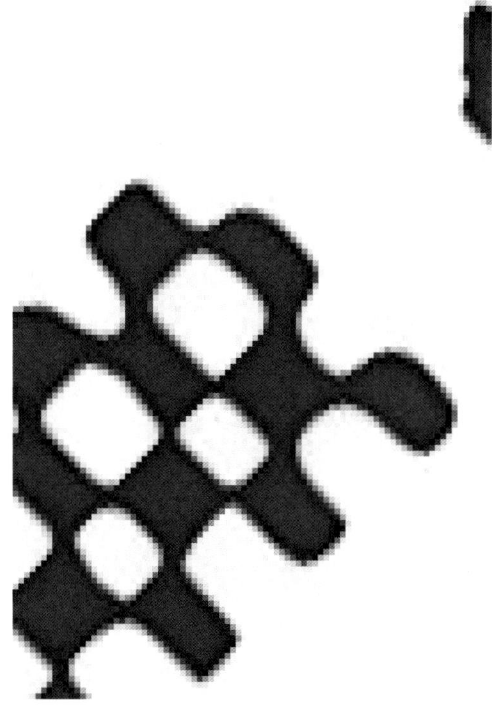

Brother, 2015, inkjet prints, each 14.8 × 10.5 cm, edition of 50 cuttings of a self-test page of a Brother printer

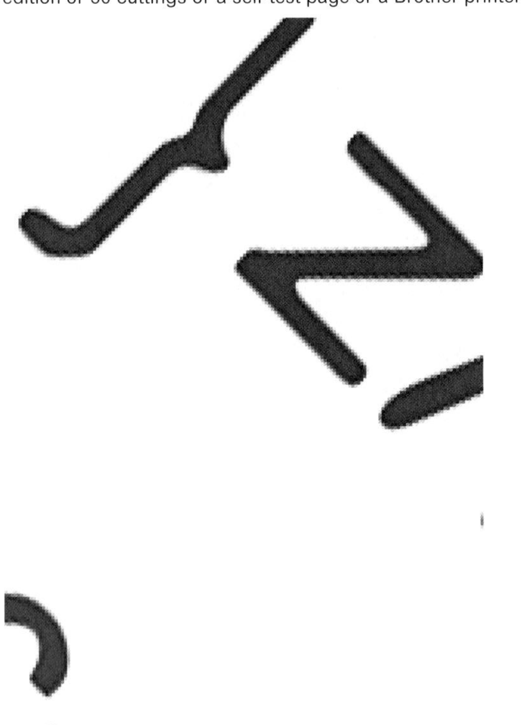

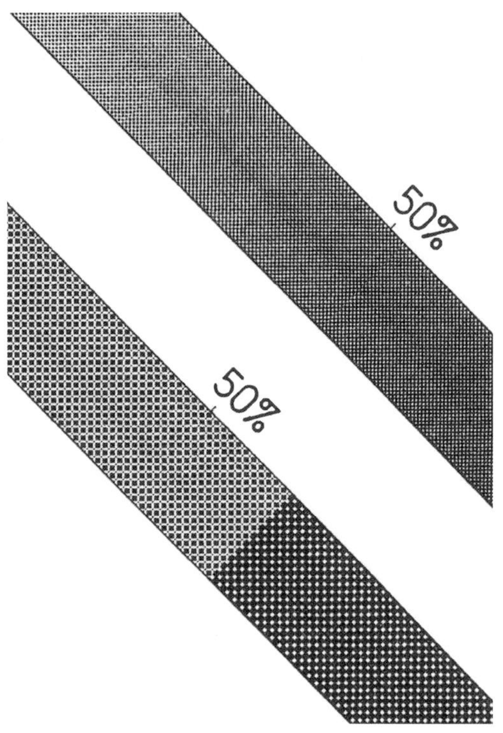

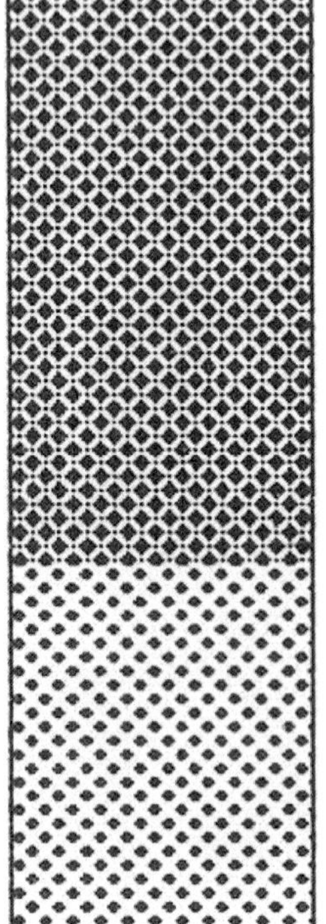

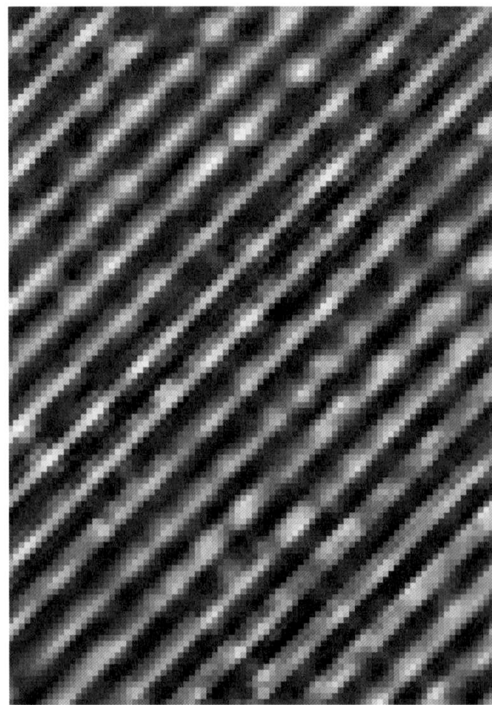

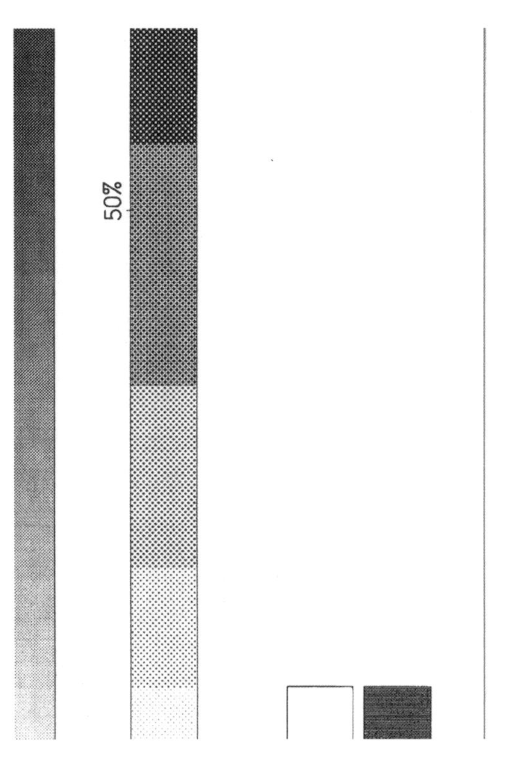
50%

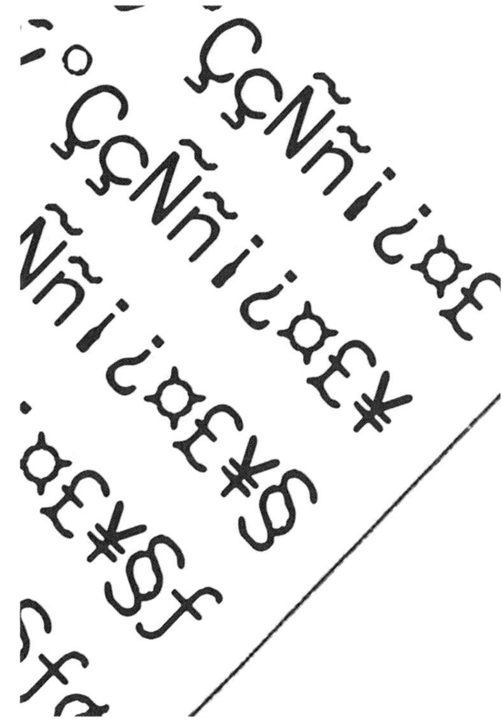

Ever since I fell down the stairs, things have changed, 2018, powder coated aluminum, 37.5 – 300 × 52 × 46 cm. Image: Dominic Michel

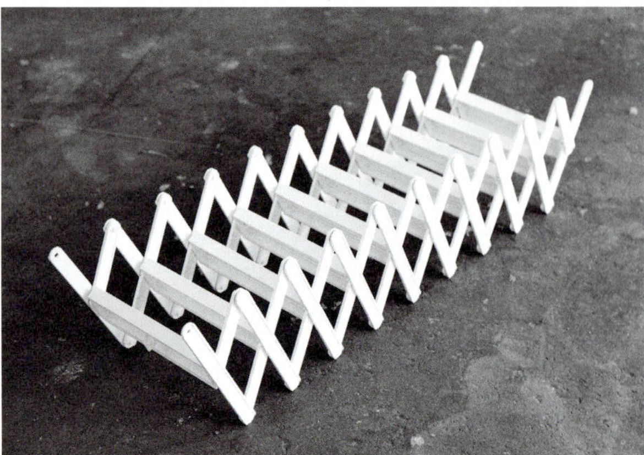

Cat stairs in Fribourg, 2018

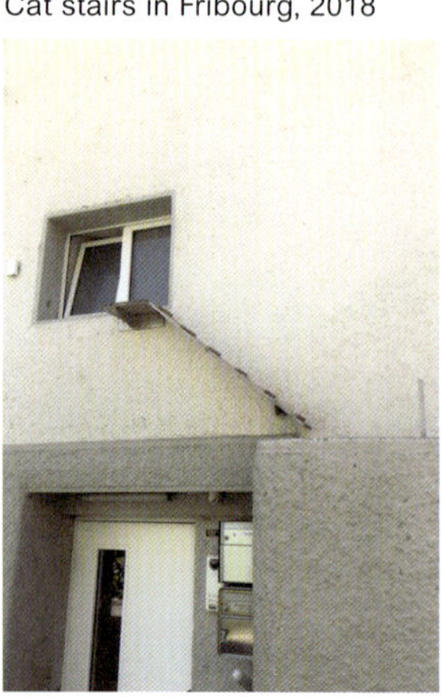

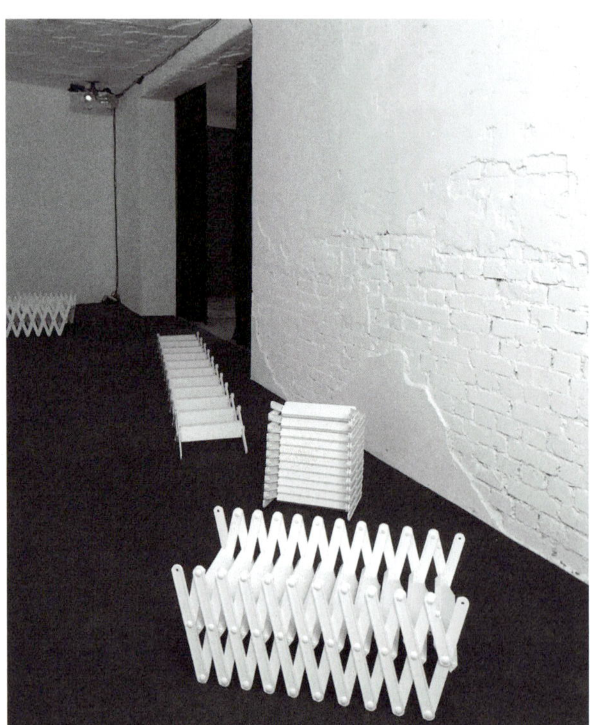

Come down the stairs to meet me; Tiramisu; Heading towards the stairs in order to go back, 2018, powder coated aluminum, each 37.5 – 300 × 52 × 46 cm, anorak at Solitude project space, Stuttgart, 2018. Exhibition view: Florian Model

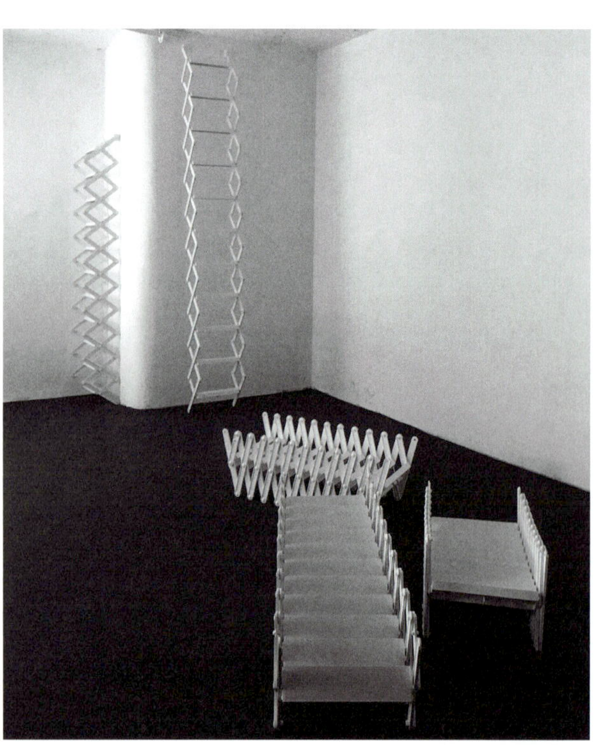

She suddenly lifted her head, stepping back at the same time; A gen ascending slope; Time and wisdom; Ever since I fell down the stairs, things have changed; Some insignificant words were exchanged in t stairways, 2018, powder coated aluminum, each 37.5 – 300 × 52 × 46 cm, anorak at Solitude project space, Stuttgart, 2018. Exhibition view: Florian Mod

Time and wisdom, 2018, powder coated aluminum, 37.5–300 × 52 × 46 cm, Hidden Bar, Art Basel, Basel, 2019

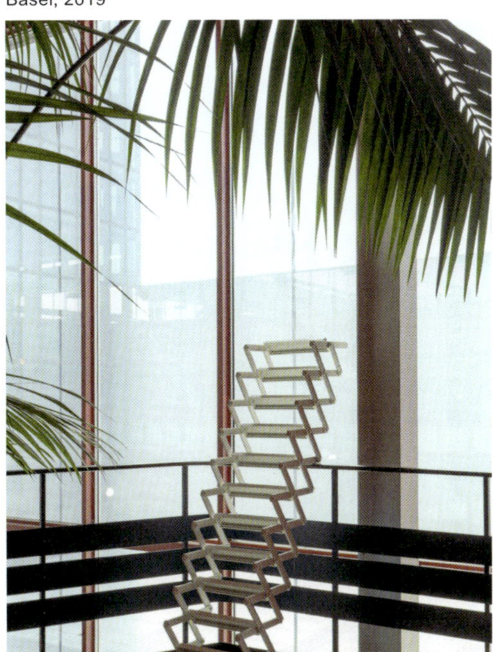

She suddenly lifted her head, stepping back at the same time, 2018, powder coated aluminum, 37.5–300 × 52 × 46 cm, Hidden Bar, Art Basel, Basel, 2019

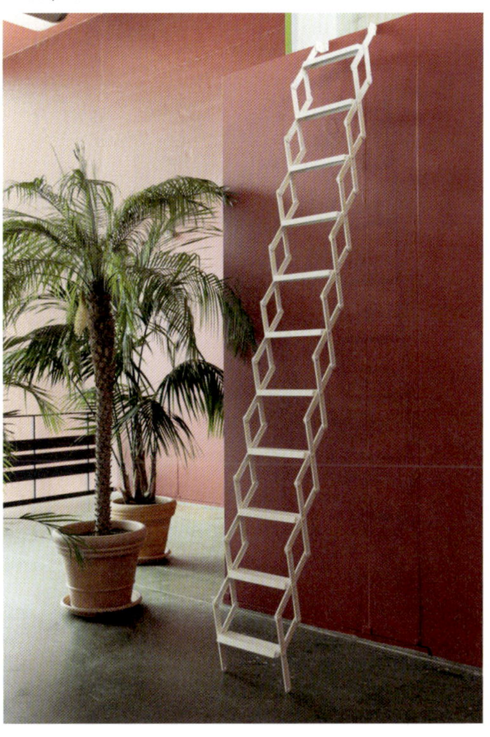

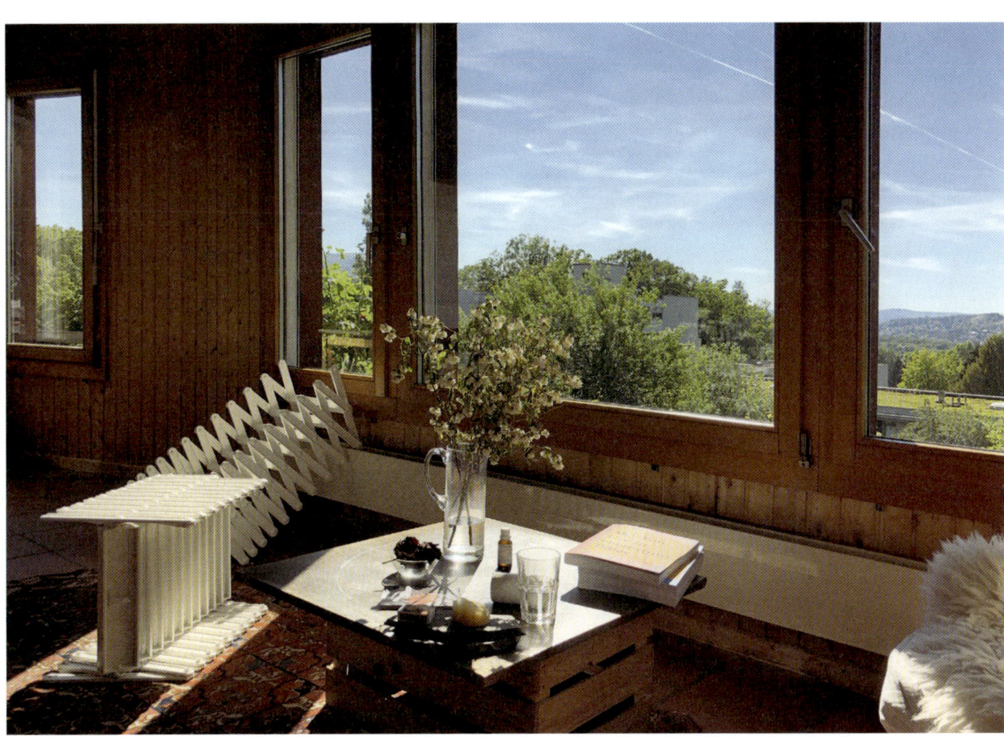

After waiting again she stepped forward; Some insignificant words were exchanged in the stairways, 2018, powder-coated aluminum, 37.5–300 × 52 × 46 cm, The Kitchen auf der Höhe, Arlesheim near Basel, 2019

Advertising images of women with attic ladders, web images, 2018

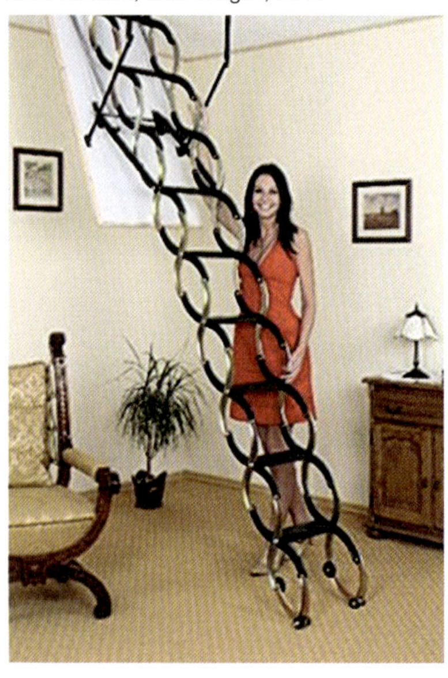
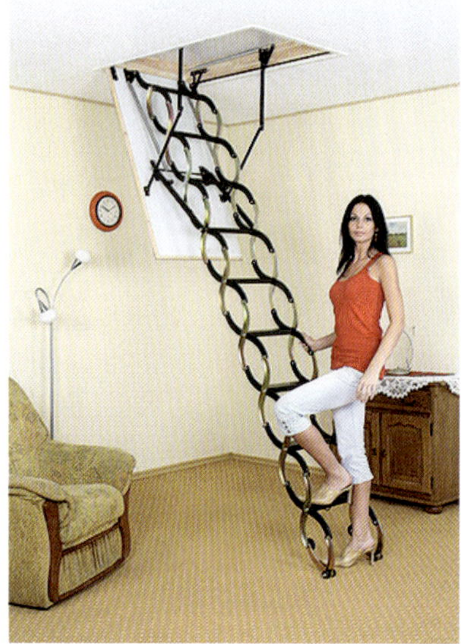
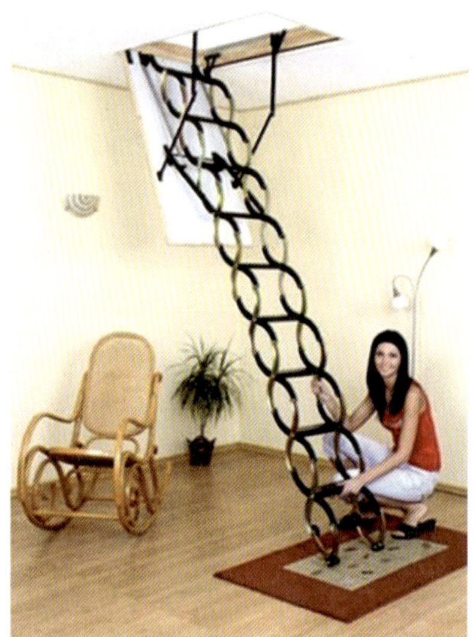
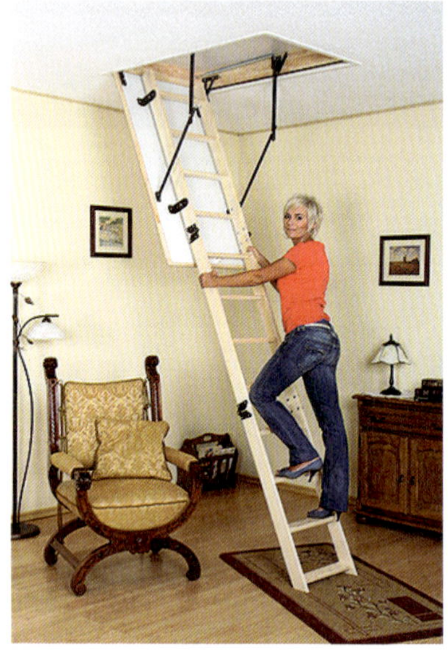
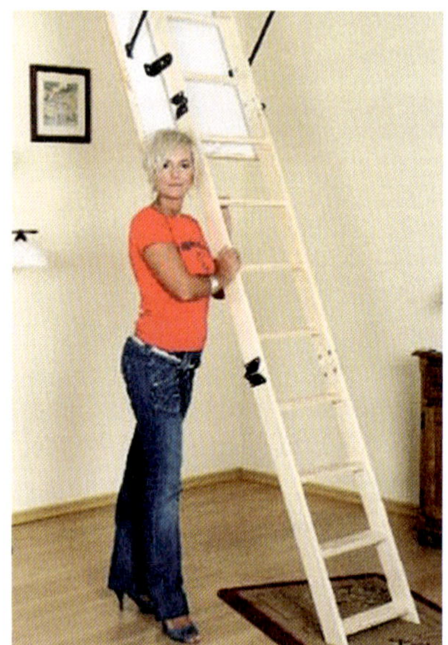
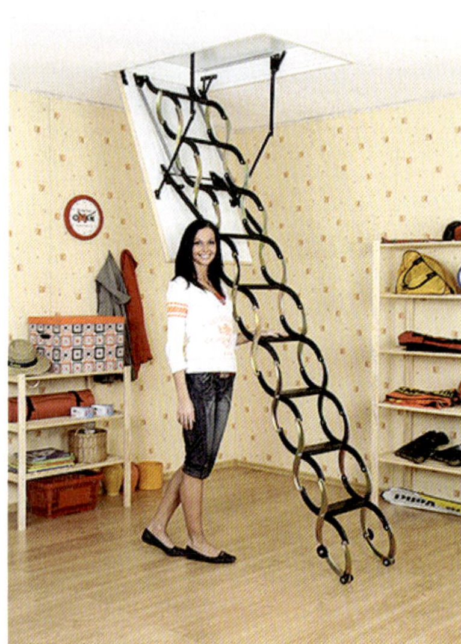
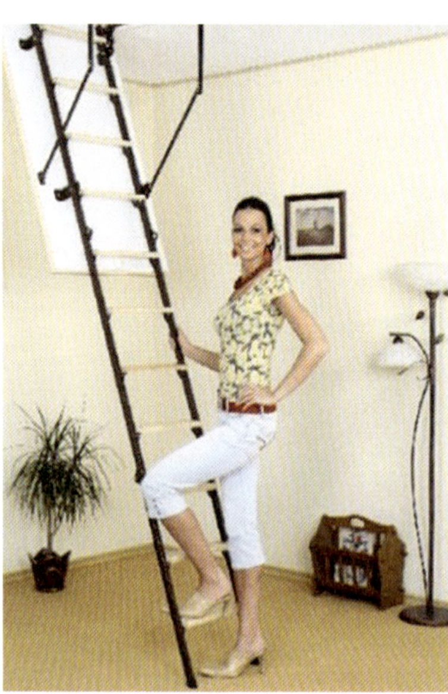

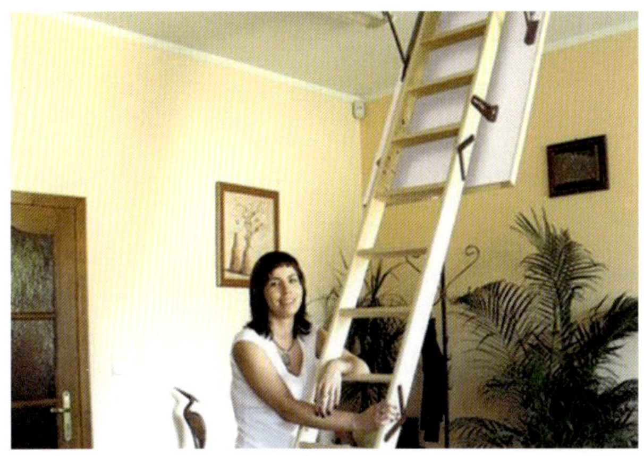

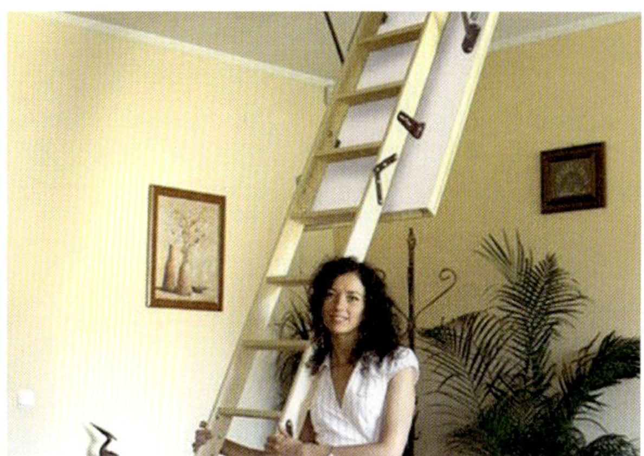

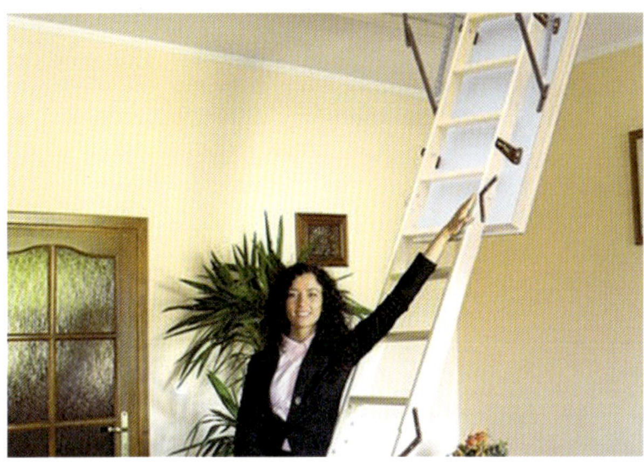

Advertising images of women with attic ladders, web images, 2018

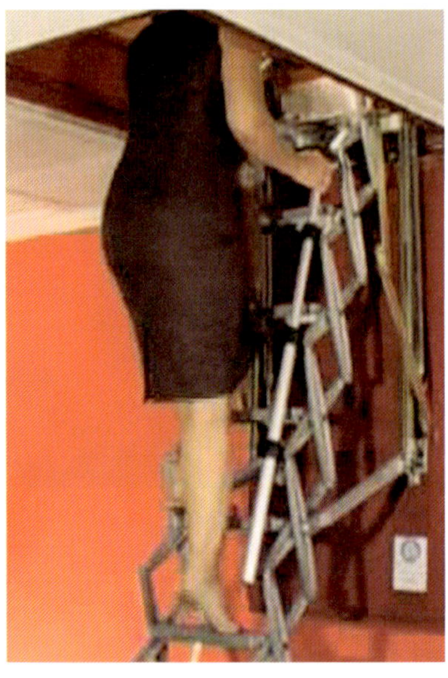

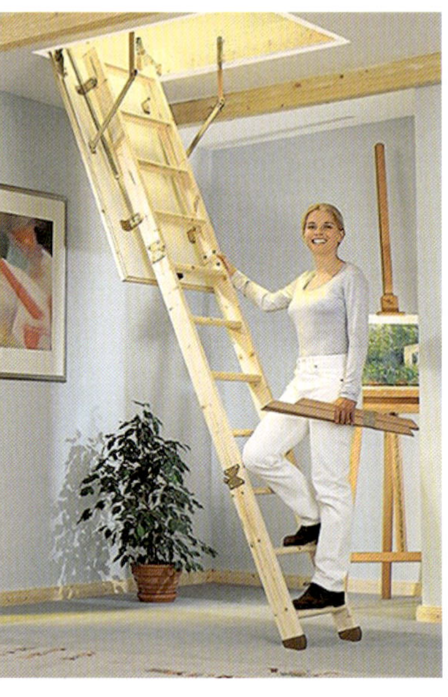

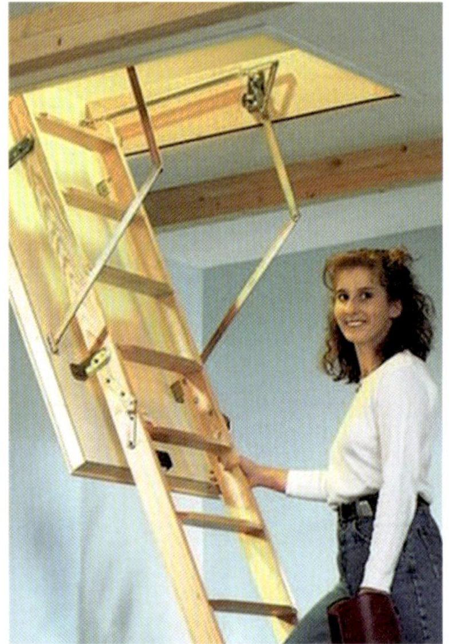

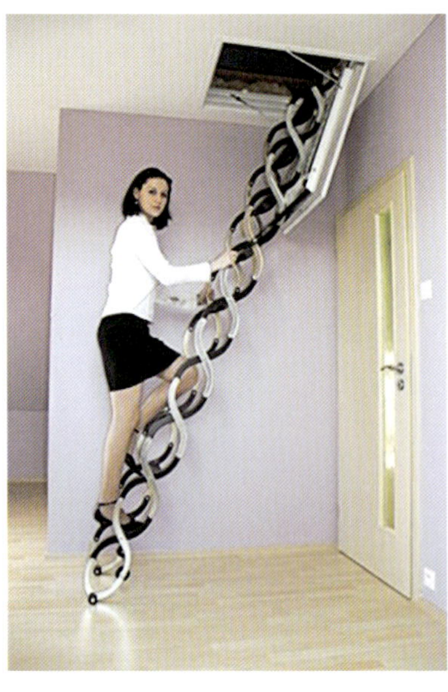

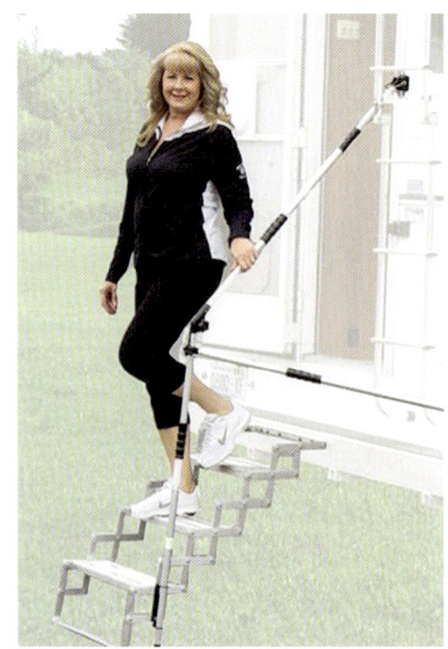

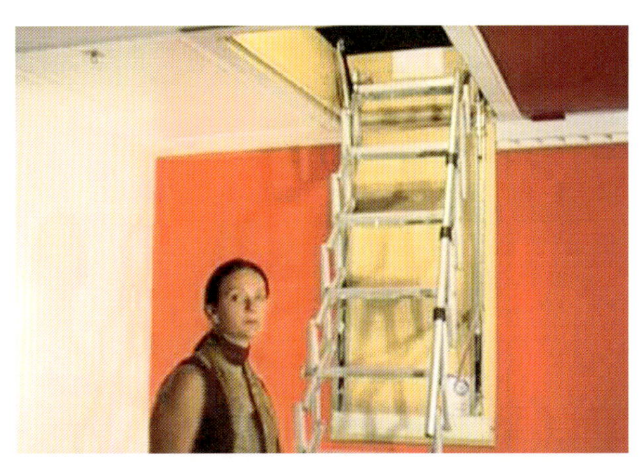

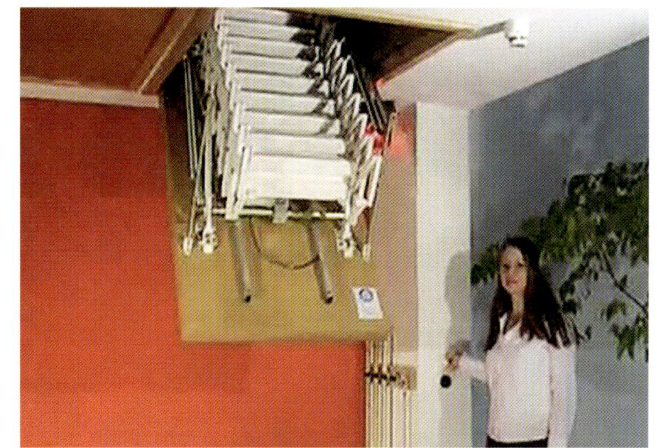

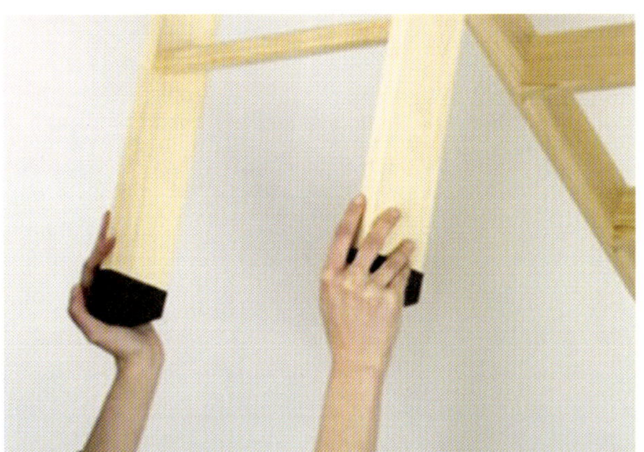

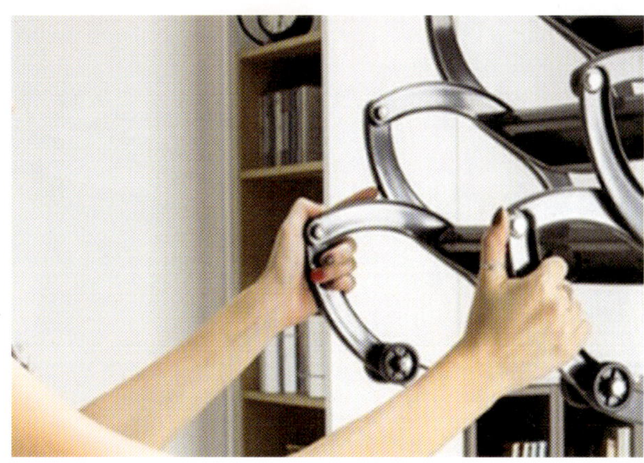

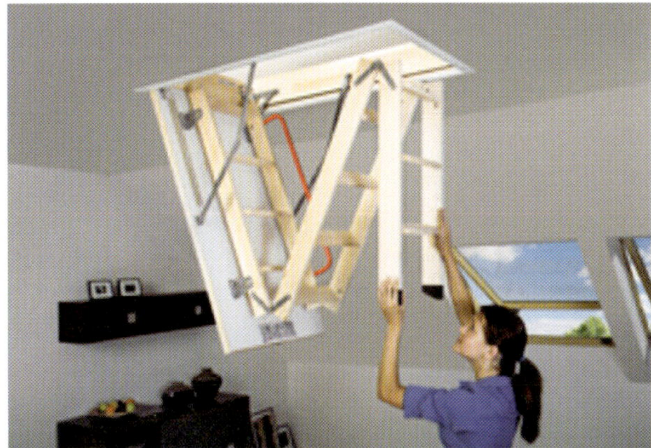

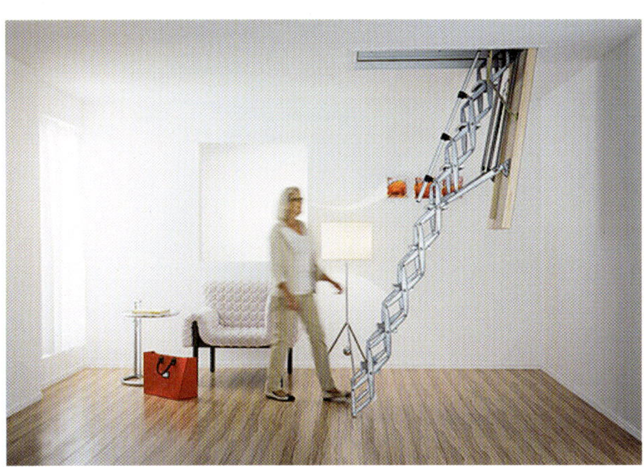

Cimitero Comunale Monumentale Campo Verano, Rome, 2016

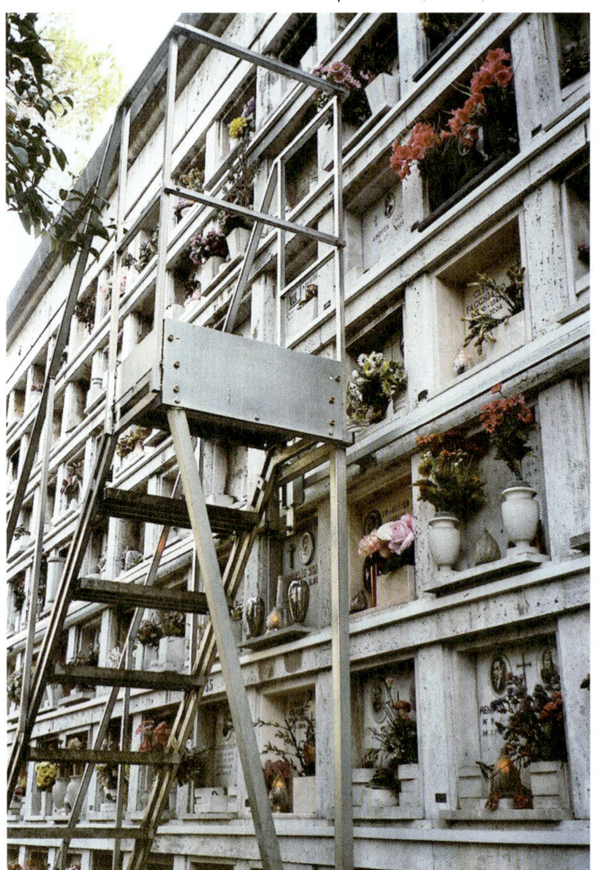

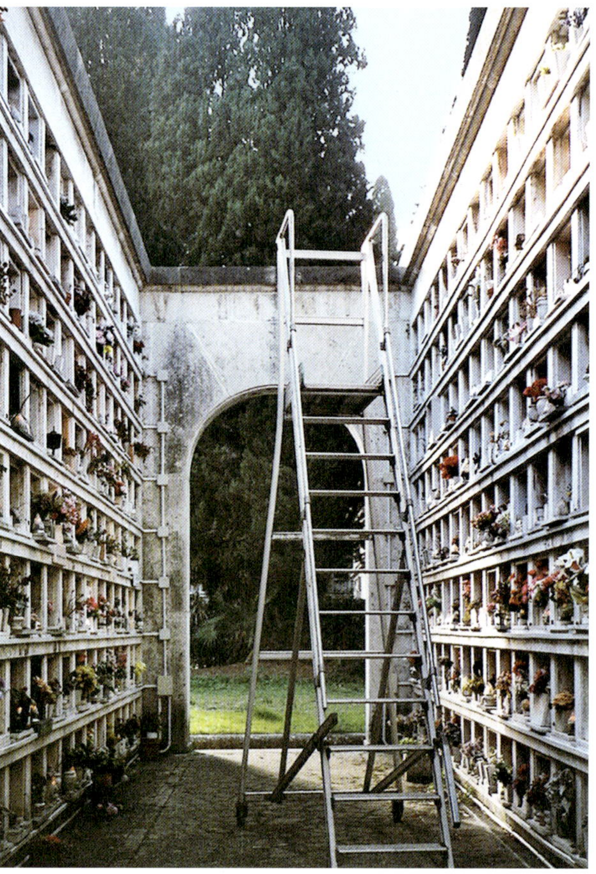

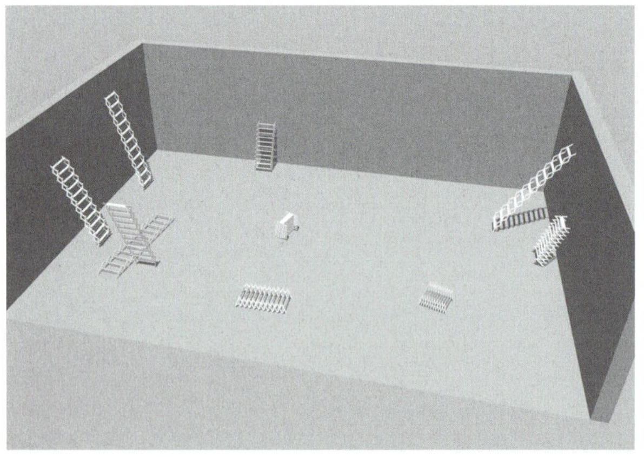

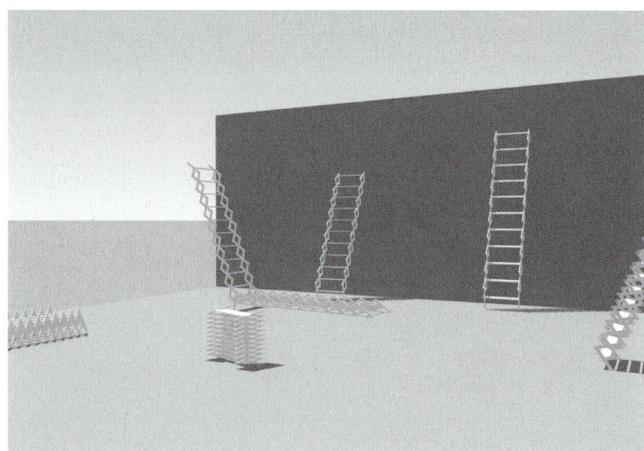

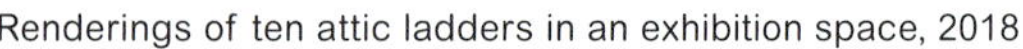

Renderings of ten attic ladders in an exhibition space, 2018

Technical drawing of an attic ladder, web image, accessed May, 2018

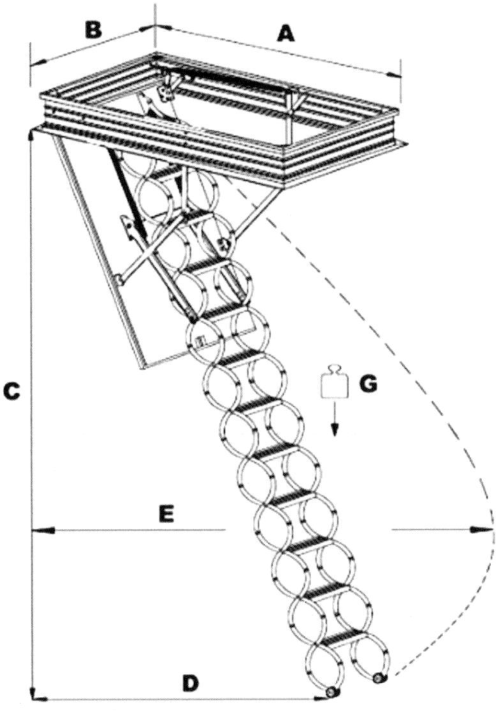

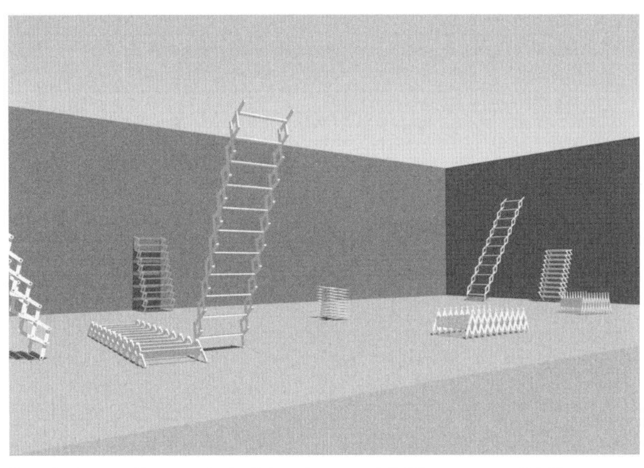

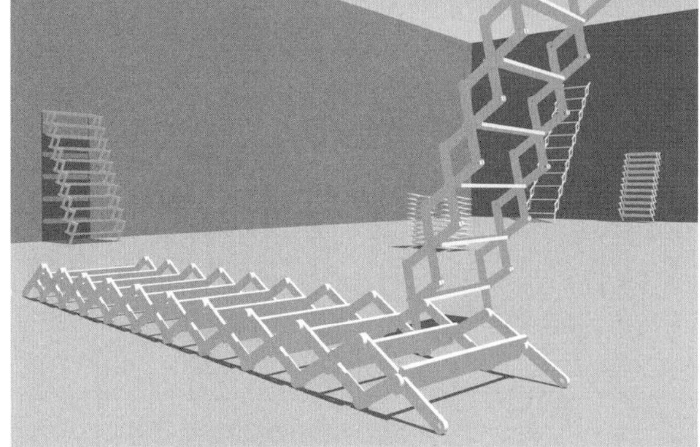

Renderings of ten attic ladders in an exhibition space, 2018

Online information on Regus, Rothschild Center, Tel Aviv, accessed December, 2018

Find > Calendar > Centre Info > Tel Aviv, Rothschild Center - Tel-Aviv

Centre information - Tel Aviv, Rothschild Center - Tel-Aviv

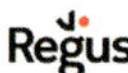

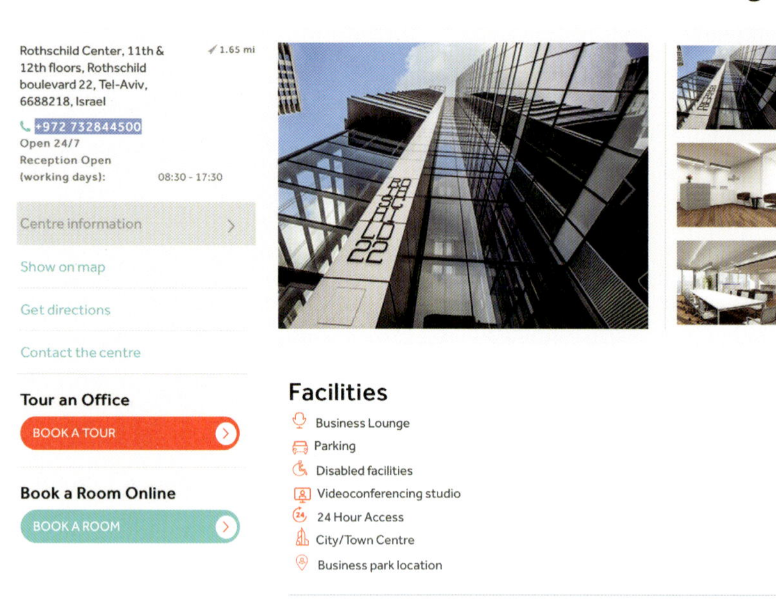

Rothschild Center, 11th & 12th floors, Rothschild boulevard 22, Tel-Aviv, 6688218, Israel

1.65 mi

+972 732844500

Open 24/7

Reception Open (working days): 08:30 - 17:30

Centre information

Show on map

Get directions

Contact the centre

Tour an Office

BOOK A TOUR

Book a Room Online

BOOK A ROOM

Facilities

- Business Lounge
- Parking
- Disabled facilities
- Videoconferencing studio
- 24 Hour Access
- City/Town Centre
- Business park location

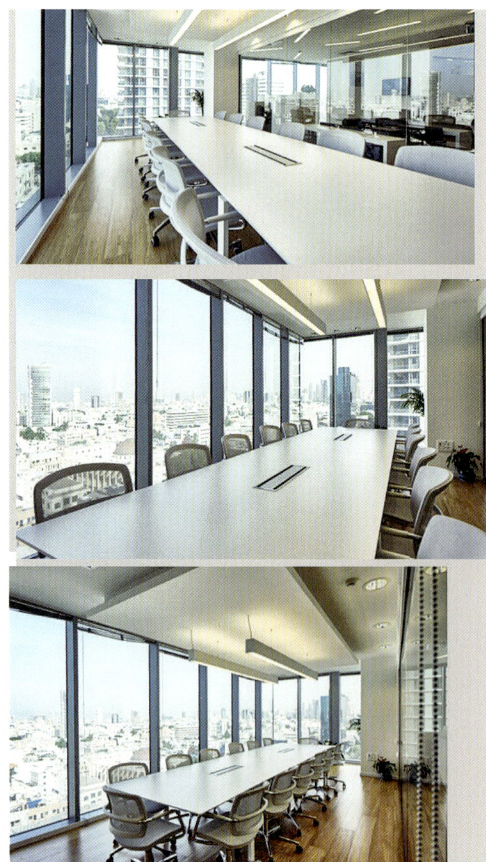

Web images of Regus, Rothschild Center, Tel Aviv, accessed December, 2018

The Untold Compromise, Ventilator gallery, temporarily at Regus, Rothschild Center, Tel Aviv, 2019

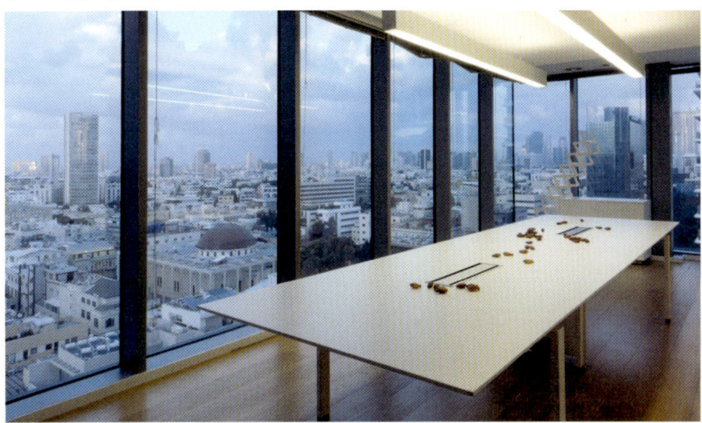

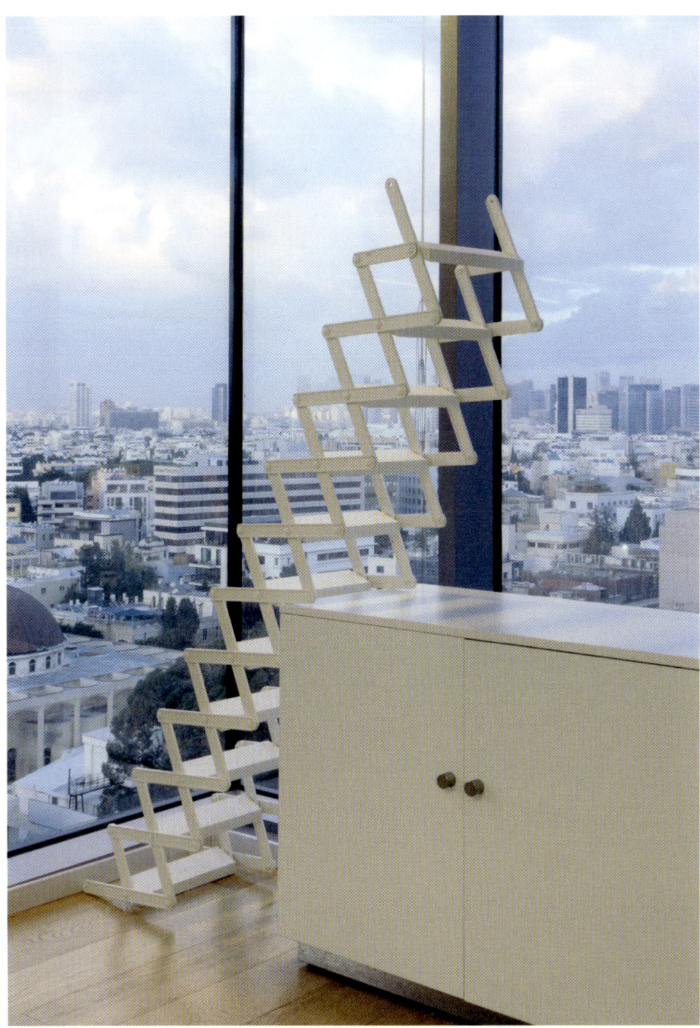

You can catch Maria on the stairs, 2018, powder coated aluminum, 37.5 – 300 × 52 × 46 cm, in The Untold Compromise, Ventilator gallery, temporarily at Regus, Rothschild Center, Tel Aviv, 2019

Ghost Tones, 2017, HD video, sound, 18', in The Untold Compromise, Ventilator gallery, temporarily at Regus, Rothschild Center, Tel Aviv, 2019

Date Series (Medjool), 2017, mold-blown glass, variable dimensions, 50 uniques, in The Untold Compromise, Ventilator gallery, temporarily at Regus, Rothschild Center, Tel Aviv, 2019

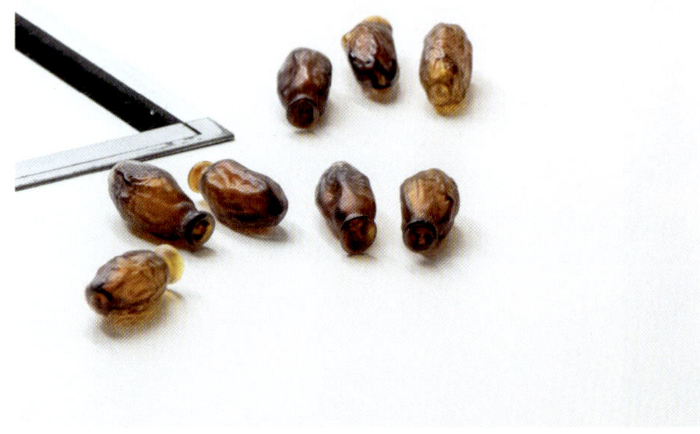

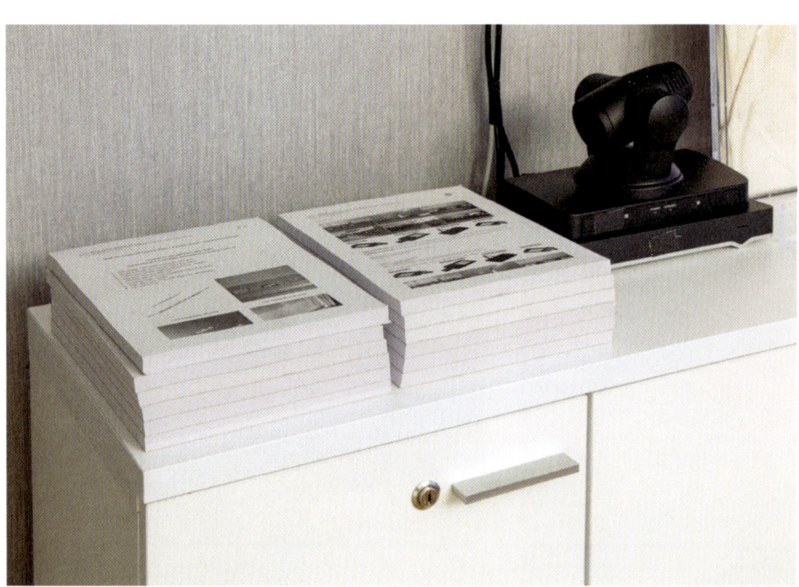

Extract from Alibaba Mails, 2017, artist book published by The Kingsboro Press, Los Angeles / New York City, in The Untold Compromise, Ventilator gallery, temporarily at Regus, Rothschild Center, Tel Aviv, 2019

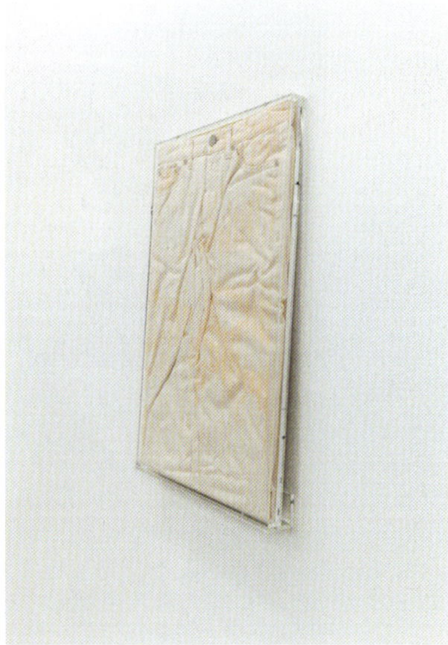

Alviero Martini, Voyage, 2016/2017, jeans, acrylic glass, 90 × 60 × 3 cm

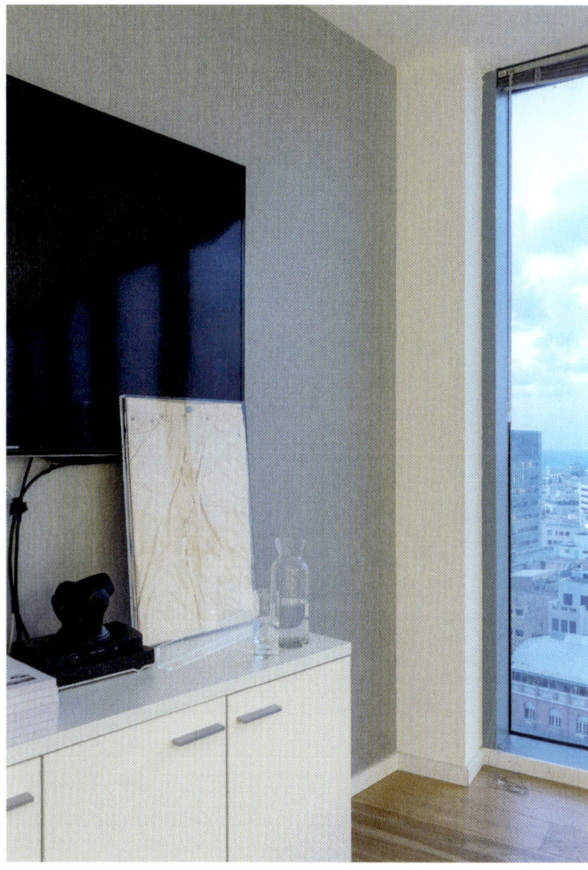

Alviero Martini, Voyage, 2016/2017, jeans, acrylic glass, 90 × 60 × 3 cm, in The Untold Compromise, Ventilator gallery, temporarily at Regus, Rothschild Center, Tel Aviv, 2019

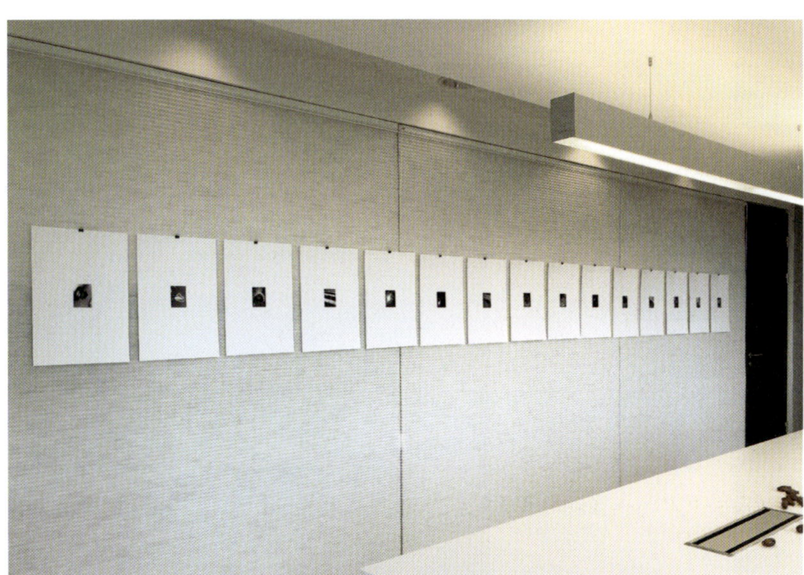

Detail of Disparate Images, 2019, in The Untold Compromise, Ventilator gallery, temporarily at Regus, Rothschild Center, Tel Aviv, 2019

Disparate Images, 2019,
inkjet prints, 22-parts, each 48.3 × 33 cm

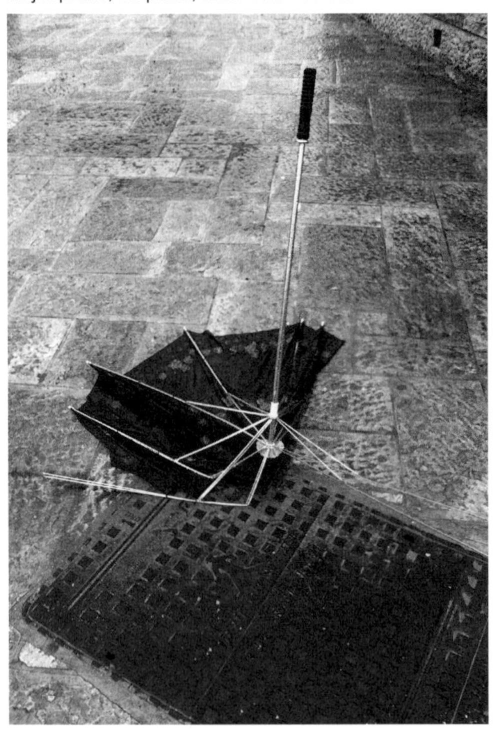

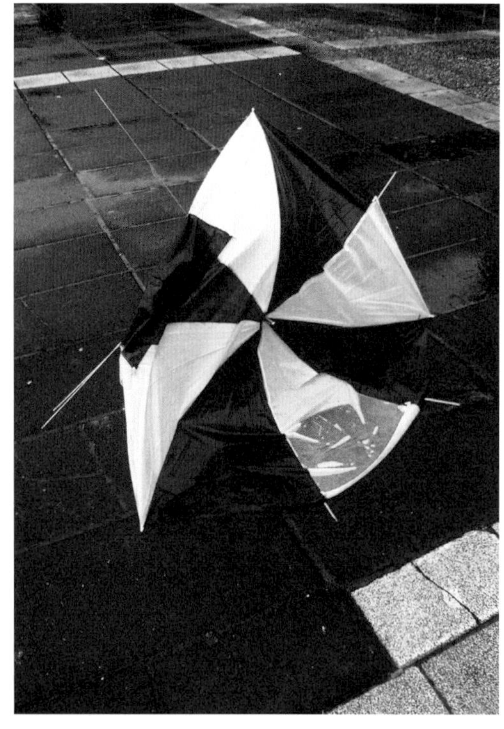

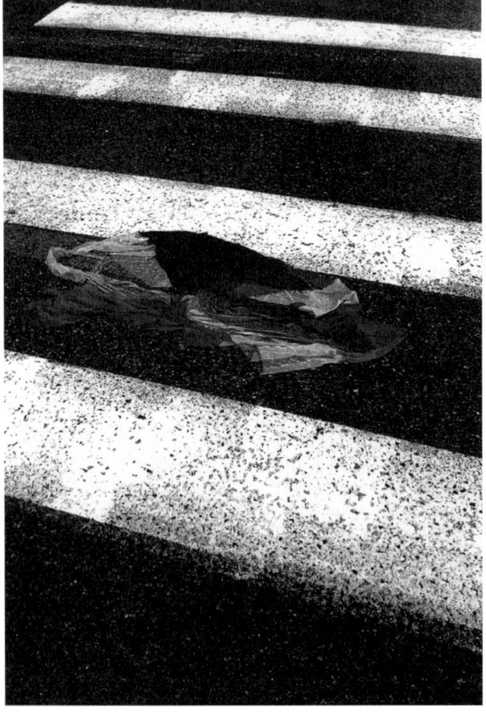

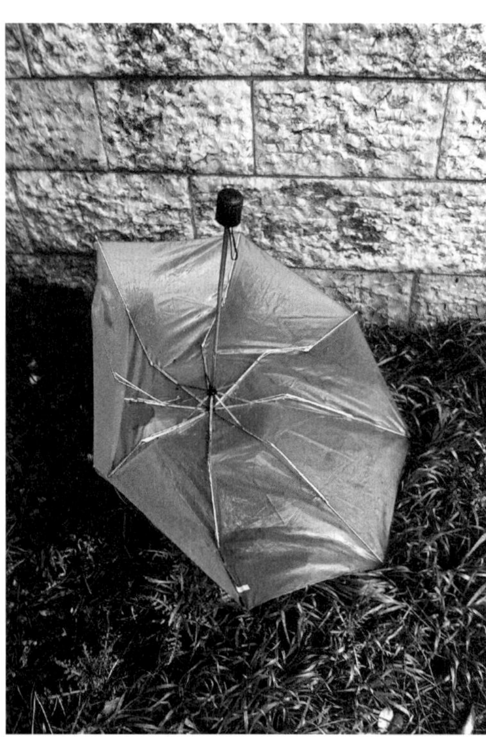

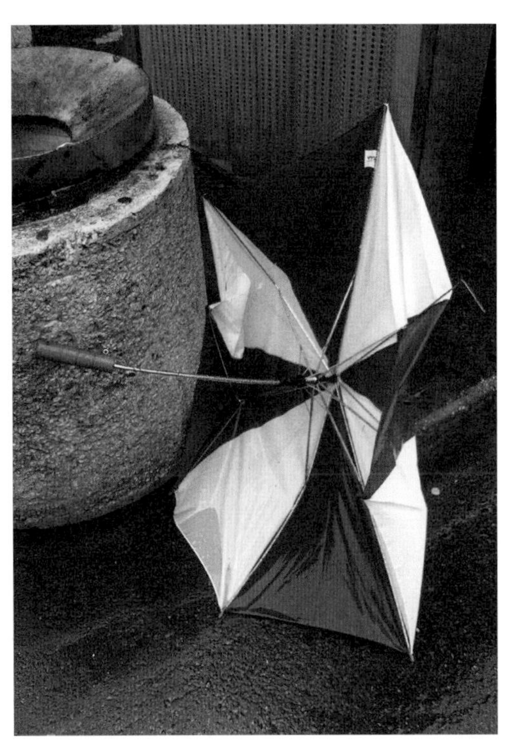
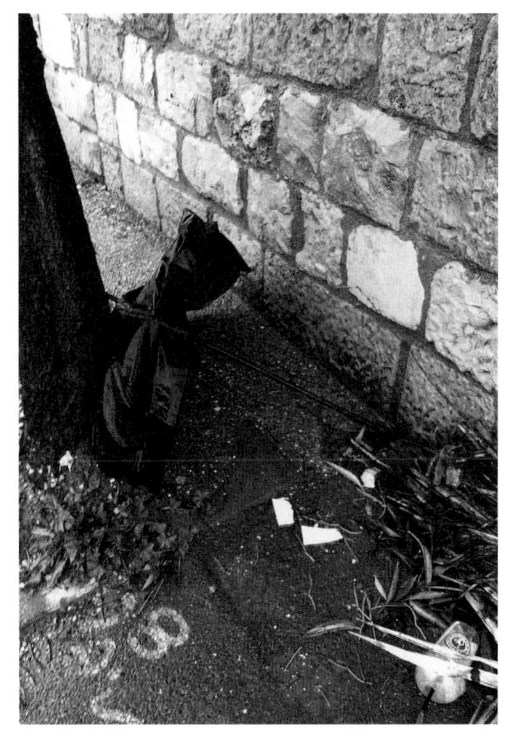

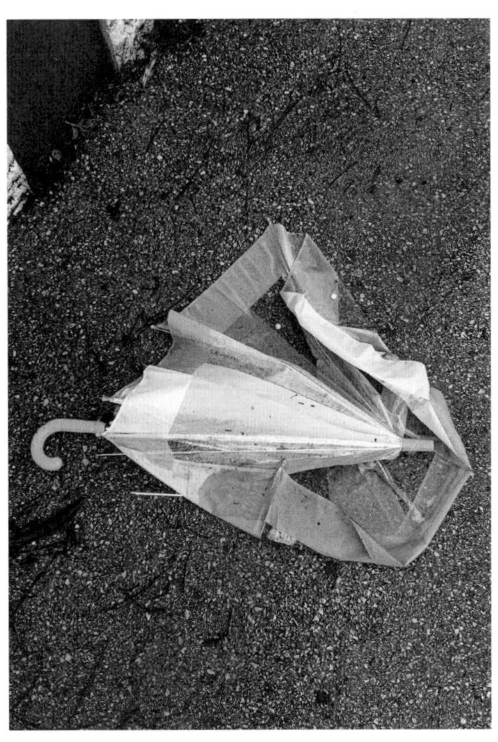
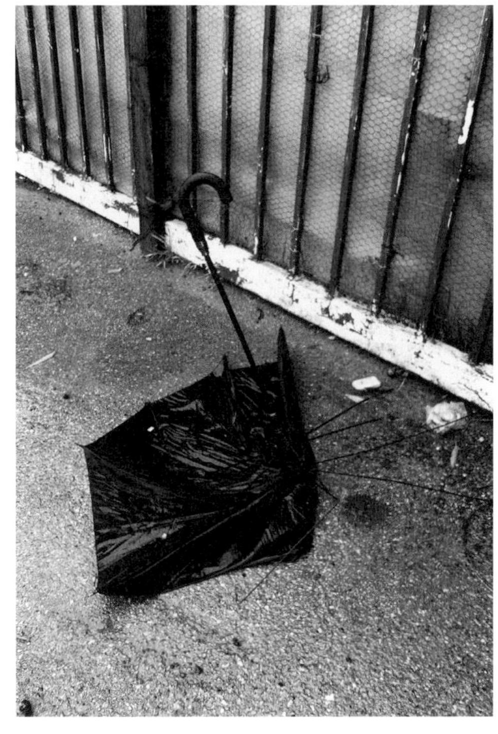

Disparate Images, 2019,
inkjet prints, 22-parts, each 48.3 × 33 cm

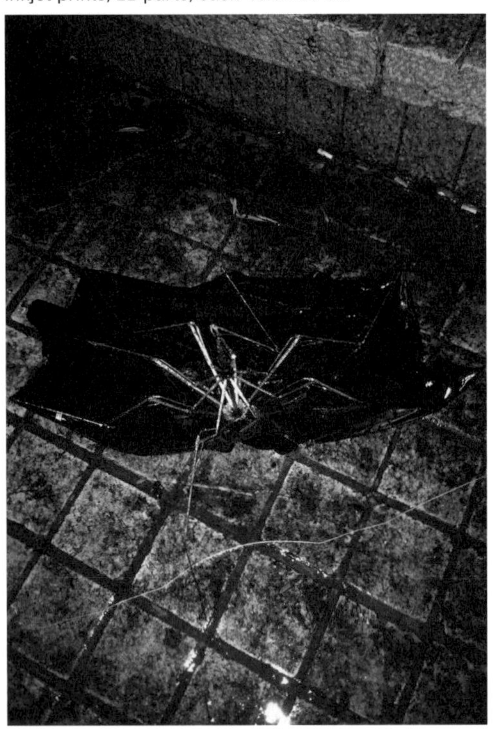

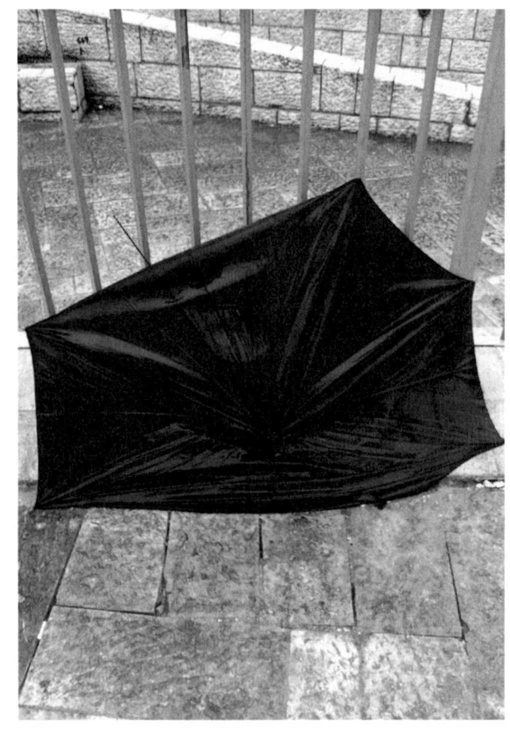

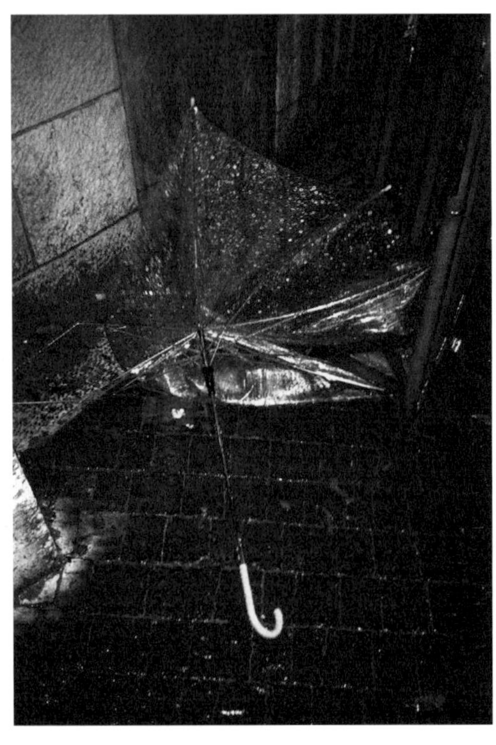

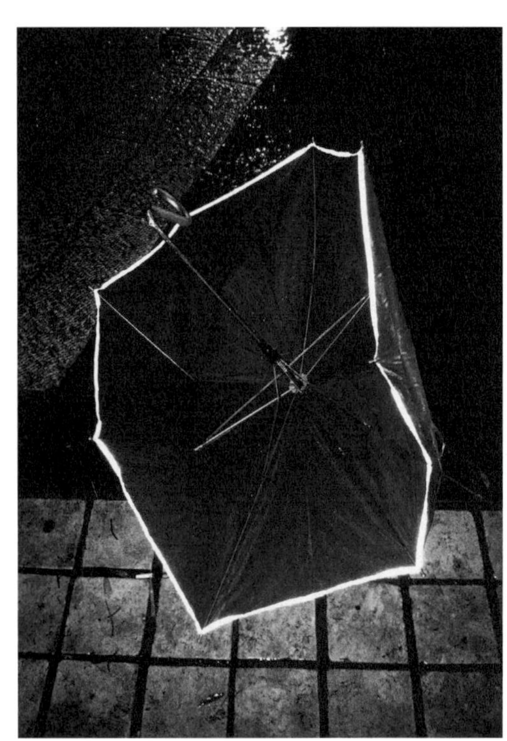

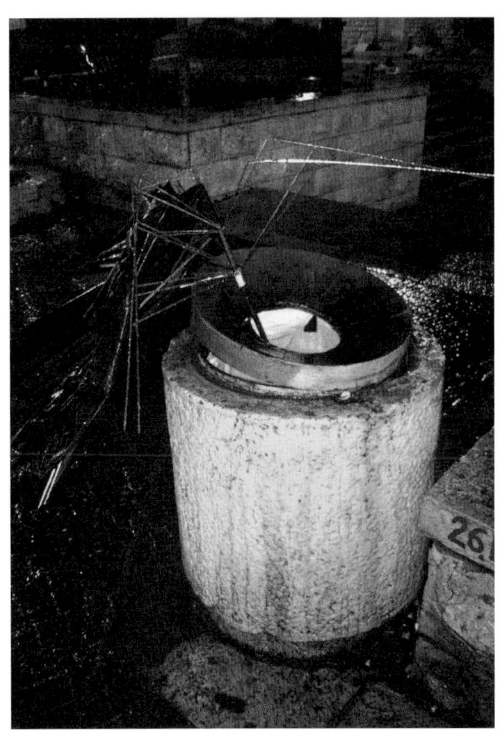

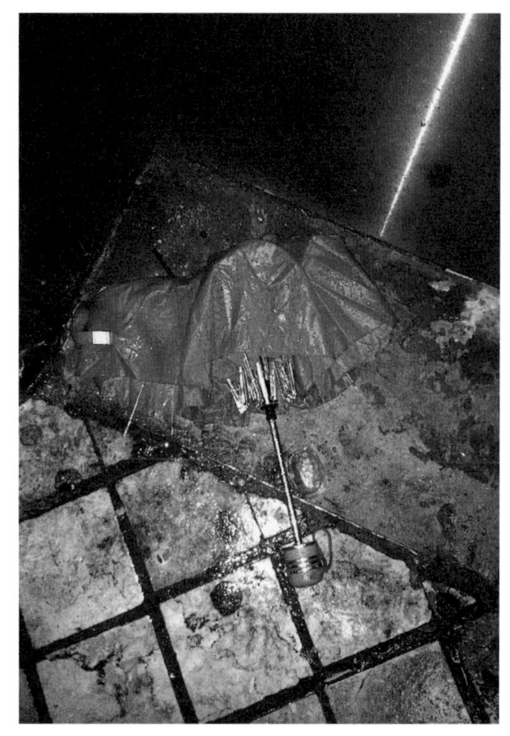

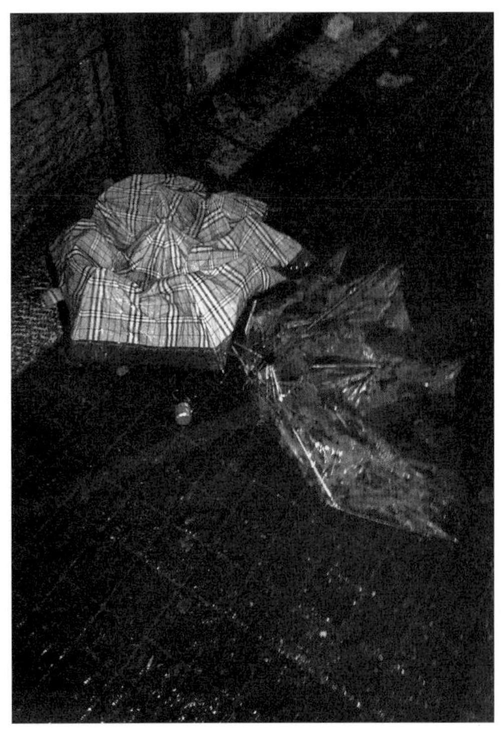

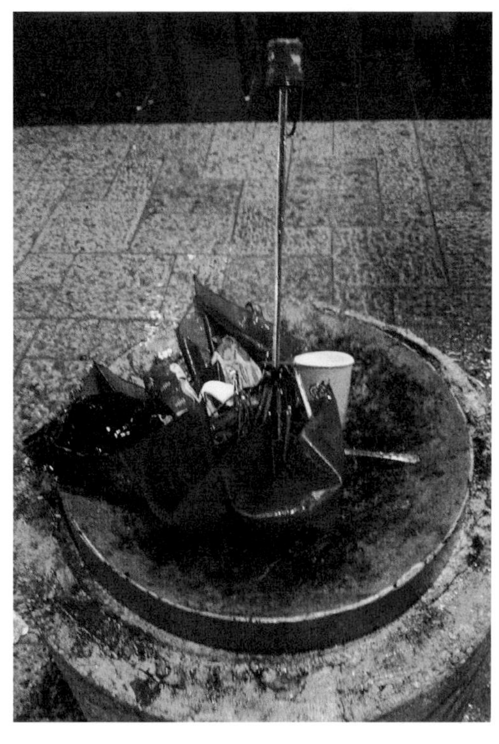

Disparate Images, 2019,
inkjet prints, 22-parts, each 48.3 × 33 cm

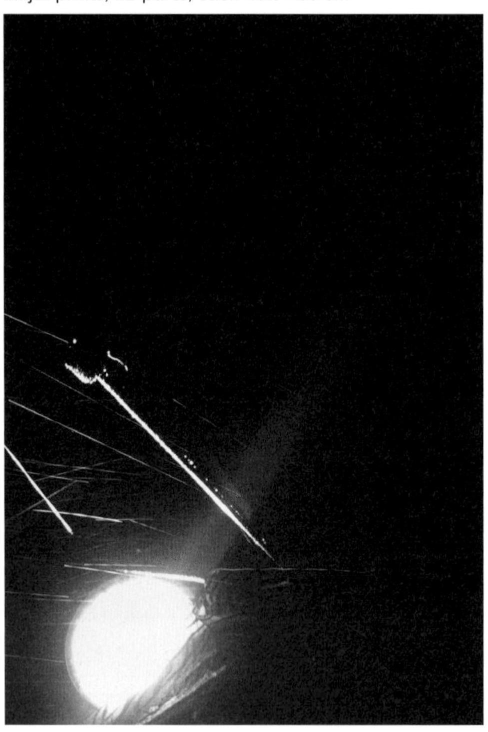

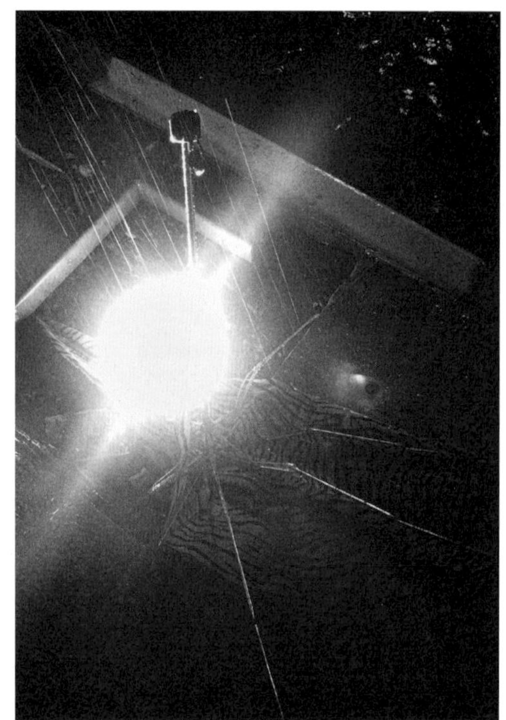

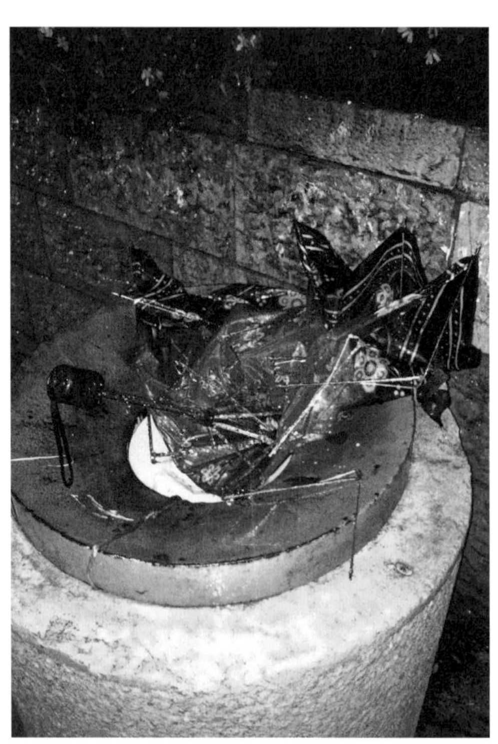

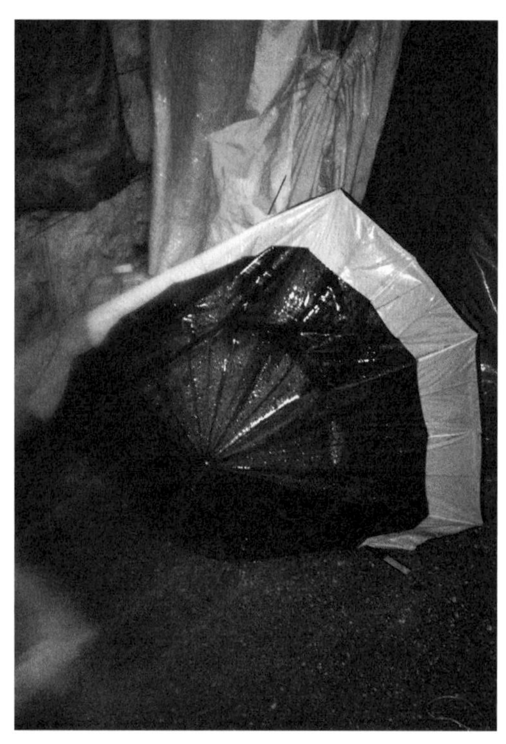

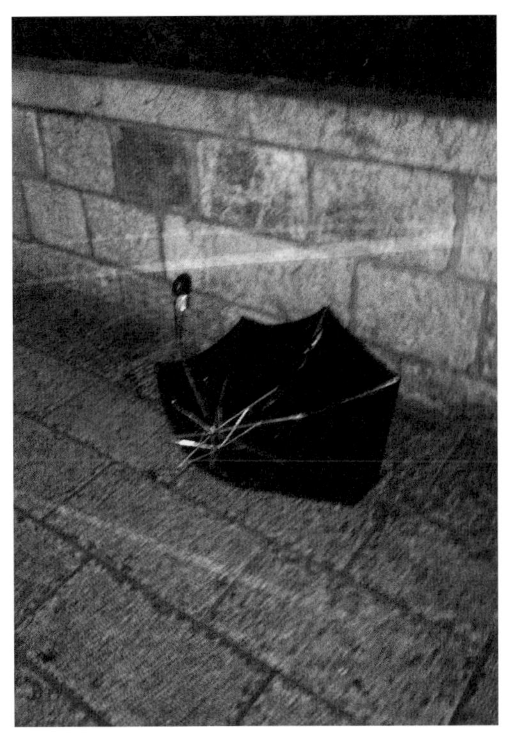

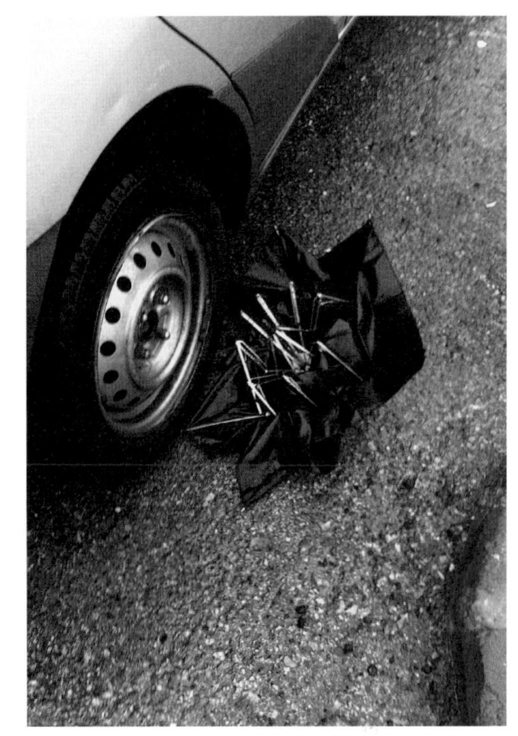

Cheap Images
On Judith Kakon's Poetics of Exchange

by Boaz Levin

The emails often come in bursts of twos or threes. Some are business-like, to the point, others include elaborate greetings, emojis, or personal notes. Most are written in the stilted English of auto-translation—an amalgam of misused turns of phrase, flawed grammar, stray commas, a wasteland of literalness—though their basic intended meaning is conveyed nonetheless, that of transaction. At times, a vague sense of proximity radiates through:

> [From Untitled (Alibaba, Stickers), 2016/2017, p. 46]
> Dear Judith,
> I hope everything goes well with you.
> Pls kindly view the attached pictures, these flowers make me want to go to the mountain. I like the nature.
> The most important thing, I hope these flowers can send my best wishes to you.
> Best Wishes, Coral

Judith Kakon started documenting her correspondence with retailers selling through the Chinese e-commerce platform Alibaba back in 2013, just as the company was about to go public in what would become the largest initial public offering (IPO) to date. At first, Kakon simply wanted to purchase a particular type of LED light panel for an art project she was working on, and Alibaba offered access to retail-priced products then still unavailable in Israel, where she was studying. But her communication with a myriad of sales representatives—some of them bots, others real living sales people, all pitching their wares assertively, often directly linked to production sites in China's industrial zones—quickly became her main focus.

The artist has long been interested in the intricacies of exchange in a world shaped by markets, and in the friction and contradictions of our everyday interactions with this world. Her works look into the ways by which commodities are brought into circulation, and the challenges of representing their flows, despite their global reach, their ubiquity, and their matter-of-factness. There's a sense of wonder and curiosity about processes we tend to take for granted, starting from that rather unassuming question: how does a commodity arrive on our doorstep? The sleight of hand of global logistics, the labor that goes into commodities' production, their afterlife as waste, in other words, the world of things in movement, hidden in plain sight, is her subject. Through these emails, we're reminded that this is not just a reality of shipping containers, ports, and freight trains (though they, too, are often either purposefully obscured, or conveniently forgotten) but also one that is steered and lubricated by mundane personal communications between suppliers, retailers and end-customers, a semblance (or vestige?) of personal relations, however tenuous or artificial.

Reading these emails now, in the midst of a pandemic that has upended global trade and exposed its logistical underbelly, I try and imagine what it would be like if I were to happen upon this trove of texts and images in some distant future, the literal and pictorial refuse of a civilization by then long lost. Images and texts attesting to commodity flows across distances, a world enmeshed by elaborate supply chains.

> [From Untitled (Alibaba, Stickers), 2016/2017, p. 44]
> Hi,
> For your reference, we already returned to normal work from the wonderful spring holiday.
> Now I am refreshed and full of enthusiasm for my work and life.
> Wish we both can make a break-through and welcome a bumper harvest this year! ^_^
> Is there anything I can do for you this moment?
> Appreciate your kind response.
> Rainey Lee

A similar impulse informs Kakon in her ongoing excavation of these emails for her work. The texts and images take on a variety of shapes and forms—becoming stickers, prints, books, carpets—echoing, in their material mutability, the flexible logic of just-in-time manufacturing. For her series Untitled (Alibaba) (2016–2020), Kakon produced stickers bearing aphoristic quotes that were then posted in public space and documented, their documentation, in turn, becoming a series of prints (pp. 42–43). Equal parts self-help platitude and business pitch, the texts are reminiscent of Jenny Holzer's iconic Truisms (1978–1987), an assortment of maxims combining contradictory perspectives and ideologies which were, also, pasted as posters in public space. But unlike Holzer's texts, with their ambivalent mix of authentic interiority and surface, these quotes are markedly outsourced, in other words, even more generic and distant—and *cheaper*.

> [From Untitled (Alibaba, Stickers), 2016/2017, p. 46 / p. 44]
> "We are confident that those lights will win more projects for you, let's work together and make money together!"
> Or, "I find that the harder I work, the more luck I seem to have."
> :-)

In this, the Untitled (Alibaba) series epitomizes a central aspect of Kakon's work: much of it deals with cultures of exchange by way of what could best be described as the legacy and logic of the "cheap image." By "cheap," I don't mean of inferior quality. Nor do I refer here to what Hito Steyerl calls the "poor image," beautifully summarized by her as the "lumpen proletarian in the class society of appearances."[1] Rather, I'm thinking of what journalist Raj Patel and environmental historian Jason W. Moore have described as the making of "the modern world ... through seven cheap things: nature, money, work, care, food, energy, and lives."[2] As they write, *cheapening* is a set of strategies to control our natural environment, to mobilize nature—be it through violence, culture, or knowledge—at a low cost. In order to survive, capitalism creates—and is in turn created by—new "frontiers," sites "where power is exercised," moving "from one place to the next, transforming socioecological relations, producing more and more kinds of goods and services that circulate through an expanding series of exchanges."[3] To their list of seven cheap things, I would add one more: "cheap images." Serial and later industrial image production—from early wood and then copper-based print-making techniques, the daguerreotype, and later photographic technologies, to today's digital images of code and cobalt—has been integral to the advent of capitalism starting in the 16th century, and it's expansion and reinvention ever since. Without cheap images with which to advertise things, landscapes, and people, with which to venerate sovereigns or surveil subjects, we wouldn't have "cheap" nature, food, labor, or energy. And vice versa: ever since its inception a vast network of trade, resource extraction, labor, and energy had to be in place for the production of the cheap image to be possible. In other words, the cheap image and the age of capitalism—what Moore and Patel refer to as the Capitalocene—are co-constitutive.

Serial and industrial image production's reciprocal relation to capitalist expansion is echoed throughout Kakon's work. For her solo exhibition The Untold Compromise (2019), the artist rented out a conference room in a luxurious skyscraper at Tel-Aviv's Rothschild Boulevard 22 for a single day (pp. 94–97). The site of the countries' stock-exchange and its economic epicenter, Rothschild Boulevard was also at the heart of the 2011 social protests, spurred by rising living costs and increasing inequality. At the time, protestors occupied the entire length of "Rothschild," as it's known, with an impromptu "tent city." Eight years later, the encampment now long gone, one of Rothschild 22's main occupants is Regus, a Swiss multinational corporation offering subleased "co-working" spaces to the city's burgeoning start-up scene. In 2017 a local newspaper revealed that the building's air-conditioned lobby is in fact one of several privately owned public spaces (or POPS) that should, in theory, be accessible to the general public.

Like Kakon's Untitled (Alibaba, Stickers), which seem to appear surreptitiously in public space, The Untold Compromise, too, was conceived as a work of stealth (pp. 94–97). From the start, it was imperative that the entire exhibition fit in a suitcase, lending the project a sort of infrastructural premise: trolley-friendly, planned for the Easy-Jet-set and their subleased co-working frontier. One of the works shown there was Disparate Images (2019), a series of 22 black-and-white inkjet prints depicting broken umbrellas (pp. 98–103). As the exhibition's curator Ishai Shapira Kalter has written, these are individual shelters with a limited shelf life, exemplifying "a global consumer product that becomes unique only once it breaks."[4] The result is a typology of mundane obsolescence. At the center of the room, on a large conference table, several dozen dates were strewn, brown and semi-opaque. Part of Kakon's Date Series (2017), these are, in fact, date-shaped glass flasks, similar to those produced across the Levant during the first century AD (pp. 113–115).[5] Among the most common mold-blown vessels at the time, and an early example of serialized production, these date-shaped flacons—molded using real dates, and thus preserving their imprint—were used to store precious liquids, such as scented oil or medicine. Archeological records suggest the date palm was domesticated in Mesopotamia as early as 3000 B.C—making it one of the oldest human-cultivated plants—disseminating from there along trade routes to the Arabian peninsula, North Africa, and India.[6] Yet the story of how dates became staples of our globalized economy, a Levantine fixture in health stores and markets from LA to Sidney, started in earnest in 1898, when a special unit of the US Department of Agriculture known as "Agriculture Explorers" was sent to Baghdad. A "date experimental station" for the "biblical fruit" was consequently established in the arid "American Sahara" of the Californian Coachella Valley. There, the fruit was advertised using the sort of "exotic imagery and fantasy many Americans associated with the Middle East."[7] Nowadays, the largest, softest, most lucrative and sought-after strain—the "king of dates"—is without a doubt the *Medjool*. Originating in a single oasis in Morocco, in recent years the Medjool has become an export of Israeli agricultural settlements and *Kibbutzim* (adopted via California) whose palm groves carpet much of the occupied Jordan Valley's arid planes, responsible for no less than three quarters of the cultivar's global market.[8] Meanwhile, in the Oasis of Boudenib, Morocco, the palm has been wiped out by disease, and efforts are being made to reintroduce it using modern strands imported from Coachella Valley.

Judith Kakon's work conjures such complex global histories of cultivation, exchange and frontier economies. Like the stickers, the date flacons are used as subtle interventions in whichever space they are shown: whether placed casually on a painting's frame, or a shelf, or strewn, as in The Untold Compromise, on a conference table. They could be remnants of some event that transpired, artifacts hinting at a drama left unseen—we tend to read them, that is, for clues. Kakon's work often functions this way, consisting of modular elements, agile and variable, which then populate exhibitions like evidence in a crime scene. In The Untold Compromise, behind the conference table, propped against a cabinet, was a semi-extended foldable aluminum staircase that led nowhere. You can catch Maria on the stairs (2018) (p. 95) consists of an aluminum ready-made expandable ladder that the artist disassembled. On her instructions, craftsmen then finished the individual components with a white powder coating before she reassembled the ladder herself. This sort of laboriousness reminds us that this thing, too, was an object of care and the product of work—that it, too, had to make the obstreperous voyage of things in circulation. Versions of this sculpture, each titled differently—displaying degrees of extension, or contraction—have been shown by Kakon elsewhere. Could this be seen as a logical conclusion of the sort of drama which began with Marcel Duchamp's Nude Descending a Staircase, No 2. (1912), itself made in direct response to chrono-photography, the industrialization of image production and its capturing of human movement? Here, in Kakon's work, the staircase reappears as a ready-made. Yet if Duchamp's gesture anticipated outsourcing with his subsequent ready-mades, the artist continues to work on the ready-made, partially outsourcing its modification to outsourced labor. In doing so, her work performs a doubling typical of our containerized global economy: the ready-made as a repeatedly outsourced artifact. As with the dates and emails from Alibaba.com, the ladder becomes a recurring motif in Kakon's work, an essential element of her personal grammar. Her works become things and images in a world made by this process of *cheapening*, by its *cheap images*—products in circulation, unique in their variability, and defined through their equivalence.

1 Hito Steyerl, "In Defense of the Poor Image," e-flux journal 10 (November 2009), 1, https://www.e-flux.com/journal/10/61362/in-defense-of-the-poor-image/, accessed May 7, 2021.

2 Raj Patel, Jason W. Moore, A History of the World in Seven Cheap Things: A Guide to Capitalism, Nature, and the Future of the Planet (Berkeley: University of California Press, 2017), 3.

3 Ibid., 19.

4 Ishai Shapira Kalter, "The Untold Compromise," exhibition press release, January 3, 2019, https://www.ventilator-gallery.com/judith-kakon, accessed May 7, 2021.

5 See for example the Roman date flask on the website of the Museum of the Bible, Washington, D.C., USA, https://collections.museumofthebible.org/artifacts/42465-roman-date-flask?&tab=description, accessed May 7, 2021.

6 Roy W. Nixon, "The Date Palm—'Tree of Life' in the Subtropical Deserts," Economic Botany 5, no. 3 (1951), 274–301, https://www.jstor.org/stable/4252037?seq=1, accessed May 11, 2021.

7 The Kitchen Sisters and Lisa Morehouse, "Forbidding Fruit: How America Got Turned on to the Date," Morning Edition: NPR, npr.com, National Public Radio, June 10, 2014, https://www.npr.org/sections/thesalt/2014/06/10/320346869/forbidding-fruit-how-america-got-turned-on-to-the-date, accessed May 11, 2021.

8 Ora Coren, "Hot Date: Jordan Valley Growers Conquer World's Medjool Market," Haaretz.com, the online English edition of Haaretz Newspaper in Israel, March 17, 2016, https://www.haaretz.com/israel-news/business/.premium.MAGAZINE-israelis-conquer-medjool-date-market-1.5418171, accessed May 4, 2021.

Date Series (Medjool, Barhi, Deglet Nour), 2017,
mold-blown glass, dimensions variable, 50 uniques of each kind,
Kunsthalle Basel, Basel, 2017

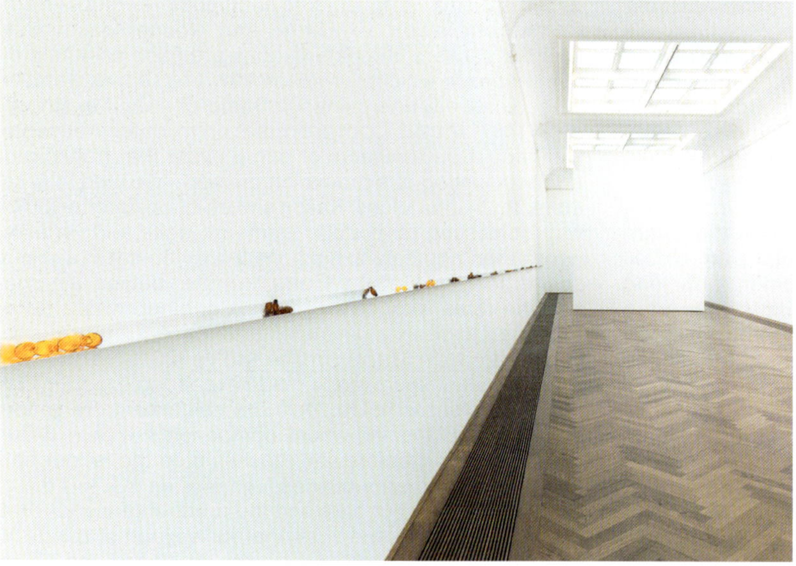

Detail of Date Series (Medjool, Barhi, Deglet Nour), 2017,
mold-blown glass, dimensions variable, 50 uniques of each kind,
Kunsthalle Basel, Basel, 2017

Still frames, Ghost Tones, 2017, HD video, stereo, 18'

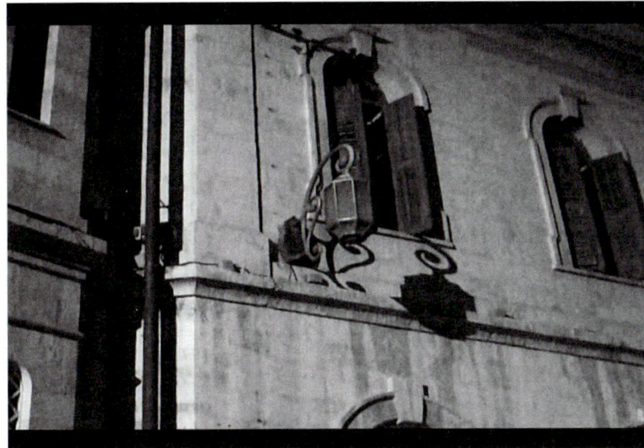

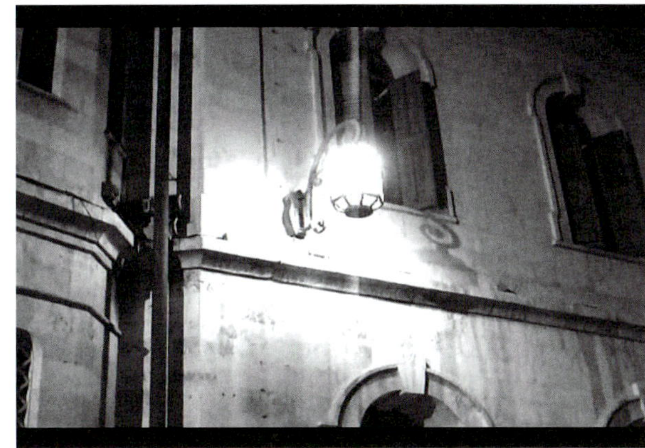

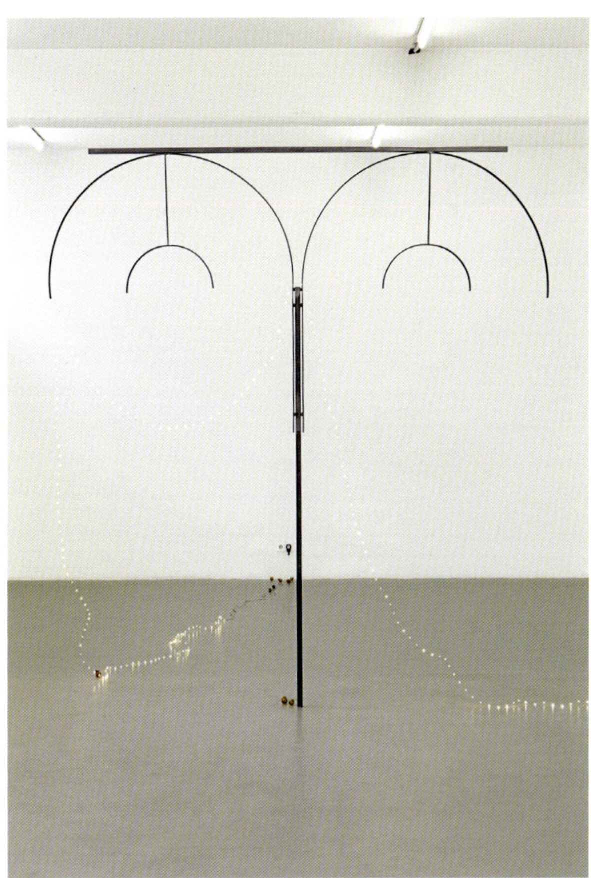

Detail of The left is formed from the right, 2017,
steel, strings of light, two-parts, each 360 × 280 cm,
Kunsthaus L6, Freiburg im Breisgau, 2017.
Exhibition view: Bernhard Strauss

Ghost Tones, 2017, HD video, stereo, 18',
Post-Disaster Residencies, Stadium de Vitrolles, Vitrolles, 2018

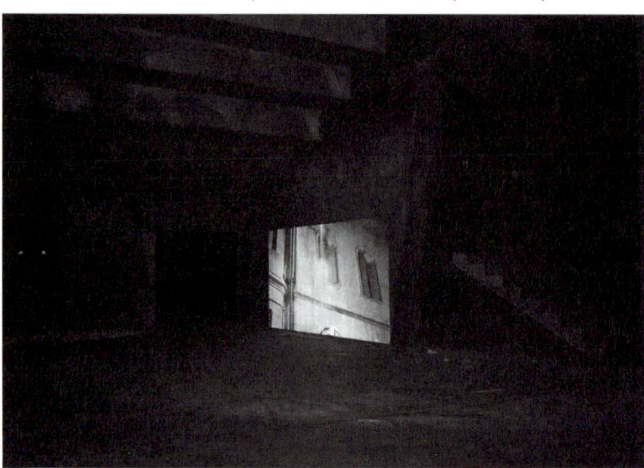

Ghost Tones, 2017, HD video, stereo, 18',
Kunsthaus L6, Freiburg im Breisgau, 2017.
Exhibition view: Bernhard Strauss

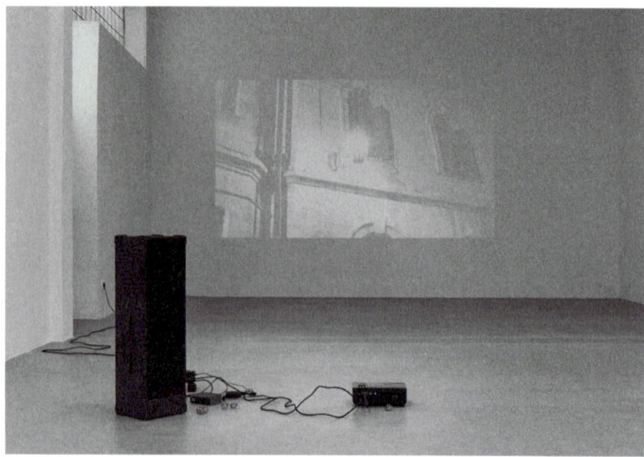

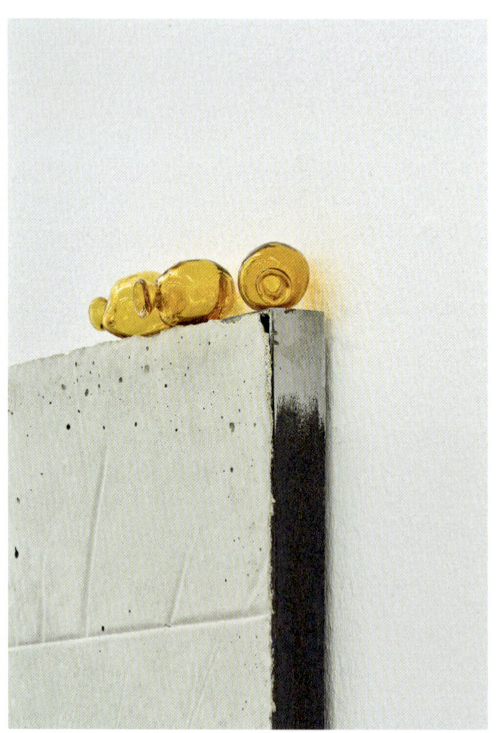

Detail of Untitled (Learn to Lay Brick) III, 2017, and Date Series (Barhi), 2017, Kunsthaus L6, Freiburg im Breisgau, 2017. Image: Bernhard Strauss

Kunstpreis Alexander Bürkle, Kunsthaus L6, Freiburg im Breisgau, 2017.
Exhibition view: Bernhard Strauss

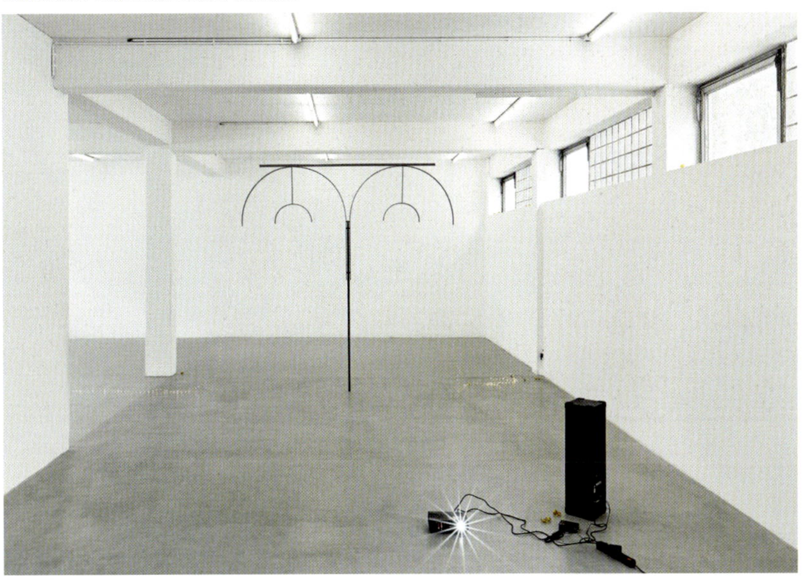

Untitled (Learn to Lay Brick) III,
2017, steel, concrete, iron-oxide, hematite, 160 × 100 cm.
Image: Bernhard Strauss

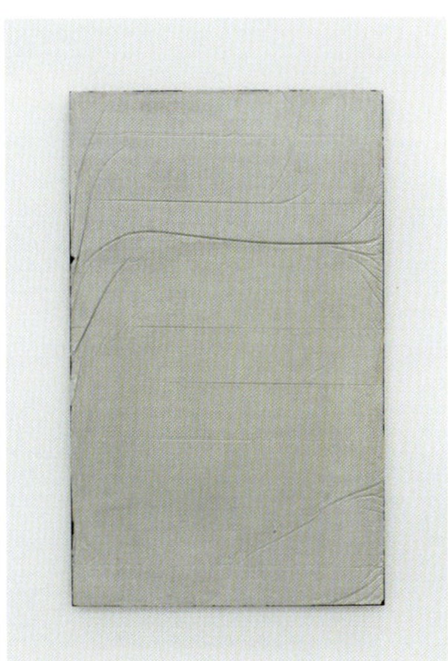

Untitled (Learn to Lay Brick) II,
2017, steel, concrete, iron-oxide, hematite, 160 × 100 cm.
Image: Bernhard Strauss

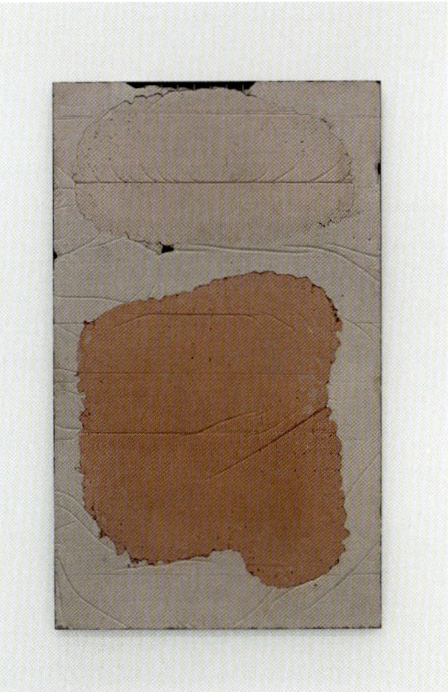

Untitled (Learn to Lay Brick) I,
2017, steel, concrete, iron-oxide, hematite, 160 × 100 cm.
Image: Bernhard Strauss

From Das Gläserne Zeitalter (1931) by Erwin Weill, found in Kunstbibliothek-Sitterwerk, St. Gallen, 2016

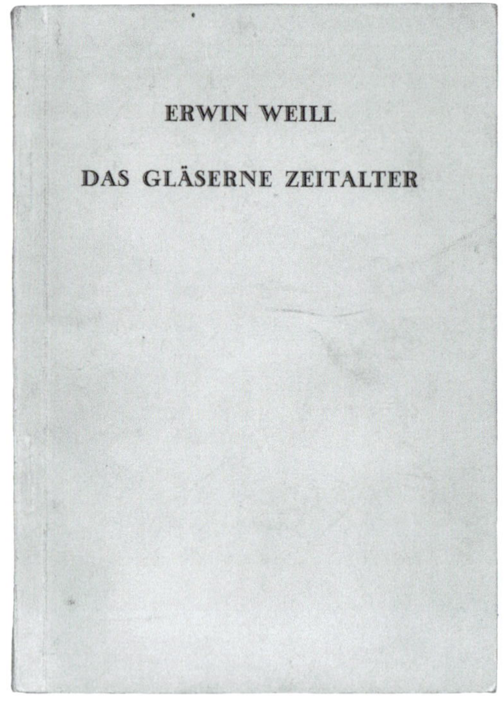

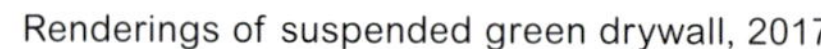
Renderings of suspended green drywall, 2017

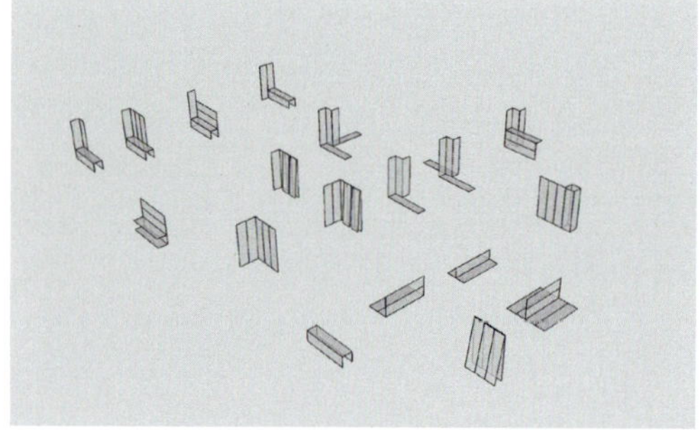

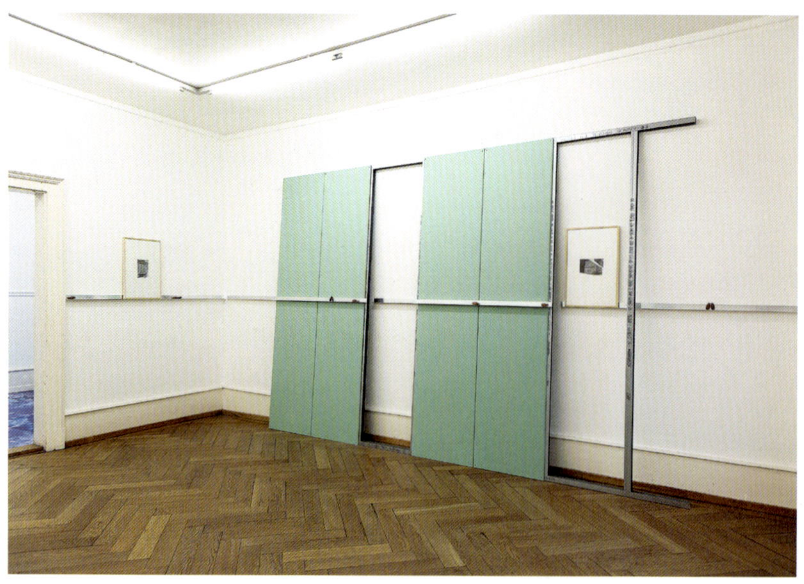

Transporting Feelings for Conceptual Objects, 2017, drywall, framework, angle sections, dimensions variable, Kunsthaus Langenthal, Langenthal, 2017

From Erwin Weill, Das Gläserne Zeitalter, 2017, Transporting Feelings for Conceptual Objects, 2017, Date Series (Medjool), 2017, Kunsthaus Langenthal, Langenthal, 2017

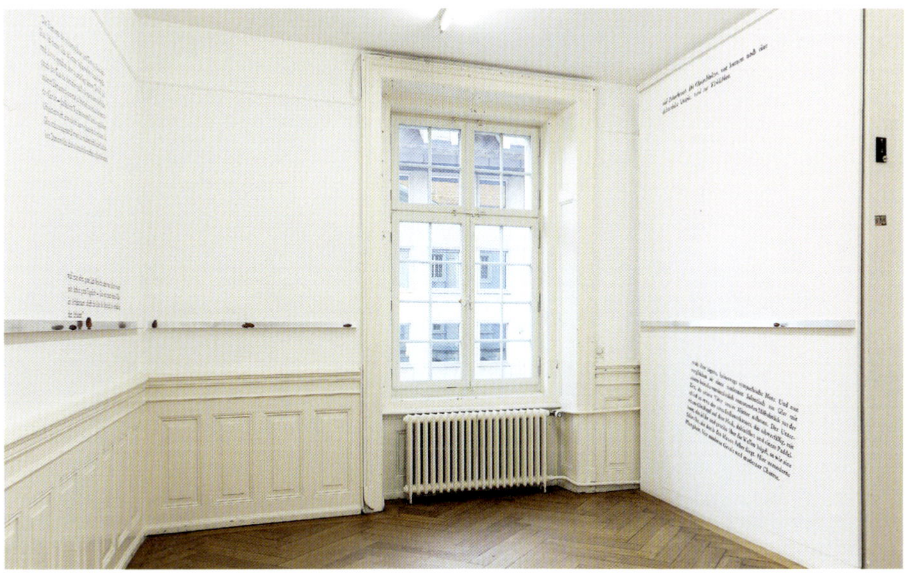

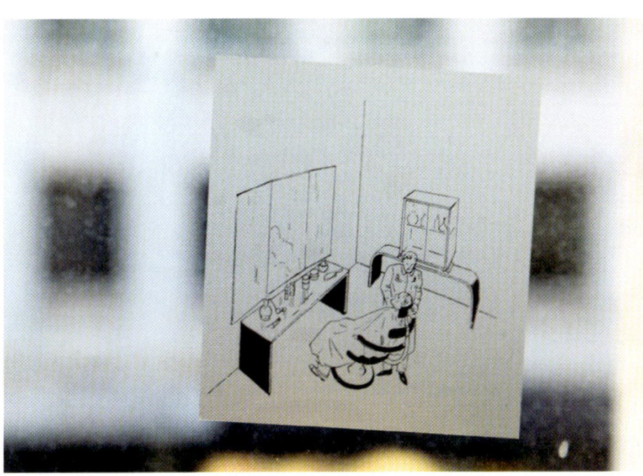

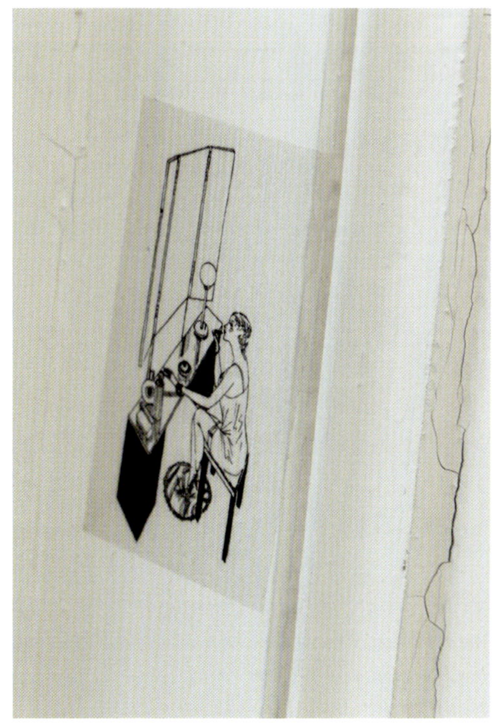

From Erwin Weill, Das Gläserne Zeitalter, 2017,
vinyl, sizes vary, Kunsthaus Langenthal, Langenthal, 2017

Guilty Containers, 2016, Transporting Feelings for Conceptual Objects, 2017, Date Series (Medjool), 2017, Kunsthaus Langenthal, Langenthal, 2017

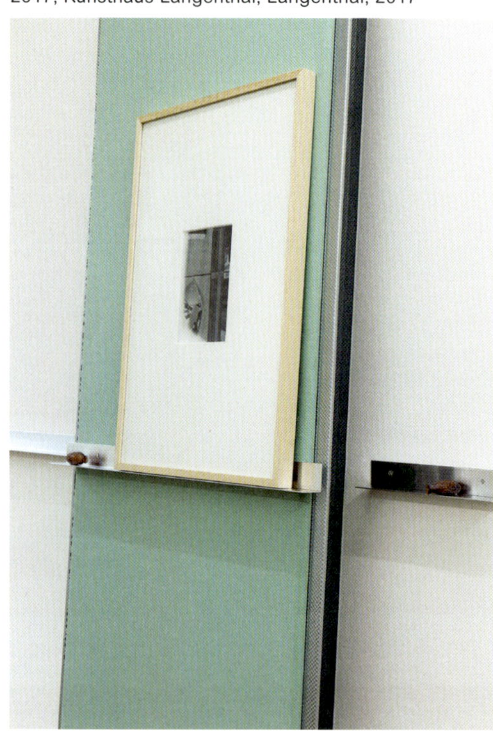

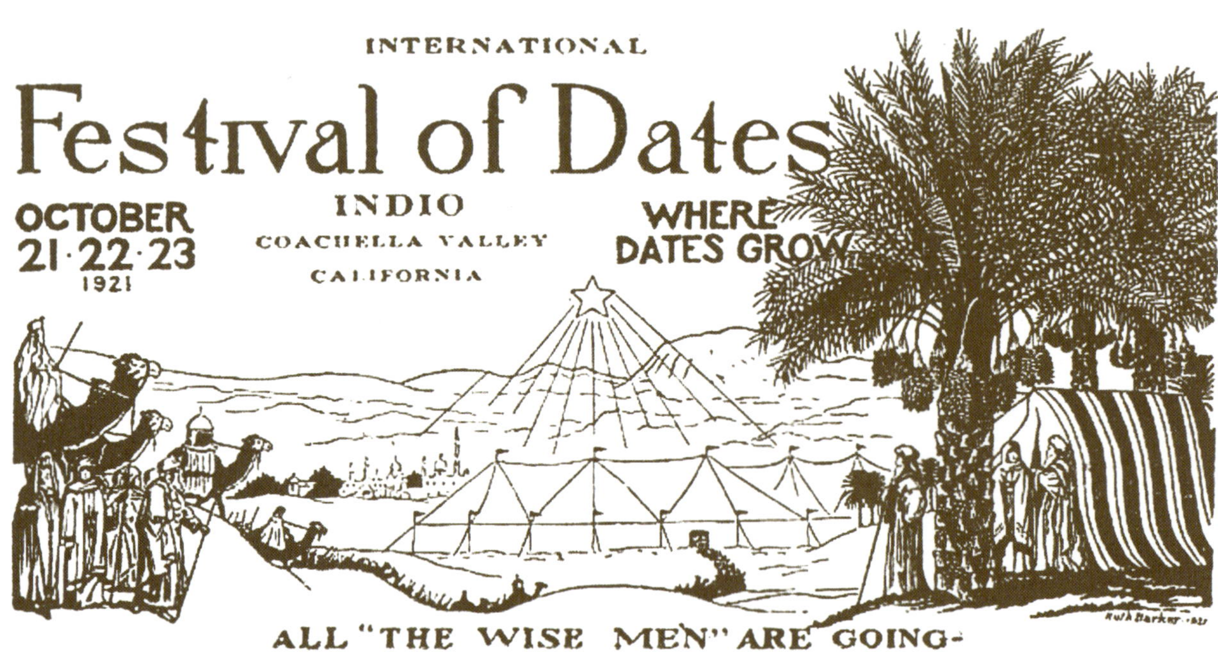

The marketing of dates grown in the Coachella Valley was based on Middle Eastern themes as America swooned over the idea of Aladdin and Ali Baba.

Courtesy of Coachella Valley History Museum

Announcement of "Festival of Dates," see description and source within image

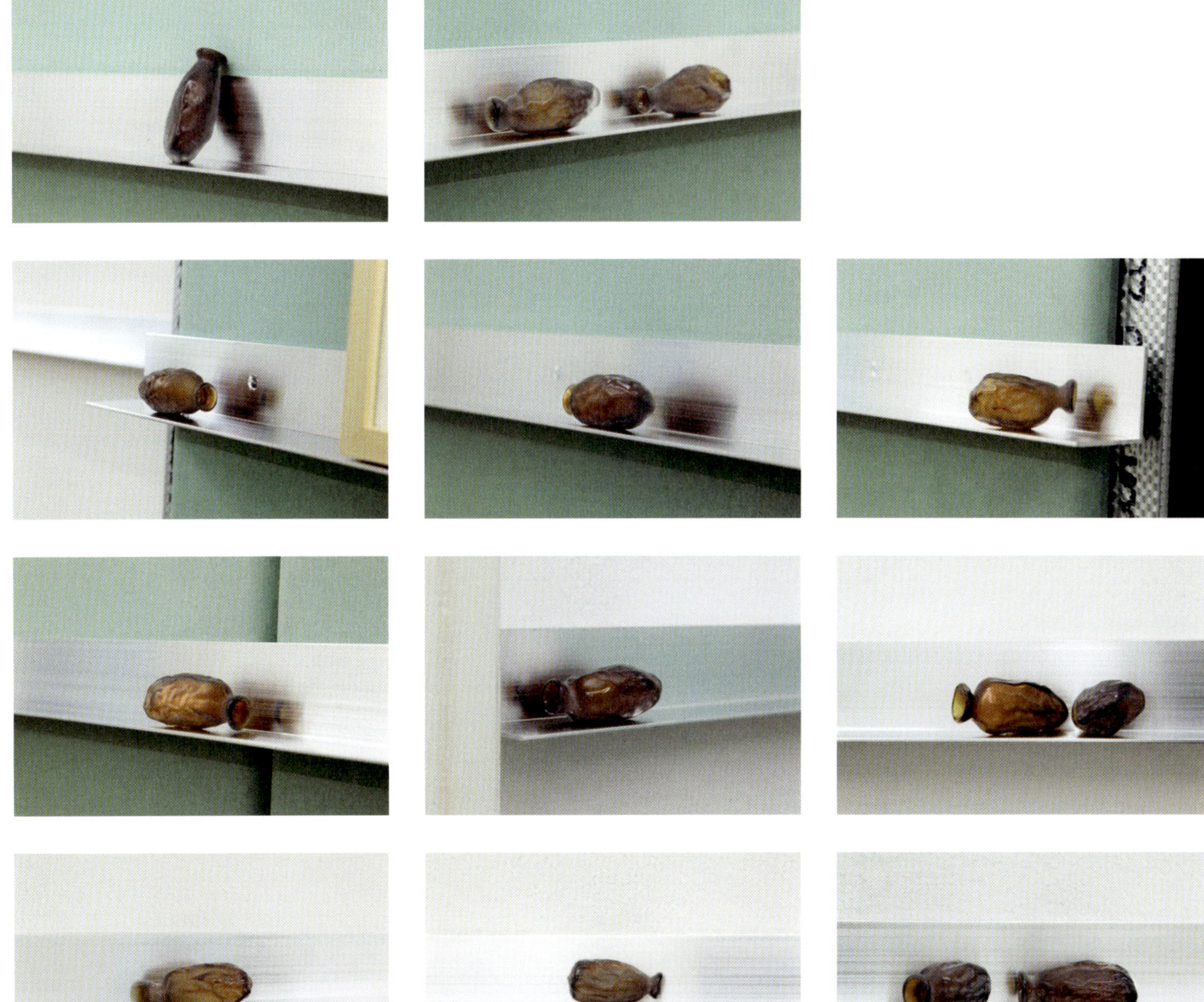

Index of all 50 pieces of Date Series (Medjool), 2017, mold-blown glass, variable dimensions, 50 uniques

Index of all 50 pieces of Date Series (Medjool), 2017, mold-blown glass, variable dimensions, 50 uniques

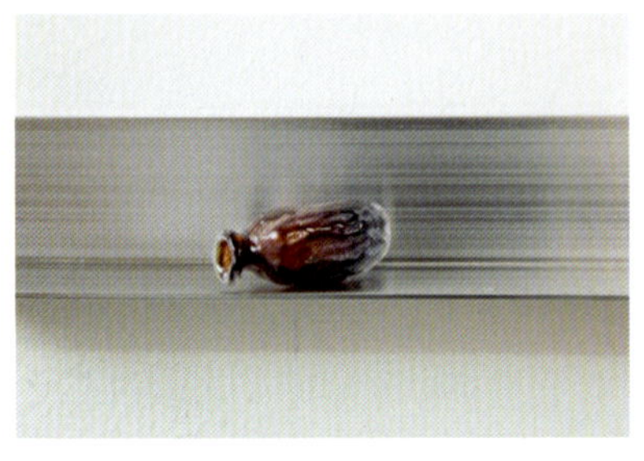
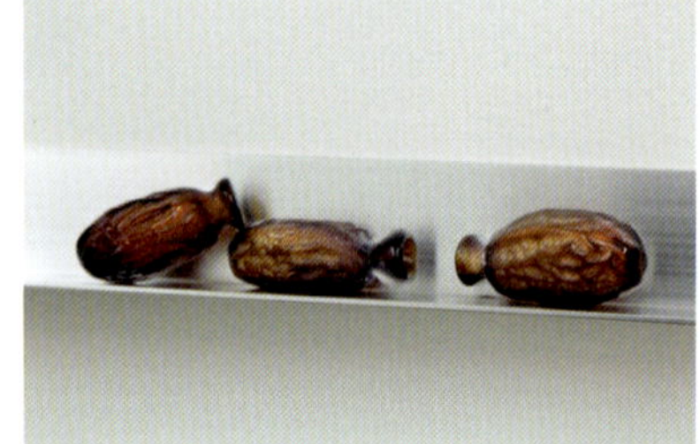
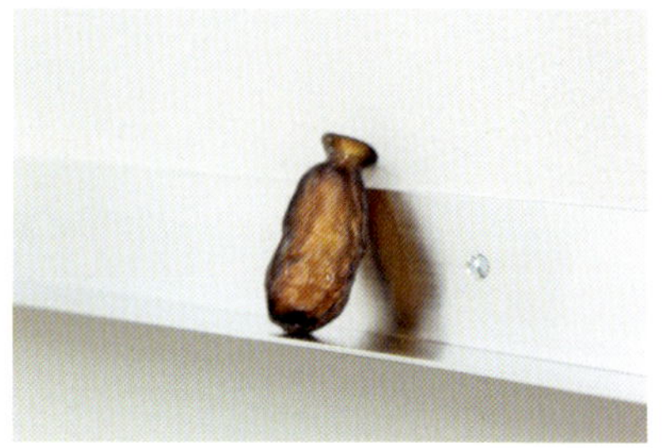
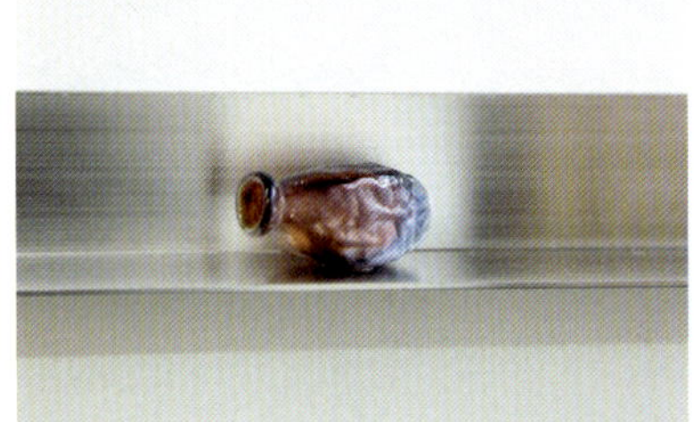
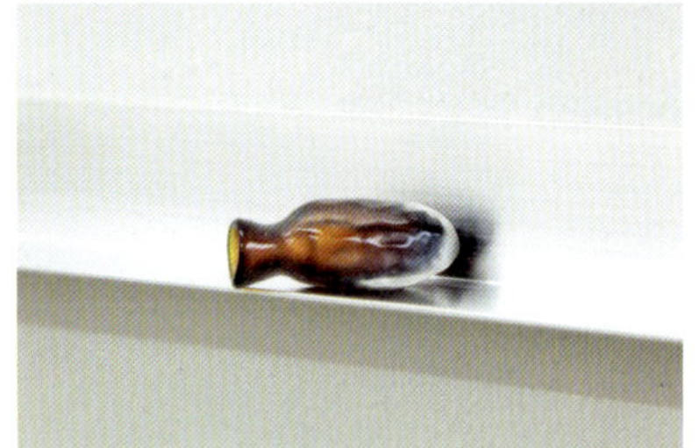
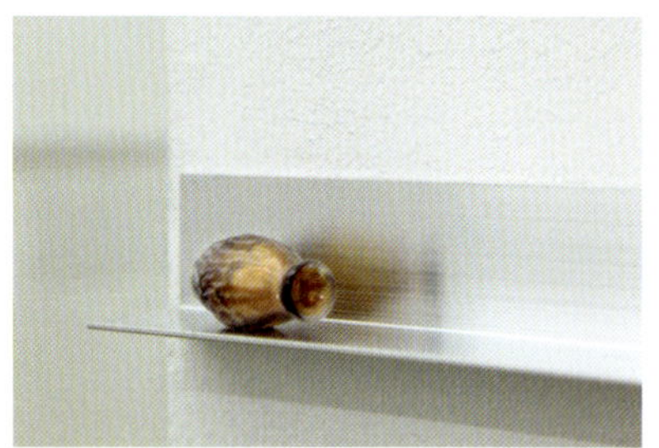
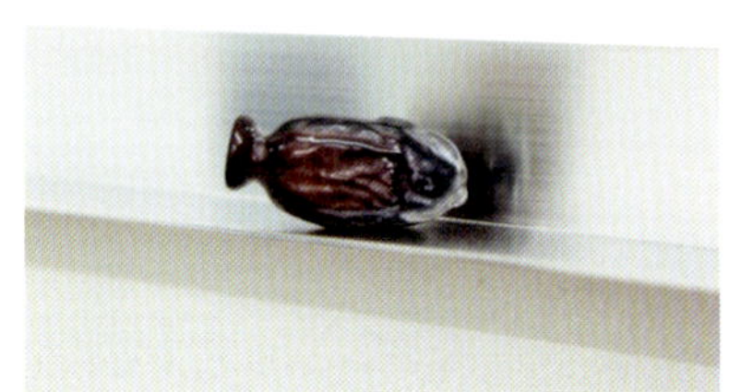
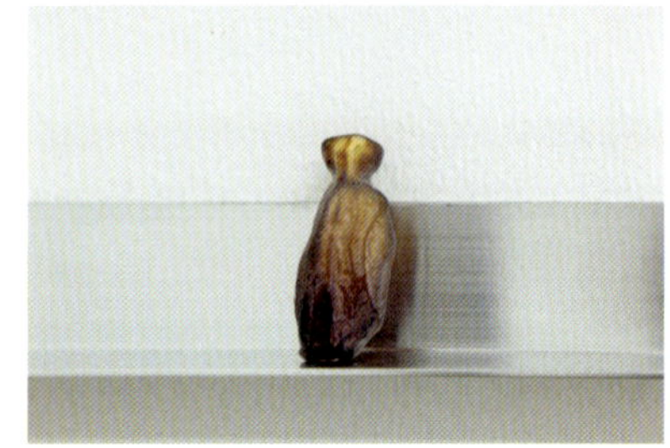
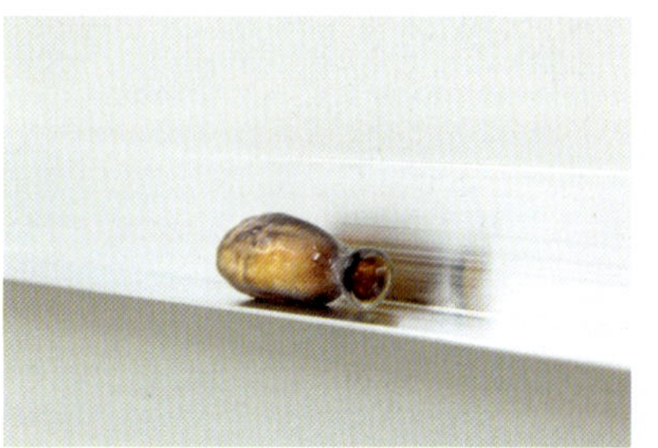
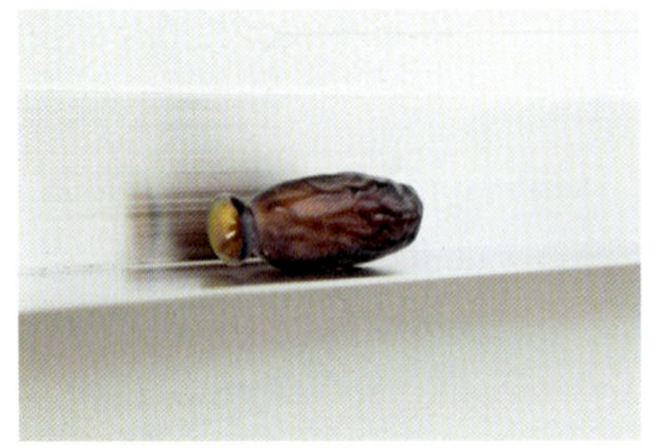
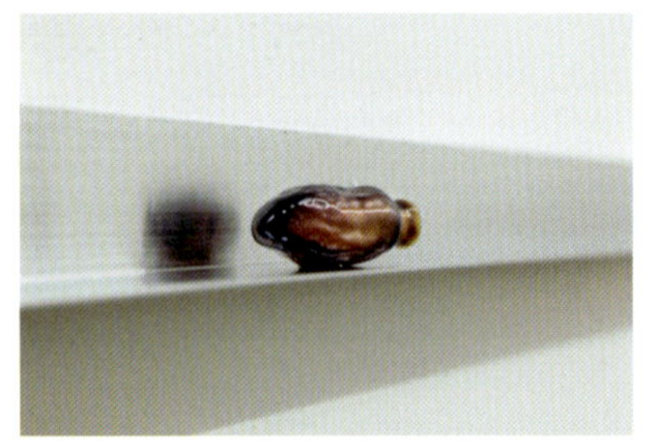
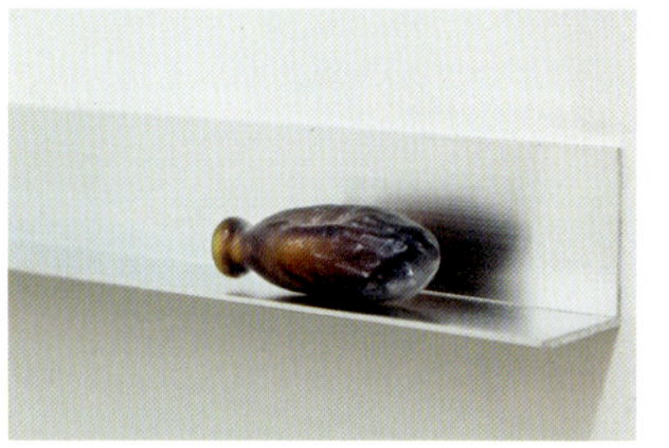
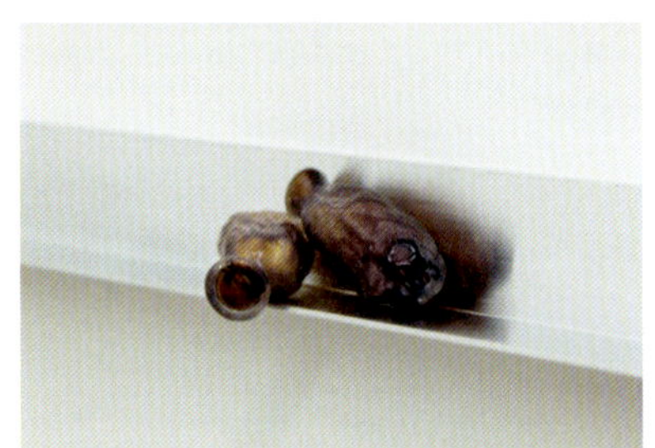
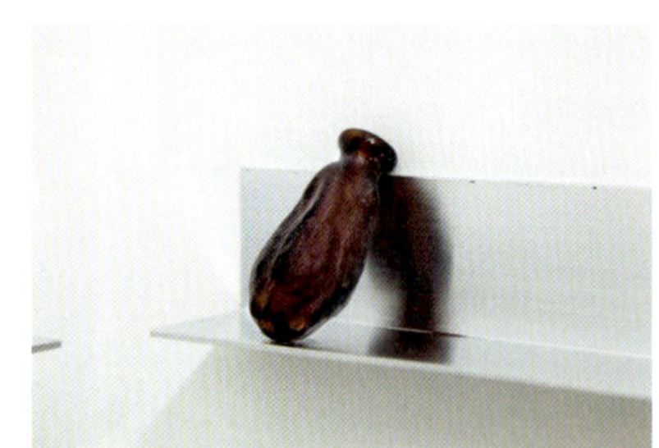
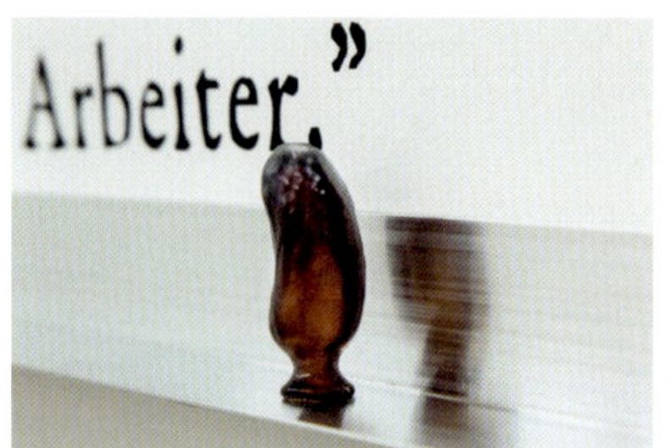

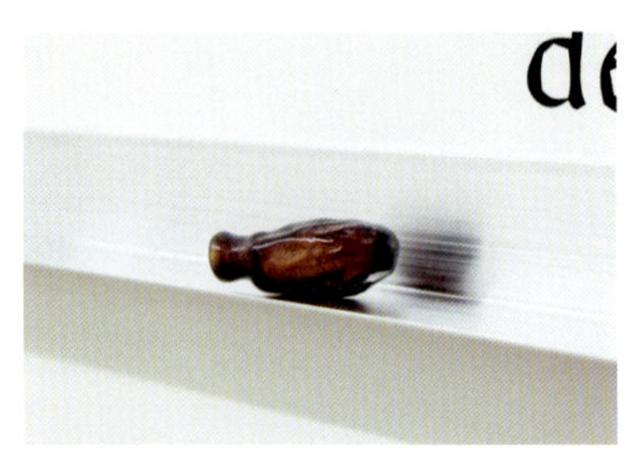
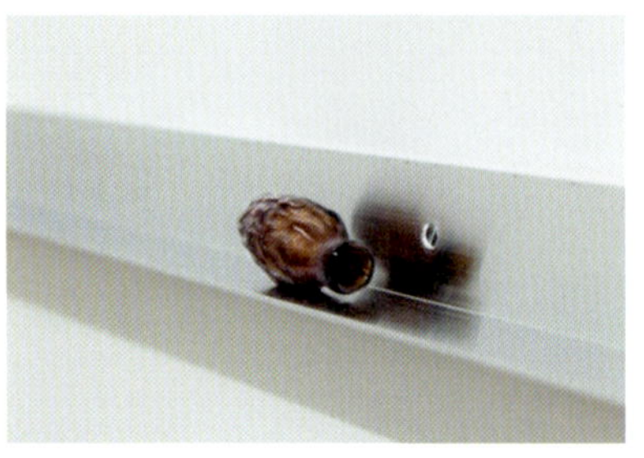
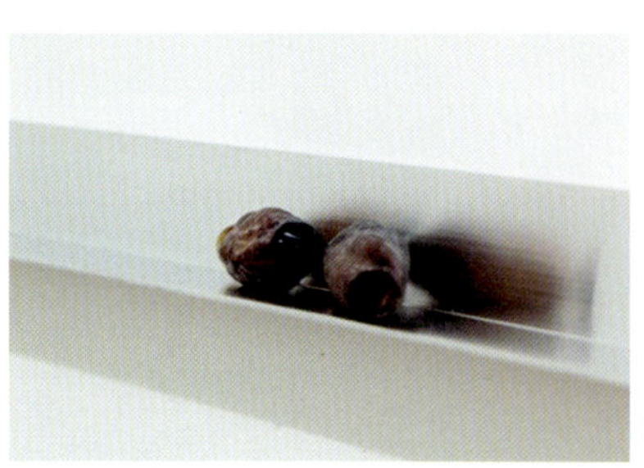

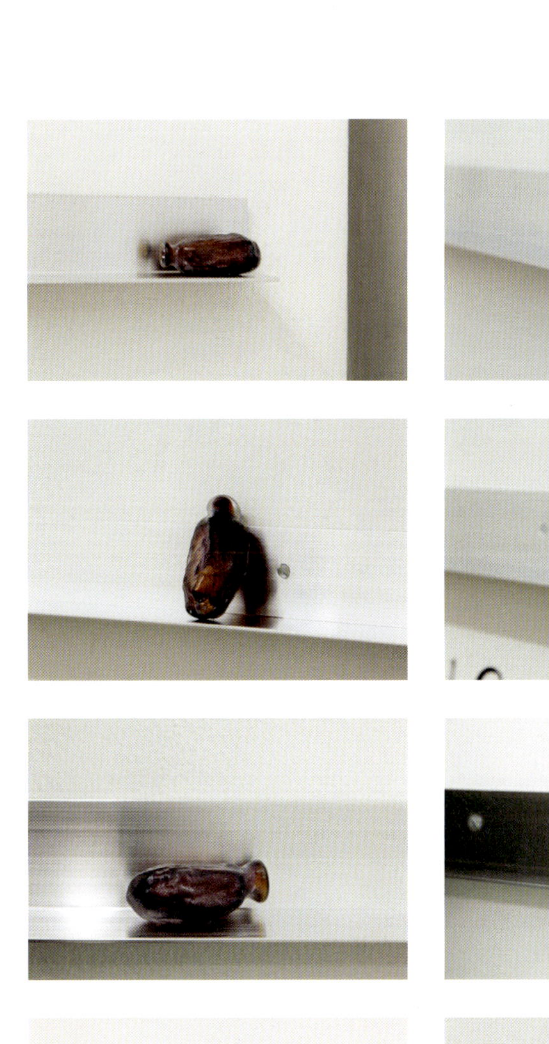

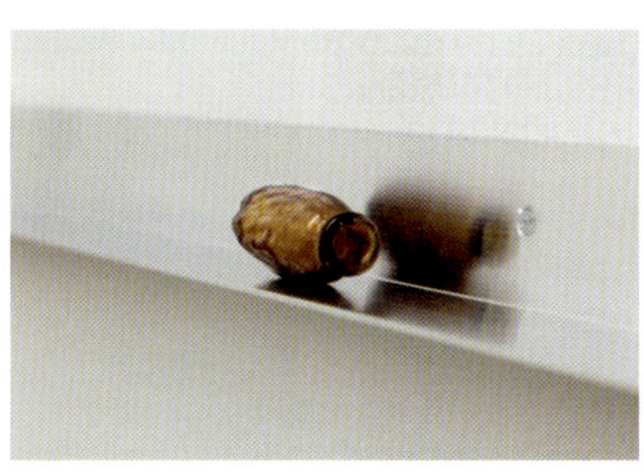

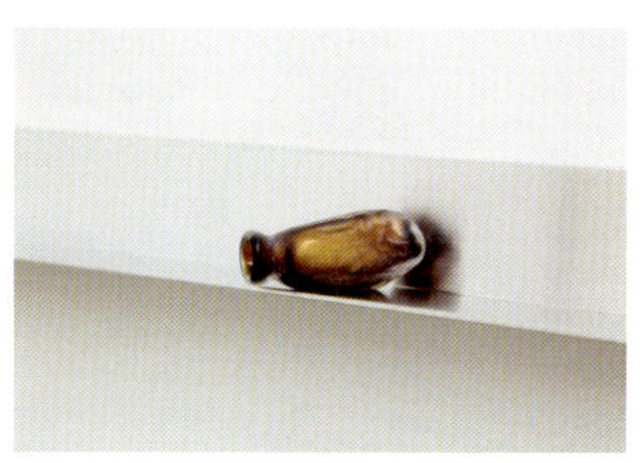

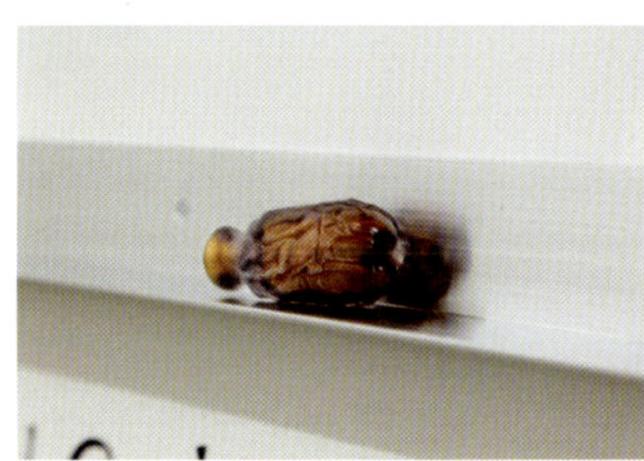

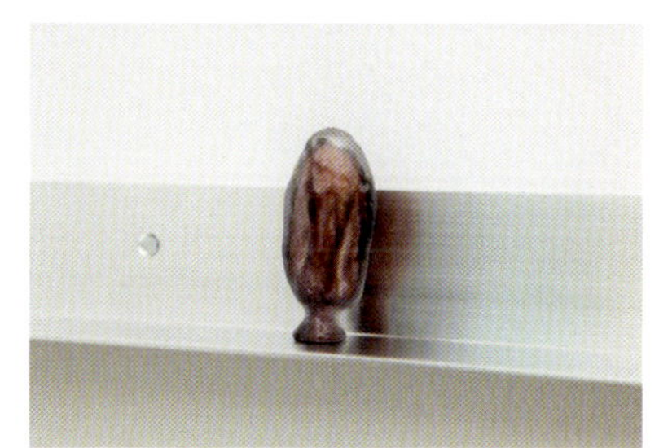

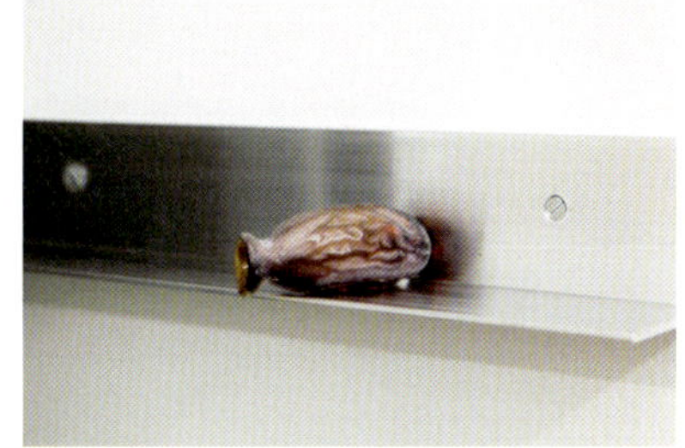

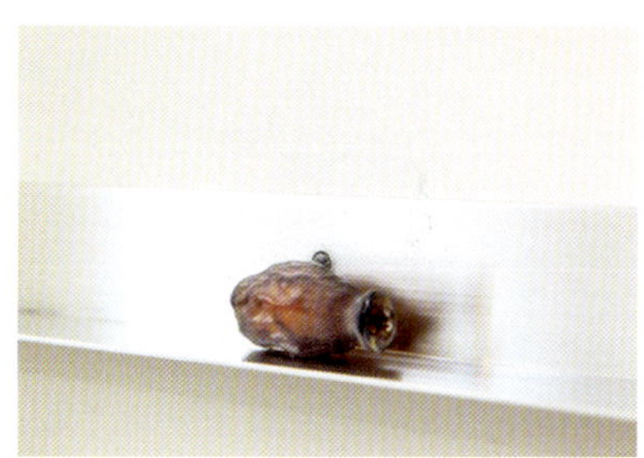

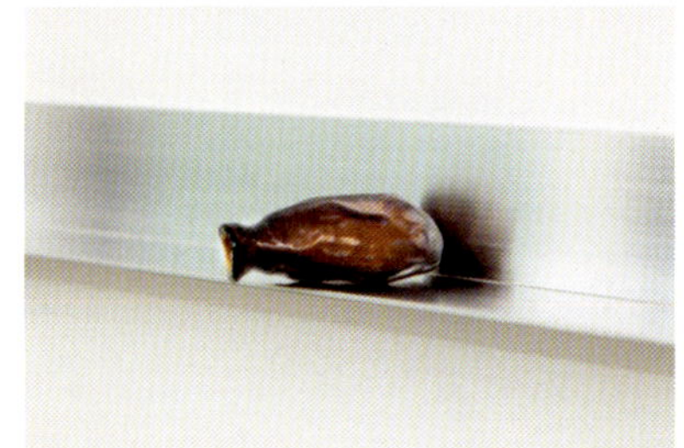

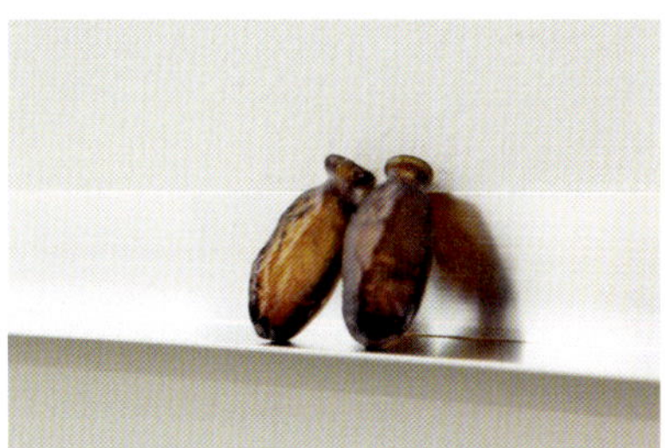

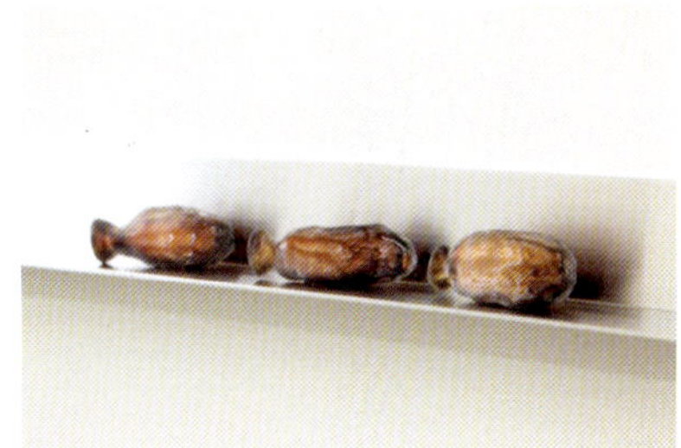

Molds for Date Series (Deglet Nour), 2017

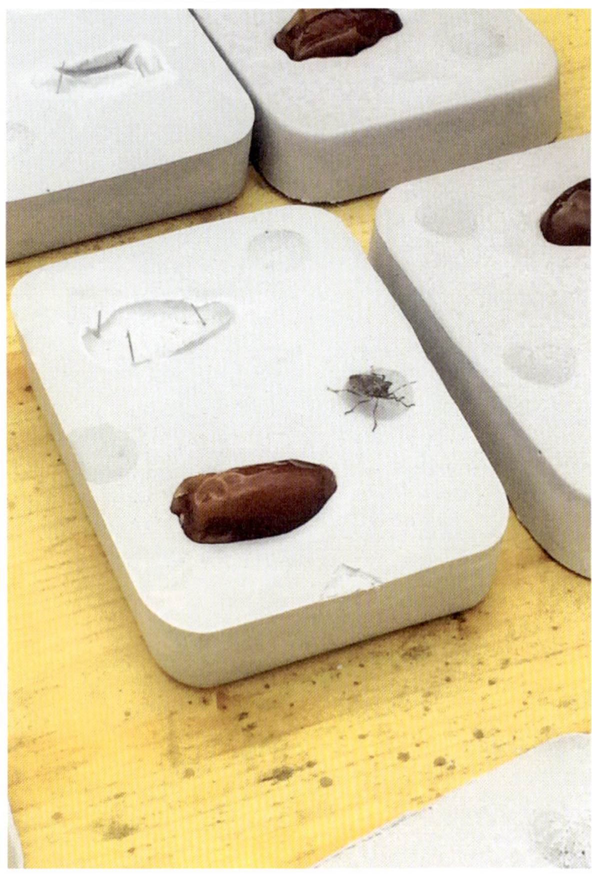

Numbering of Date Series (Barhi), 2017

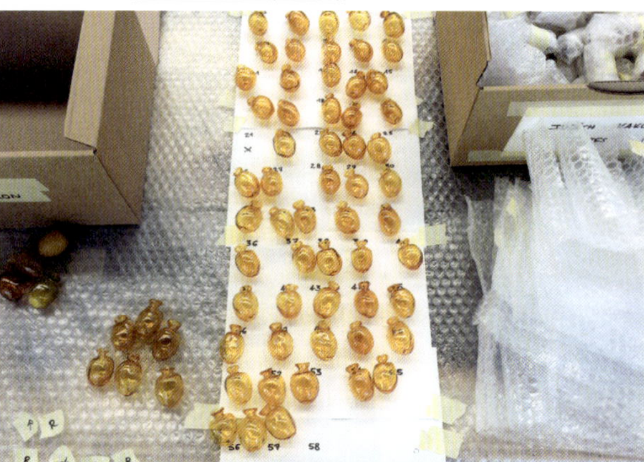

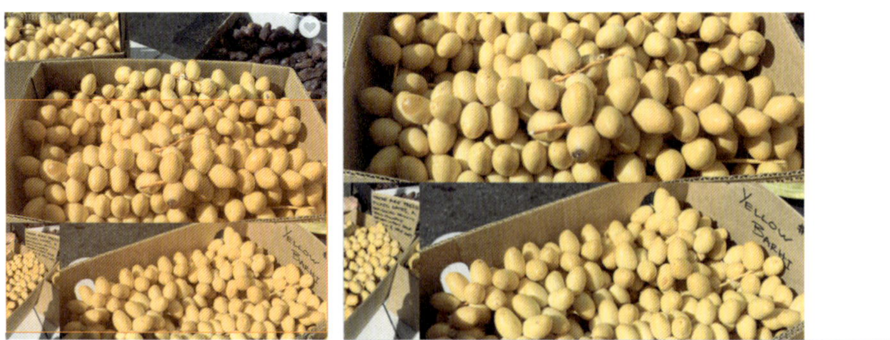

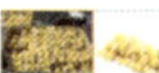
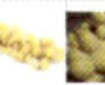
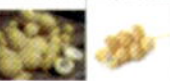

Barhi dates for sale on Alibaba.com, accessed May, 2021

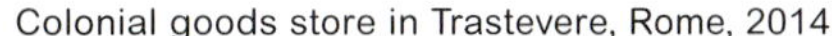

Colonial goods store in Trastevere, Rome, 2014

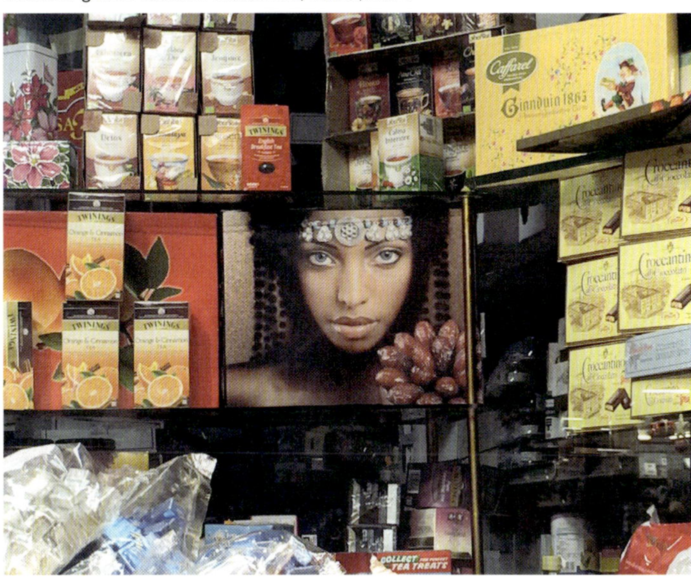

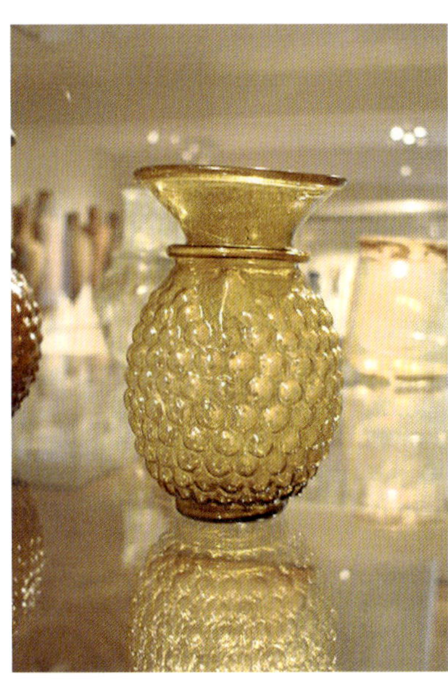

Amber Grape Flask, The Metropolitan Museum of Art, New York City, web image, accessed September, 2018

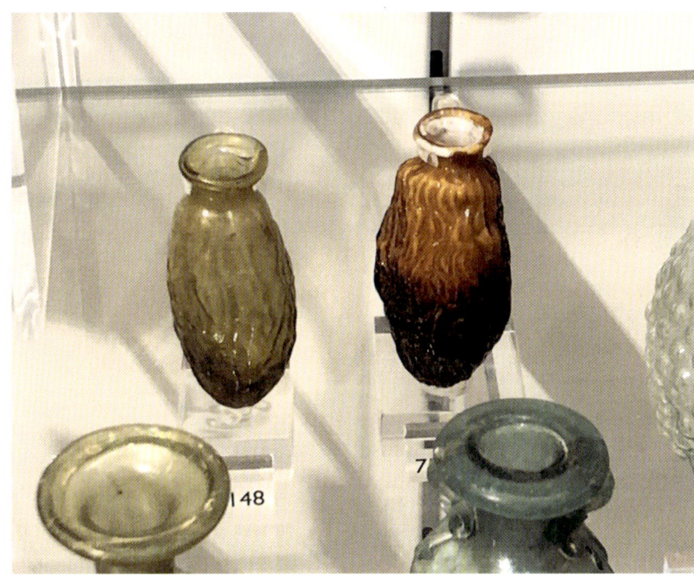

Roman Date Flask, web image, accessed September, 2018

Date Flask, The J. Paul Getty Museum, Malibu, 2016

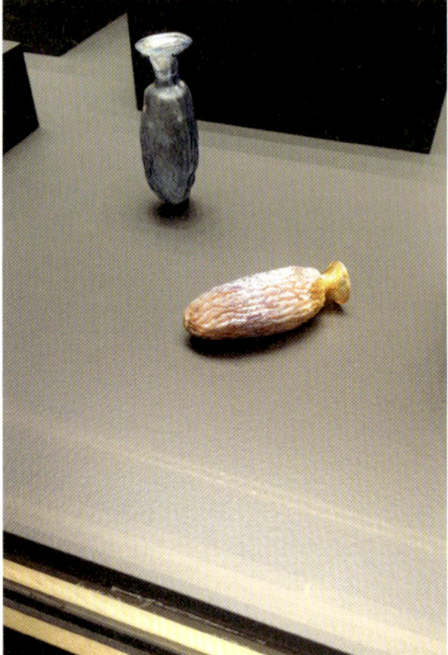

Production of Date Series (Medjool), 2017

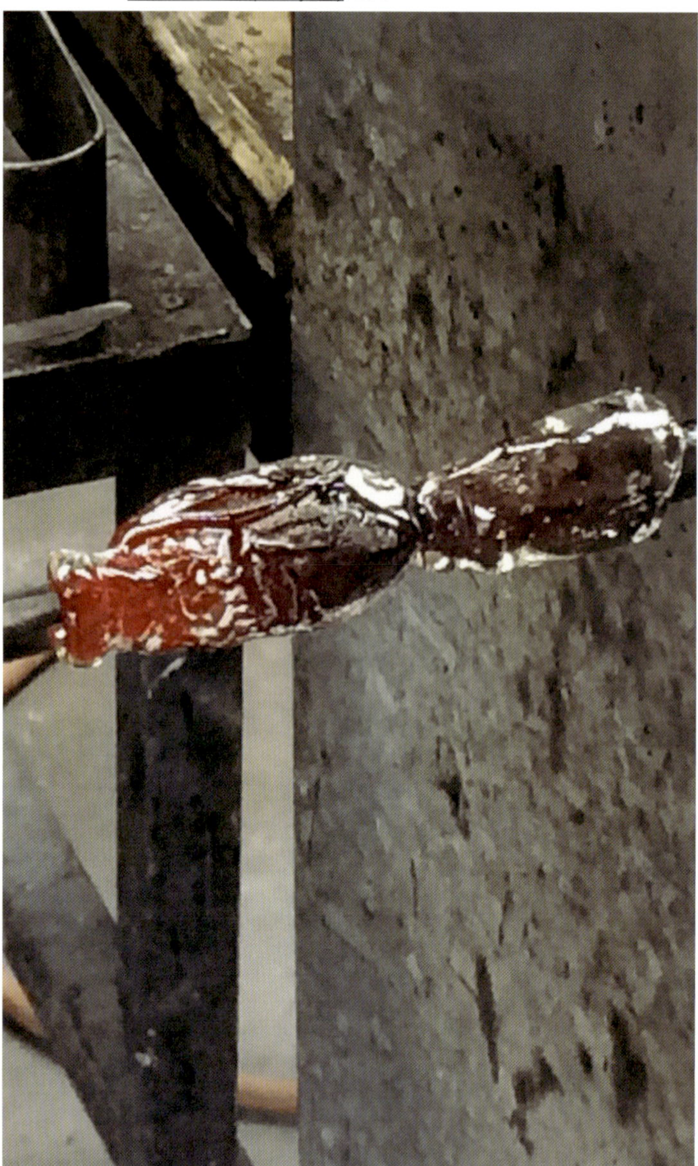

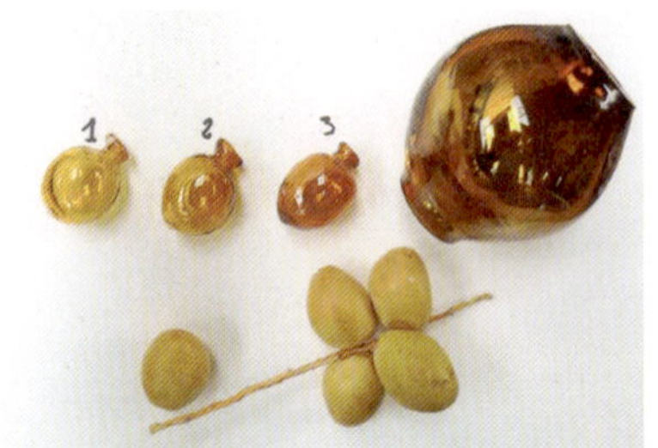

Color matching of Date Series (Barhi), 2017

Bronze wings (of a marble archangel by Raffaello da Montelupo), Castel Sant'Angelo, Rome, 2016

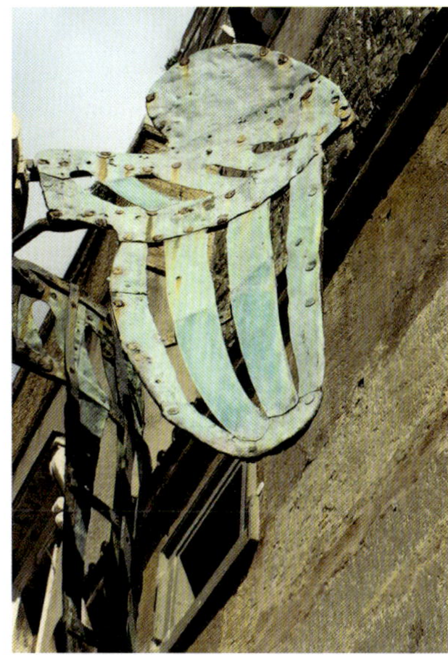

Antennas disguised as palm trees for sale on Alibaba.com, accessed May, 2021

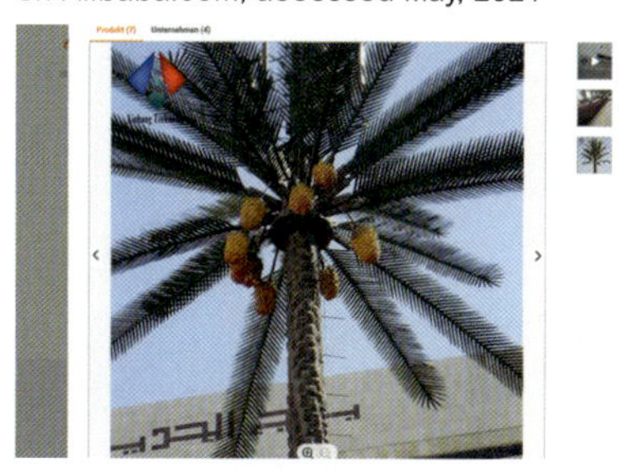

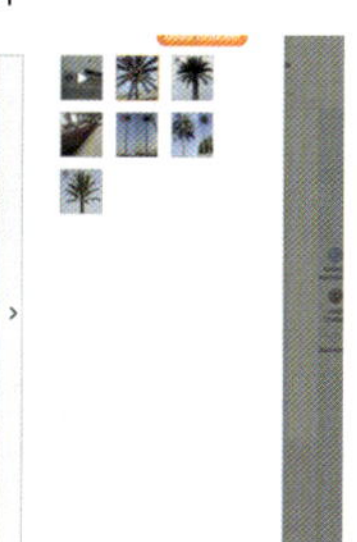

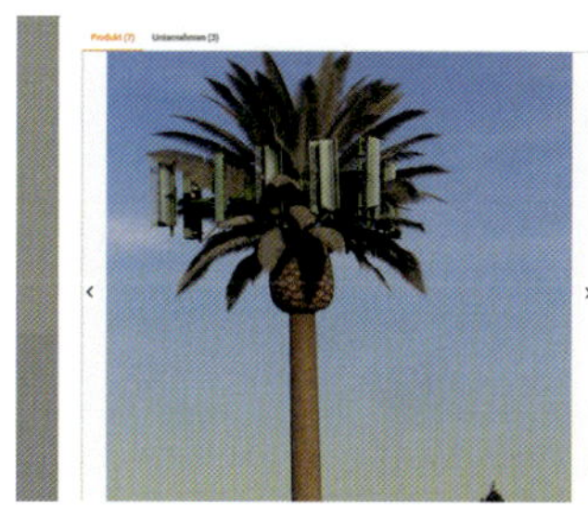

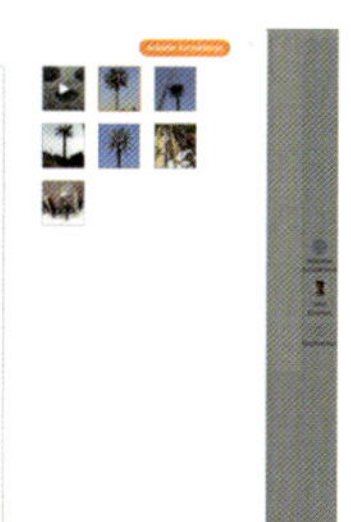

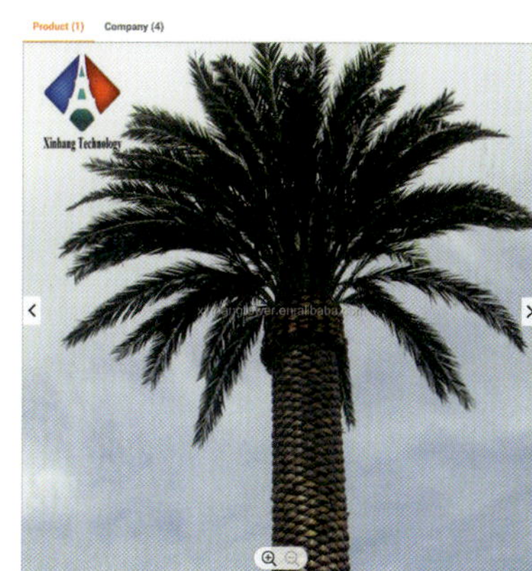

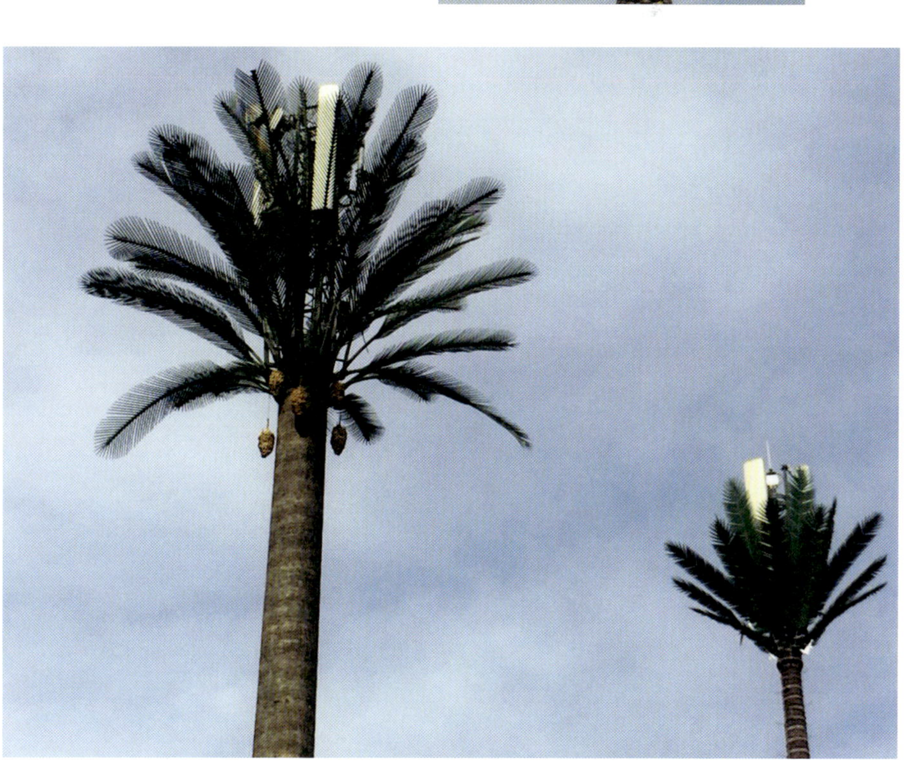

Antennas disguised as palm trees, Marrakech, 2018

Street lamp in Sabaudia, 2015

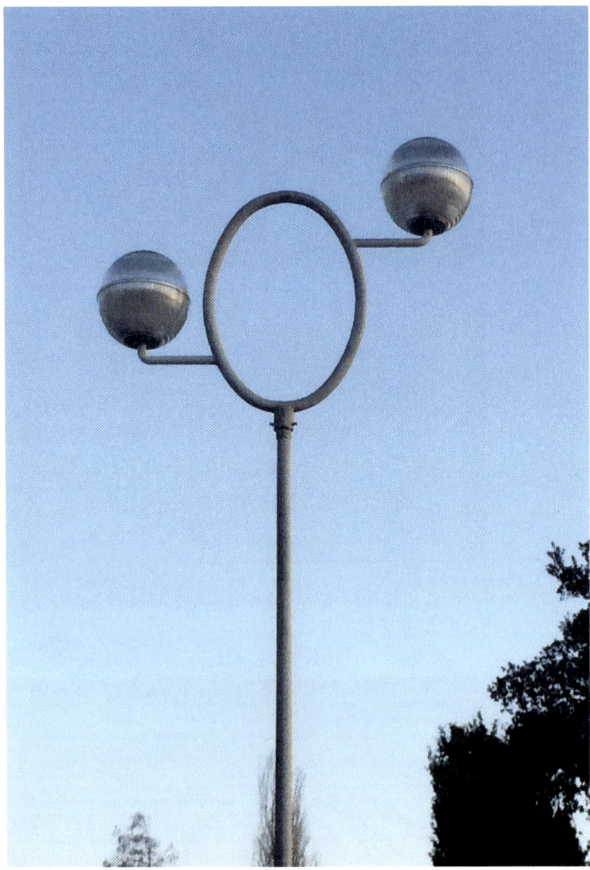

Street lamp in Marrakech, 2018

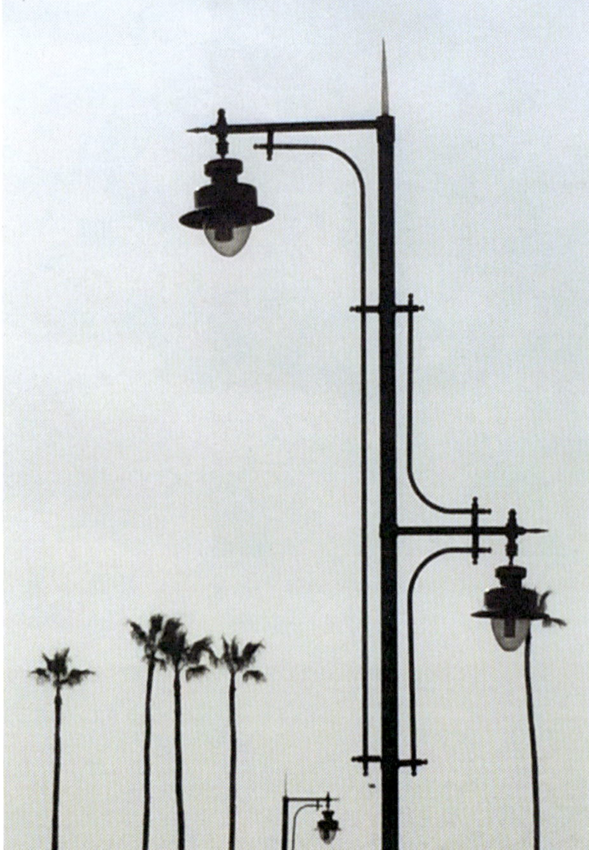

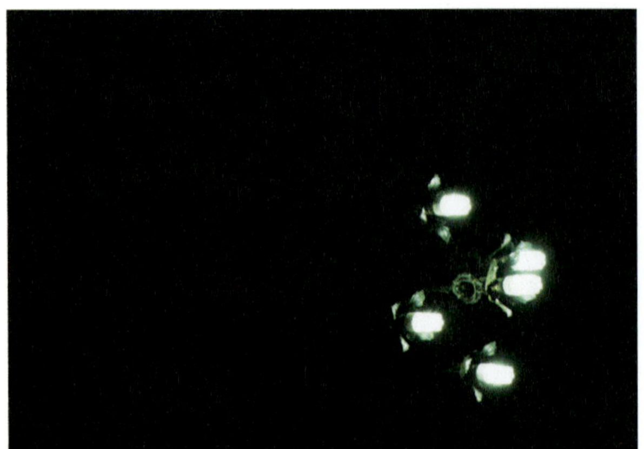

Halogen chandelier, Port of Genoa, 2016

Christmas lighting of Basel's Society for Christmas Lights, Basel, 2020

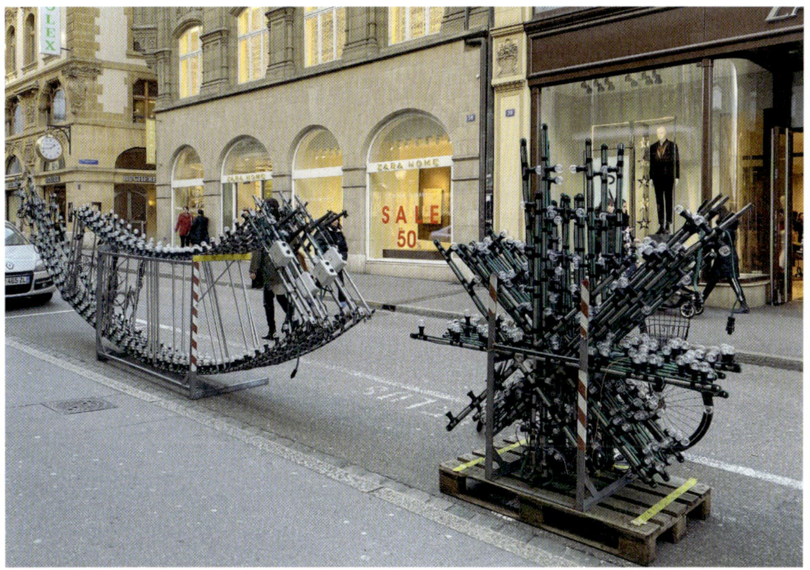

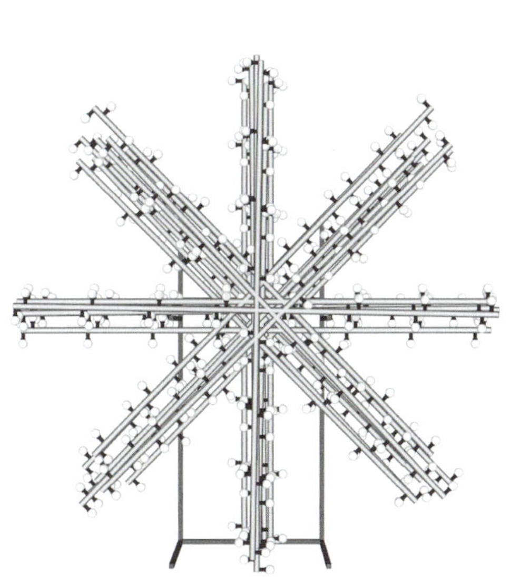

Rendering of the star of Basel's Society for Christmas Lights (in stock condition), Basel, 2020

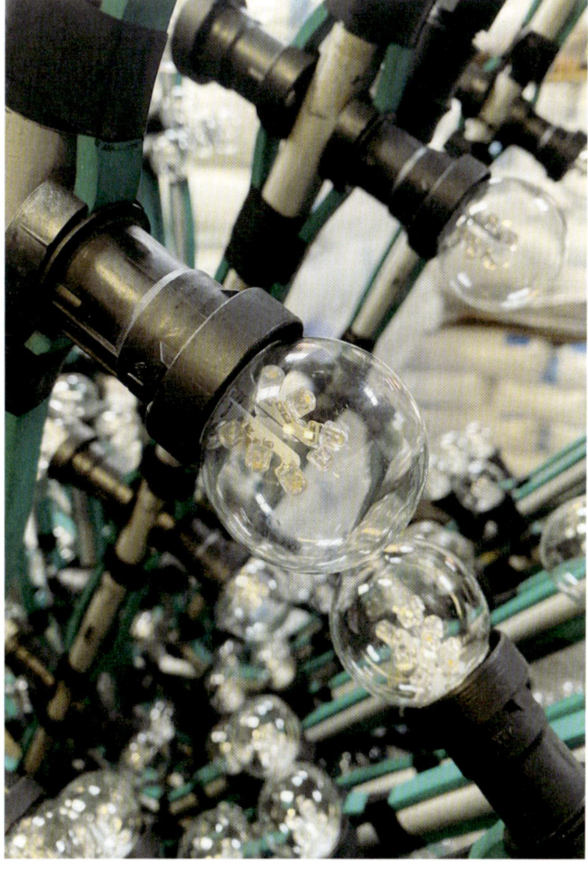

Detail of Christmas lighting of Basel's Society for Christmas Lights, Basel, 2020

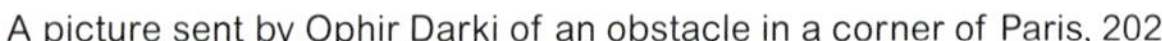
A picture sent by Ophir Darki of an obstacle in a corner of Paris, 2021

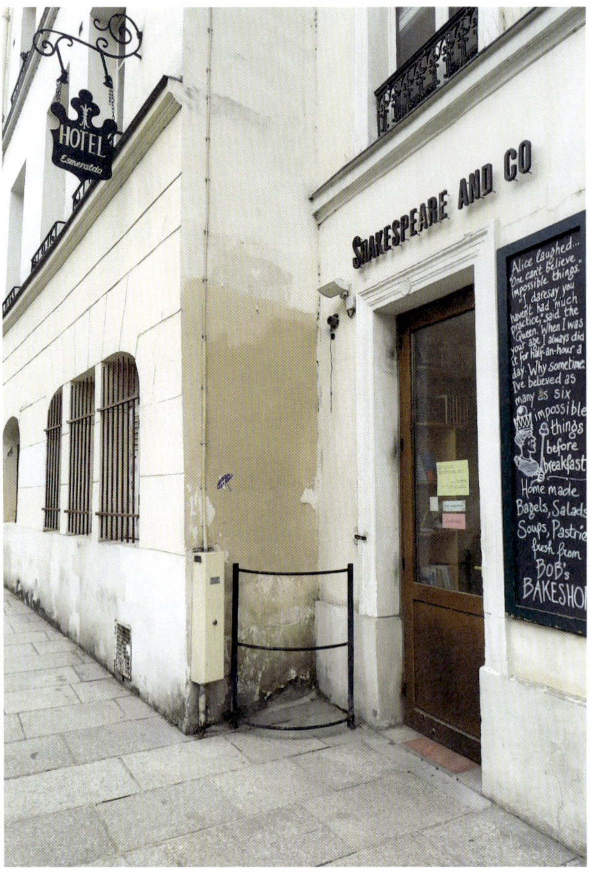

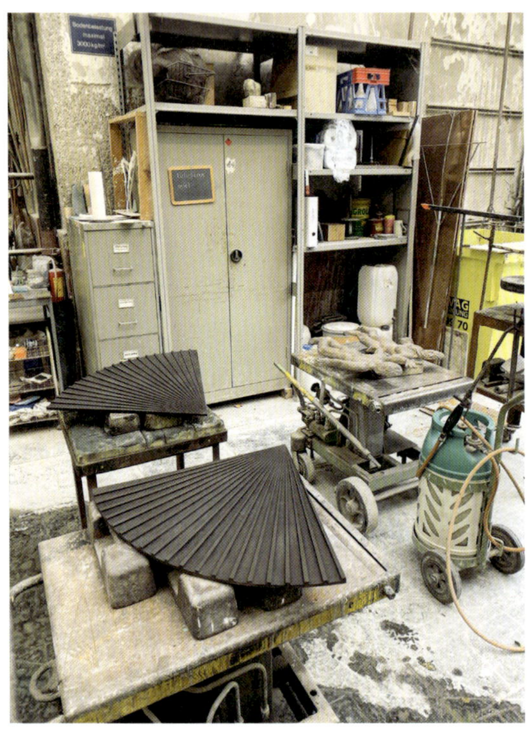
Production of Commons, Basel, 2019

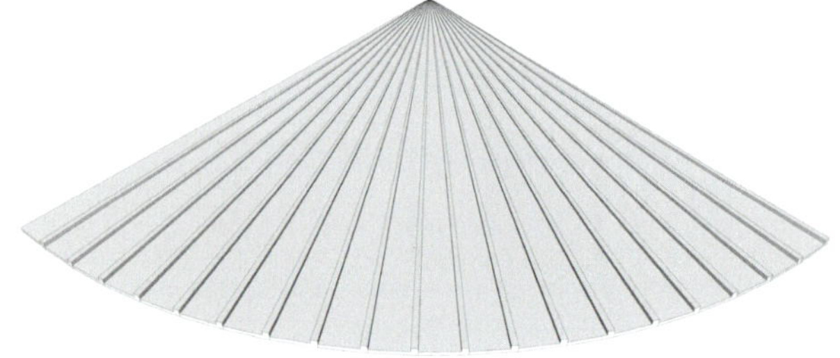
Rendering for Commons, 2019

Commons (1/4 – 2/4), 2019, bronze, each 60 × 80 cm.
Exhibition view: Mischa Schlegel

Commons (3/4 – 4/4), 2019, bronze, each 60 × 80 cm.
Exhibition view: Mischa Schlegel

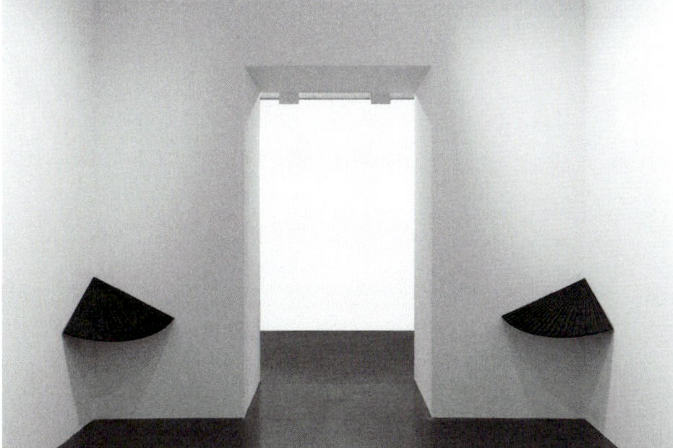

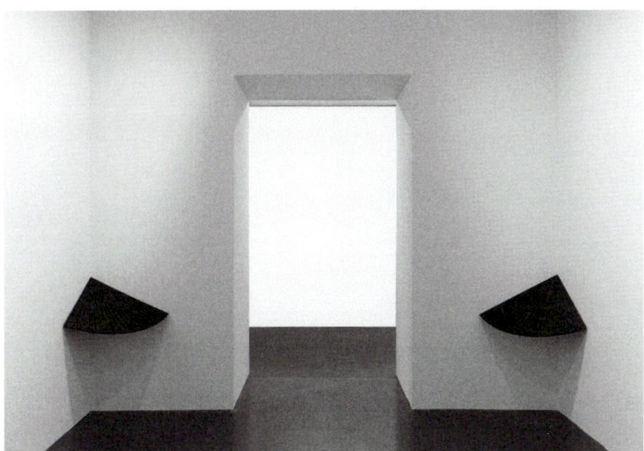

Commons (1/4), 2019, bronze, 60 × 80 cm.
Exhibition view: Mischa Schlegel

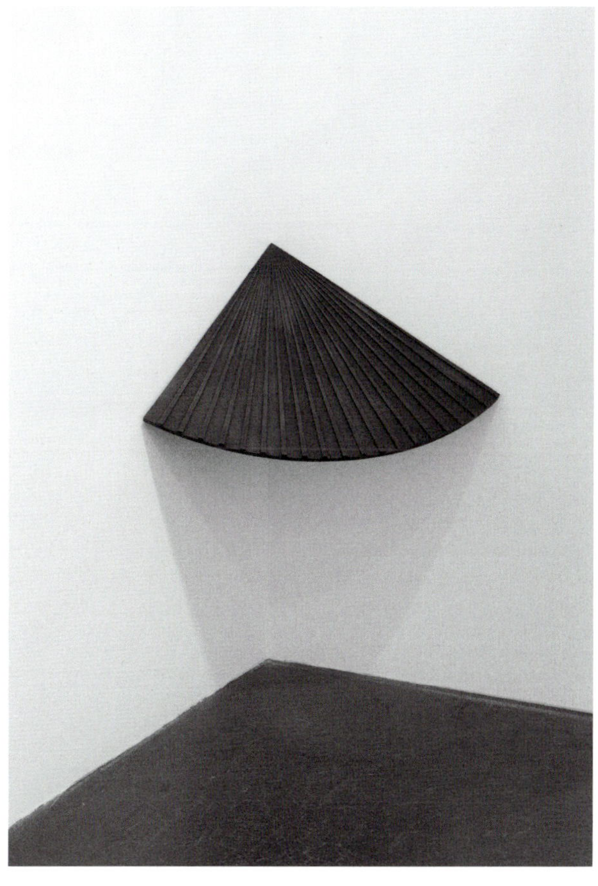

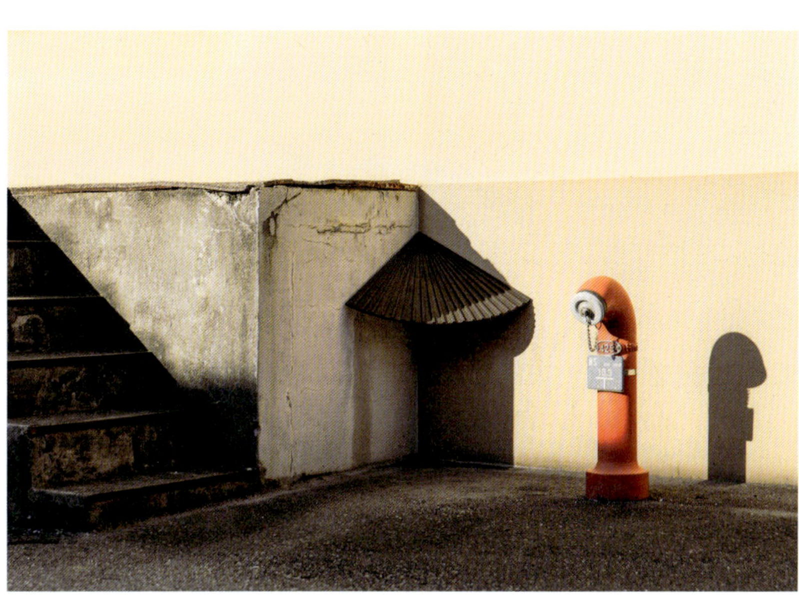

Commons (1/4), 2019, Kunsttage Basel, Helsinki-Strasse, Basel, 2020.
Installation view: Damaris Thalmann

Commons (2/4), 2019, Kunsttage Basel,
Florenz-Strasse, Basel, 2020. Installation view: Damaris Thalmann

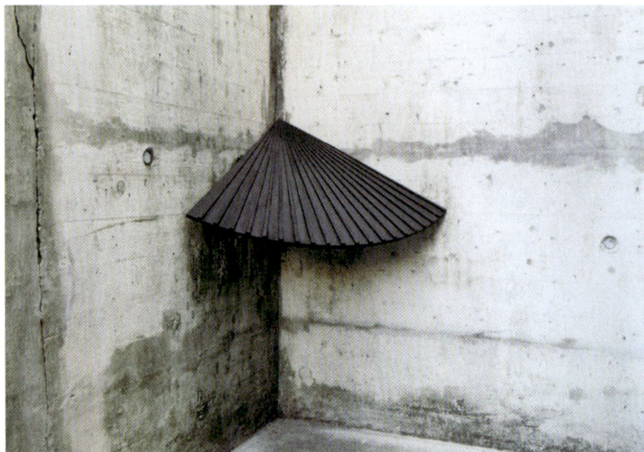

Commons (3/4), 2019, Kunsttage Basel,
Steinenberg, Basel, 2020. Installation view: Damaris Thalmann

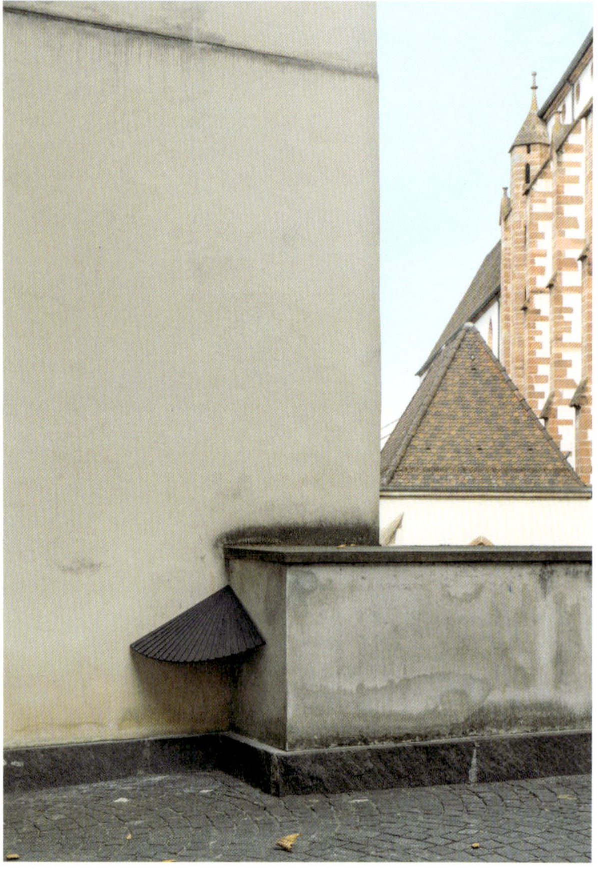

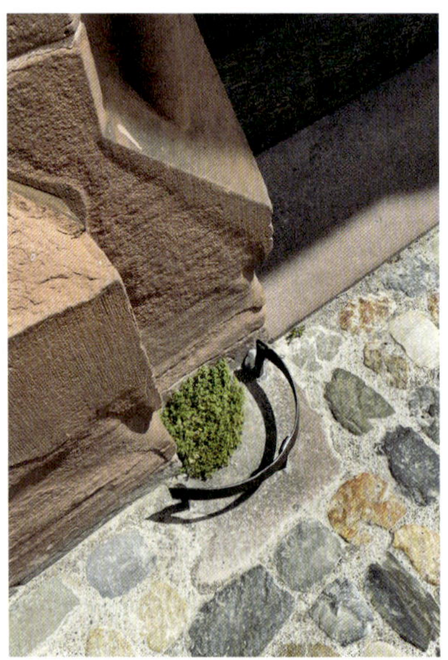

Shoescraper at the entrance of the
Basel Minster, Basel, 2020

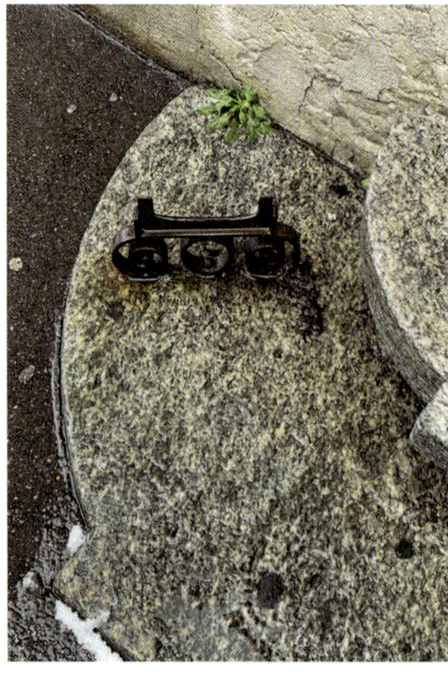

Wet shoescraper on Elisabethenstrasse,
Basel, 2021

Commons (4/4), 2019, Kunsttage Basel, Restaurant Kunsthalle, Basel, 2020

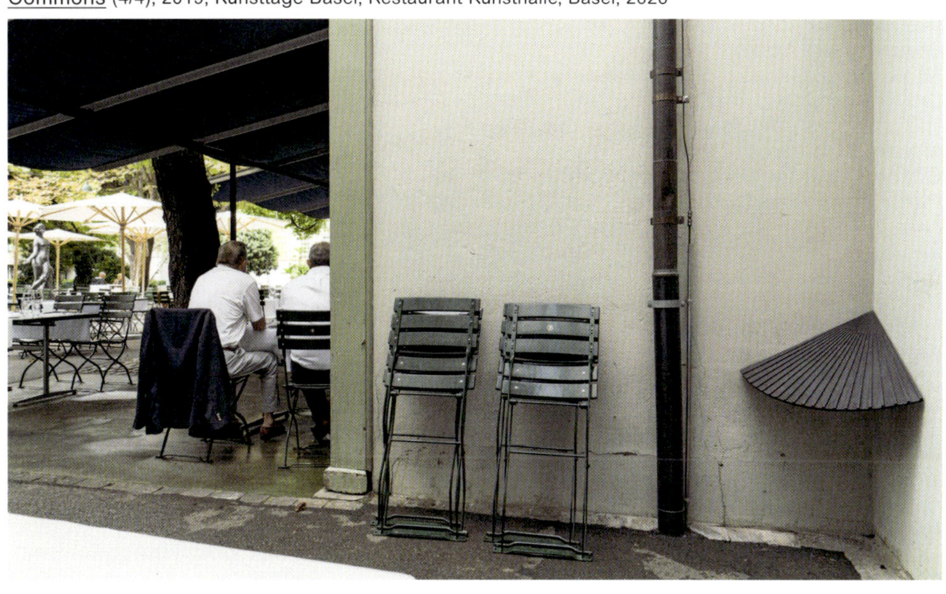

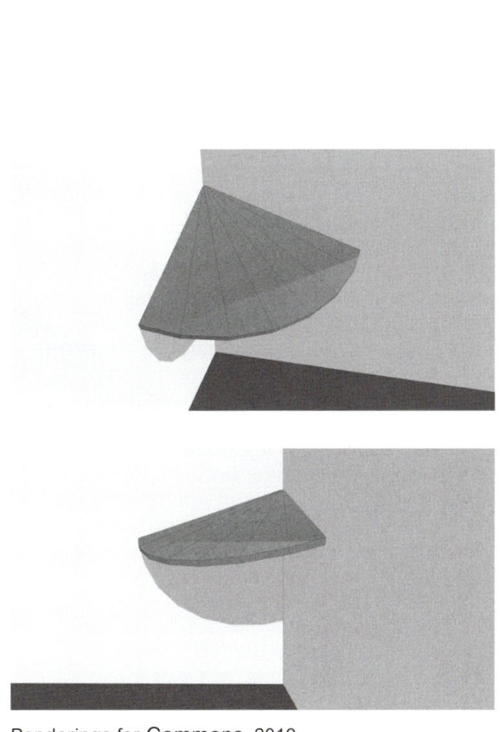

Renderings for Commons, 2019

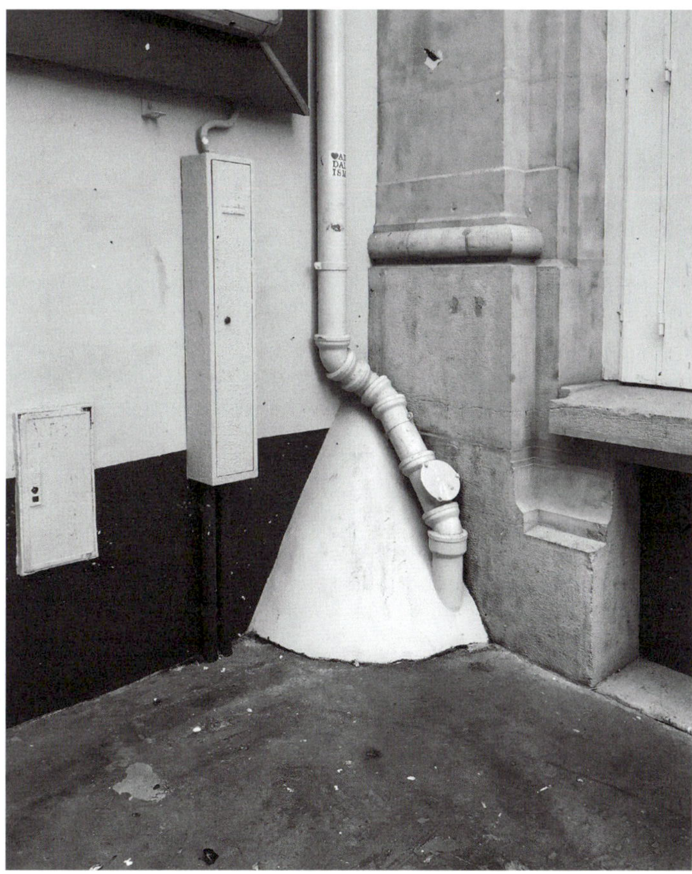

Another picture sent by Ophir Darki of an obstacle in a corner of Paris, 2020

The corners open like fans—
Bronze, waist-high
No powdered faces hidden discretely behind them
Only the empire of that expectation
The piss-poor politics of privatized commons and
discarded empires of urinals
Queerness of the occluded pale powdered cheek
Dark pleats of eyelashes, lowered, that brush against it
Then open wide, like a scalloped fan, bronze, waist-high—

It's the summer of 2020, no 2021, and trust in empire
Is at an all-time low—our social screens tell us so.
We lower our eyes and open our overheating screens
Troops and currency are being withdrawn like faces
behind fans
Like liquid bodies from the carceral commons
We will spend the heatwave writing about the real
Which takes many literary forms:
pharmaceutical prescription,
Animal essay, lyric arson, emailed test result sonnets,
televised testimony of
Flood as poet's novel. Sculptural dystopian nonfiction
Strobes the institutional and architectonic corners
Scalloped forms genuflecting some idea of deterrence,
all glittery mineral
Violence, corporate and corporeal, aimed for a populace

Visit the same restaurant. They hydrate with
plastic bottles
In every shaded corner. Their imaginary always pointed
to this blinding
Whiteness, shade they require from it, this golden
west-ness,
Marble tablets of treasury—etched with ancestral debts
and colonial riches—
Their natural inheritance. They'll take it—

Look up
Bronze skies streak the coast, fires flaring like fans
In the mountains. Flames lick at foothills that surround
The capital, burn through the wide, twisting fronds
And rosettes—the fountainlike leaves and flesh—of
Ancient agaves, what the locals call immortals
Designed to last, giant ornamental succulents
Studding the hills for millennia, their form taken for
Ionic columns and archaic and classical red-and-black
vessels—
Smoke turned the painted motifs black during firing in
5000 BC—
If our summer's fires lick at the agaves' tongues of leaves
The smoke in the city center remains occluded
Particles breathed as microscopic as our
commonly held

After Commons

by Quinn Latimer

Whose bodies remain visibly public,
constantly opening
And seeking relief. What form of life is this?
Why palmettes
Not pissoirs? Not commons. Each form, fanlike, each
body, an autofiction—

The reader points to the selfsame names of author
and narrator
The reader points to temples, treasuries, and ruins they
remember visiting
To the narratives offered as parables about the natural
Liquidity of capital and the unnatural liquidity of bodies
The former circulating, "naturally," the latter
judged harshly
For their desperate circulation across borders,
their visibility
In cities that would deny their rights to existence, that is,
to any space
Behind such fanlike reports, in our pale and
pressed imaginary
Like some blush-bound face obscuring its desire
With feathery forms that open with a snap
Eyes not lowered, lashes spiderlike, pupils dilated
Are golden real estate opportunities for those
From the north or east spending a few days in the south—

This is empire now: golden visas, golden temples, golden
Showers striking golden urinals, some faceless sun god
In a pandemic summer tourist advertisement.
Sunsets over ancient sites are first class, gradients
of mineral
Color fanning out like lotuses or palmettes above
Columns, islands. The gold prospectors sweat out
the temples,

Secret, our common understanding
of some hazy difference—
We all breathe it, we'll all lose the forest, we all
Swim the poisoned waters, but only some swallow
Some allowed shade and relief in the corners while others
Die by fire with the trees, the animals, the nonhuman
spirits—

The corners open like fans—
Bronze, waist-high
No powdered faces hidden discretely behind them
Only the empire of that expectation
The piss-poor politics of privatized commons and
present empires of urinals
Queerness of the occluded pale powdered cheek
Dark pleats of eyelashes, lowered, that brush against it
Then open wide, like a fan, bronze, waist-high—

On the island, in the small archeological museum
In a high-ceiling room that once stored tobacco—
A room in the Venetian style, built during the Venetian
occupation—
Tablet after tablet is carved with the form of a fan,
a palmette.
Each tablet a stele, some funerary stone, for a citizen
Wealthy or famed enough to commission it. Scalloped
Or feathered or flamed, each palmette motif crosses
Cultures and periods: Greek, Roman, Indo-Greco,
Byzantine, Renaissance, Baroque, Empire.
In ancient Egypt palmettes invoked lotus flowers
Or a stylized tree of life, the lotus rising
From the black swamps to touch the sun or a palm
Reaching from earth to heaven. Indeed, I read:
"The palmette carries the characteristics of the
Axis mundi or world tree."

Likewise, the fleur-de-lis, "enigmatic emblem
Of the divine right of kings," also a variant of the
fanlike form
Conferred on early French rulers by an angel.
In ancient Greece, the design was called anthemion,
Flower or keepsake, and decorated friezes, columns.
In Hellenistic architecture, such motifs
Formed "flame palmettes," twisting and rising—
Flames or flowers? The deterrent designers of
later empires
And their hostile architectures—ours, for example—
Wonder as they stare at the hills amid the
endless heatwaves
And corporate-state fire sales of late capital—

It's the summer of 2020, no, 2021, and trust in empire
Remains real and ecstatic. As does the real estate
market
No matter the climate, the collapse of common systems
Of weather, no matter flood and fire. In the city, restless
With debt and hunger and pandemic, along the
overbuilt river
Long and dry as a sentence, only tourists and riot police
And addicts roam the heat-stricken streets of daylight
Refugees and developers, some figured desire, take to
shaded corners
In the papers, which we open like fans on our
overheating laptops
We read of the constant elections of death cults
Each regime bringing favored urban planners and
"heat specialists"
Vast new police forces and cutting austerity measures
Each administration offering a stream of language
We recognize in its cadences and edges of smooth or
scalloped violence—

So it is that the fire season is divided between tenants
And owners, the hourly waged and the grandchildren's
inheritance
From ancient shipping routes that trace the scalloped
lines of
Centuries of empire: forced displacement, slavery,
and migration
Or perhaps an inheritance come from opioids flooding
The common market somewhat later, that is, this decade
Or the last extant ancient forests disappeared by arson
and policy
What is common, I mean, is not the event of expropriation
Nor the sharp scent of its violence, the ammonia
Odor of ships and boulevards, the private practices
Of their corners and corridors, what is notable
Is that such death, such necropolitics, should be
decorated with palmette
Designs gleaned from immortal agaves and lotus flowers
And a stylized tree of life in early iterations of what some
call society
Though others claim it does not exist.
We exist. Those palmlike fans, genuflecting, are records
of so—

The corners open like fans—
Bronze, waist-high
No powdered faces hidden discretely behind them
Only the empire of that expectation
The piss-poor politics of privatized commons and erotic
empires of urinals
Queerness of the occluded pale powdered cheek
Dark pleats of eyelashes, lowered, that brush against it
Then open wide, like a fan, bronze, waist-high—

Should spikes line the pavements so we might not
Sleep, should fans frame the corners so we might
Not feel relief, should our lands be set aflame
So they might be seized and developed, should our
Waters be bottled or poisoned or turned to new and
ancient graveyards
Black Atlantic, Black Mediterranean, Black Athena
Bodies of water marked for death or tourism
Choose, they say, as if from behind a fan, its flames
almost reaching
Should each policy be enacted to make
movement smaller
Bodies smaller, bodies should disappear—

So inoculated but not immune
We are figured by desire and its denial
Trespassing corners designed to deter
They are teaching sustainable design and
decolonial aesthesis
At the universities but this is not it
Should bodies take their pleasure with each other
in pissoirs
As they always have, this is also the history of empire
And of the life that blooms in the shade of its violence—

It's the summer of 2020, no 2021, and the fashion for the
Commons in language has dully departed the theory
Departments but not our common need for relief
Dying bouquets of flowers wrapped in cellophane
Like some poor offering are tucked into the wrought-
iron words
Scripting a long exterior wall delineating some narrow
city square
Who placed the flowers there, limp against language
That gages our exteriority to or complicity with its
coded brutality:
ESTATE, REAL, TRUST, PRIME, GAME, EMPIRE, 2020
Plus some percentage sign suggesting the total inequity
And expert expropriation of our present conditions
Or the violence of the language that has brought us here
Or maybe that's just pure speculation—

Even so we will spend the heatwave writing about the real
In a medieval font then fashioning it in iron in our
thoughts
By real is meant perhaps some testimony to the irreality
Of certain bodies, common desires, and the elimination
of them
From social and public life, of language as algorithm
And code for violence against the true liquidity of bodies
What we have in common, or in commons, and what we
do not
Not trust, not prime, not game, not empire, not estate, but
Air, water, forest, valley, mountain, tundra, stars, sun,
desire, grief
Some solidarity against ornamental iconography
gleaned from the natural
That is, vegetal life, and our denied place within it
For nature only exists if you consider yourself outside of it
Testimony to the feathery and flaming blooming of
the lotus
Used to commemorate the refutation of those
still existing—

In the city, all its spaces newly vast or narrow
But in every case designed to discourage gathering
Still there remain bodies, as ever, and language.
In the stream of words I hear a hiss of judgment,
Rhetoric, emptiness, and cruelty, then only a trickle.
In the dark corners ornament to disguise:
The fiction of debt
The illusory narrative of austerity and authority
The deceit of architecture
The speculation of desire
And the violence of the necropolis—

In what style should I tell this? To design is to desire
And so the stylized lines of the epic poem or
Romantic lyric or sober autoethnography
Like leaves twisting upward as smoke to some sun
Feathered and fleeing and now falling
Like a boy, a son
In ink or marble or stone, or the scalloped form
Opening wide as a lotus in bronze
Bending at the waist and greeting you
In the shade, touching each corner
Of the public square, that common
Architecture for a common form of life, its inheritance
Discipline and expropriation, not very romantic
There is no shelter no shelter no mercy either
Still there is some yearning
Still you come closer, seeking shadow
And requiring relief
And it is touching each corner, and your
Knees, your waist, you
Gently, gently

Chiba, 2021, C-prints, framed, 3-parts, each 40 × 60 cm

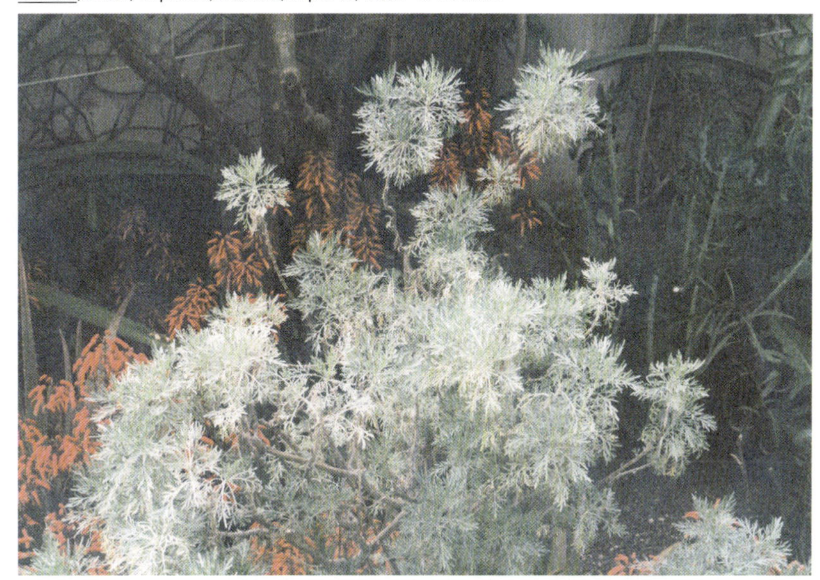

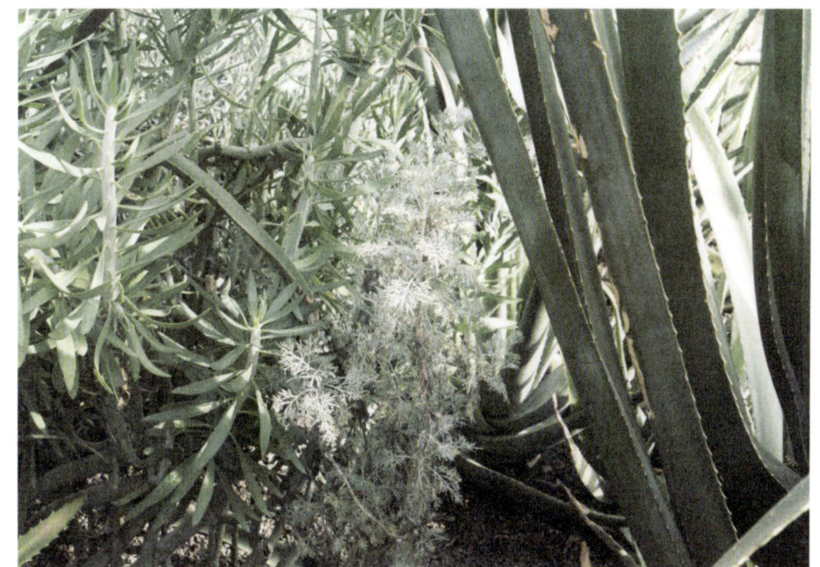

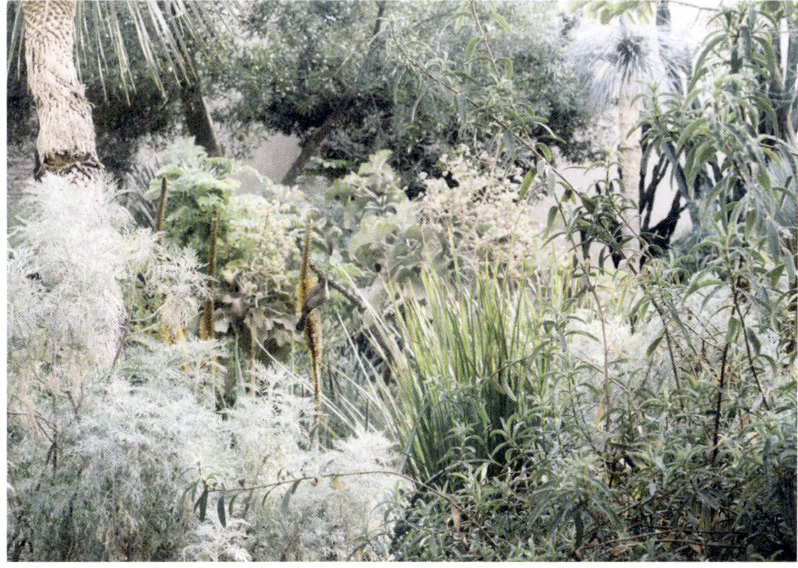

SWISS-LI, 2019, digital prints, 4-parts, 118.9 × 84.1 cm

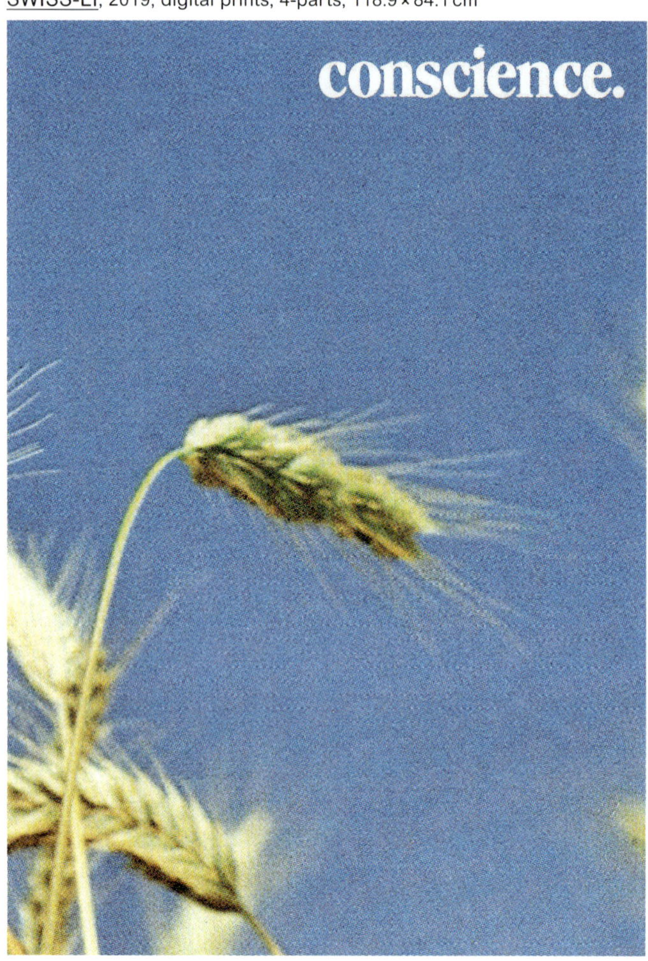

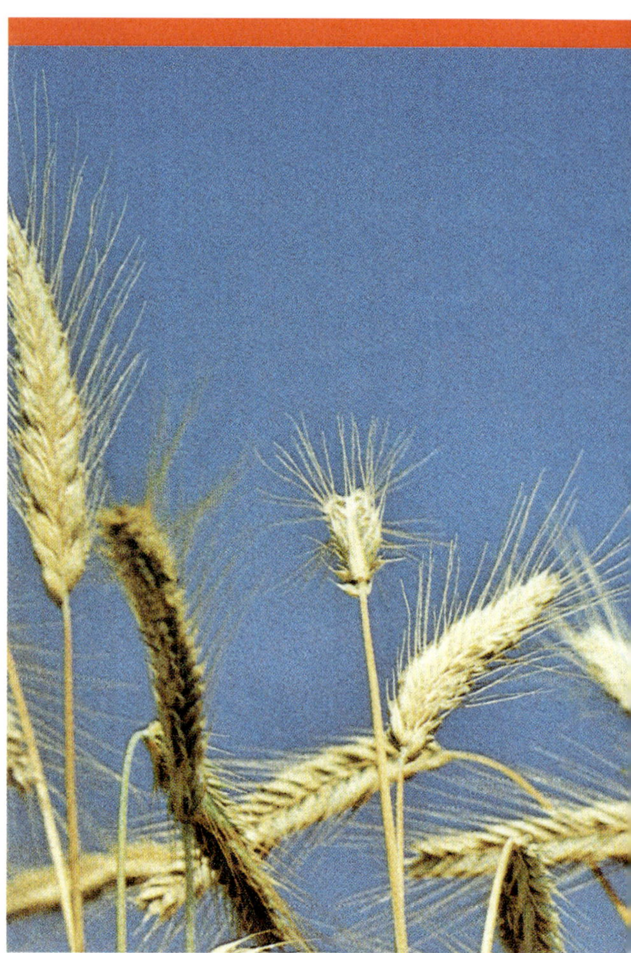

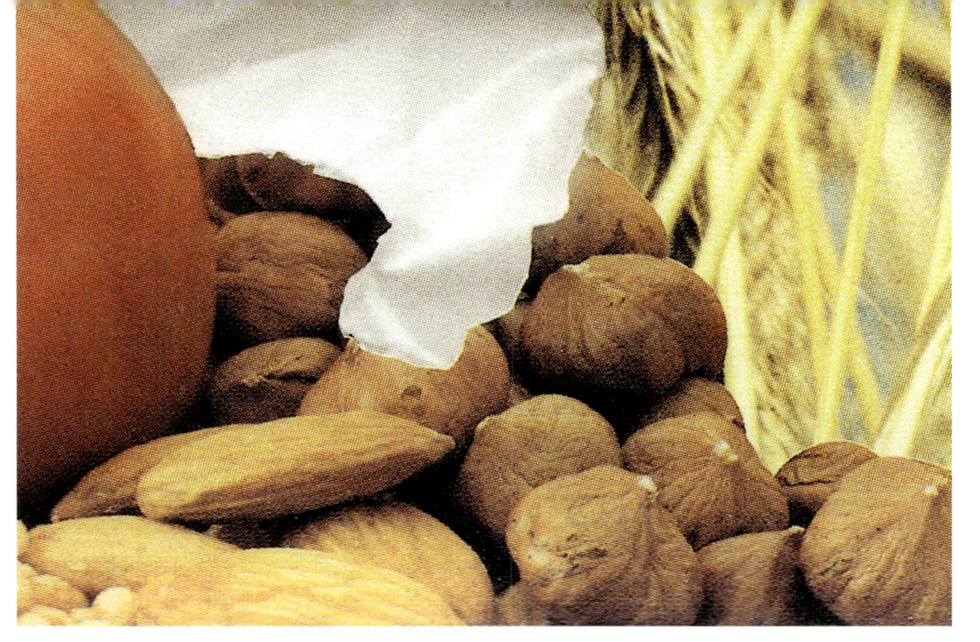

'SWISS-LI'

Mr. Bamba, 2019, inkjet print, 100 × 75 cm

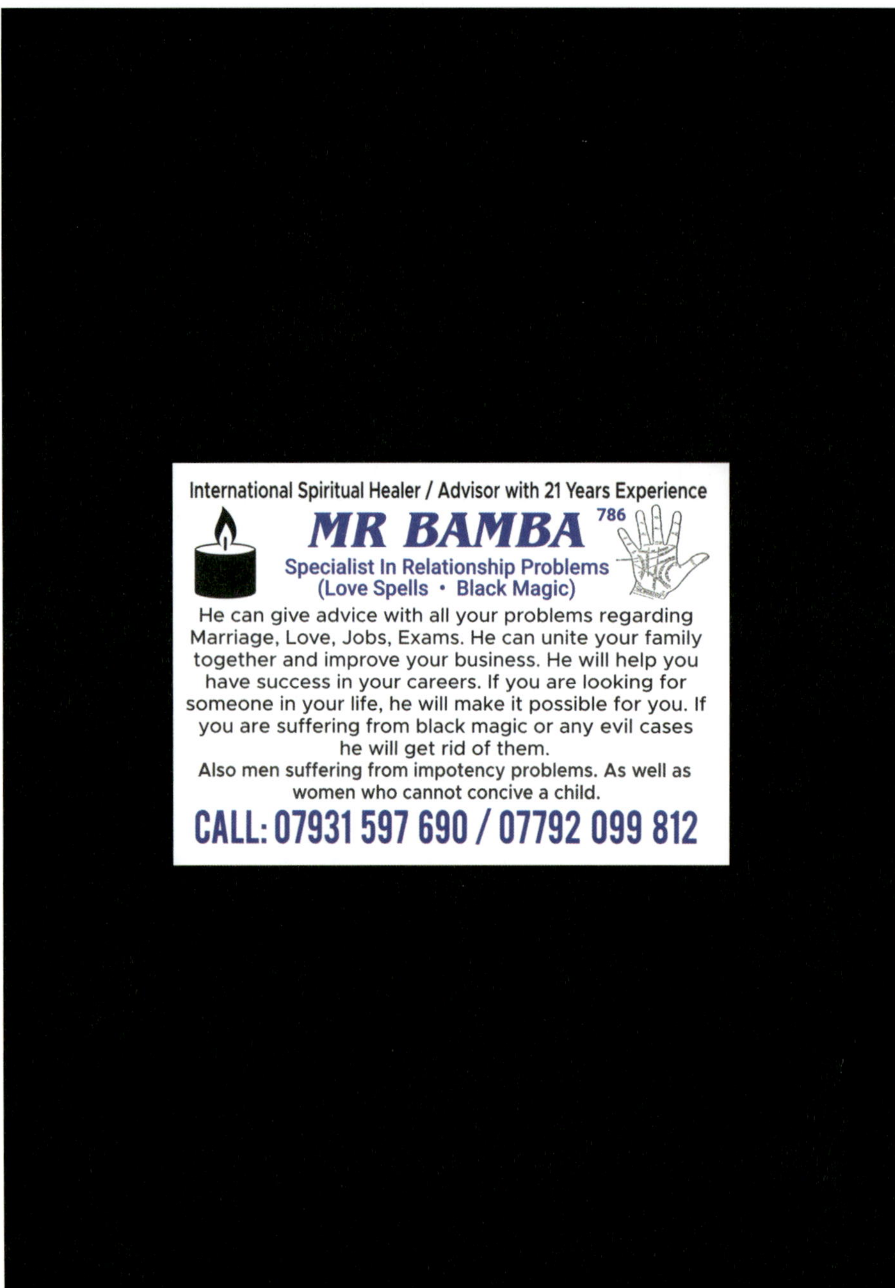

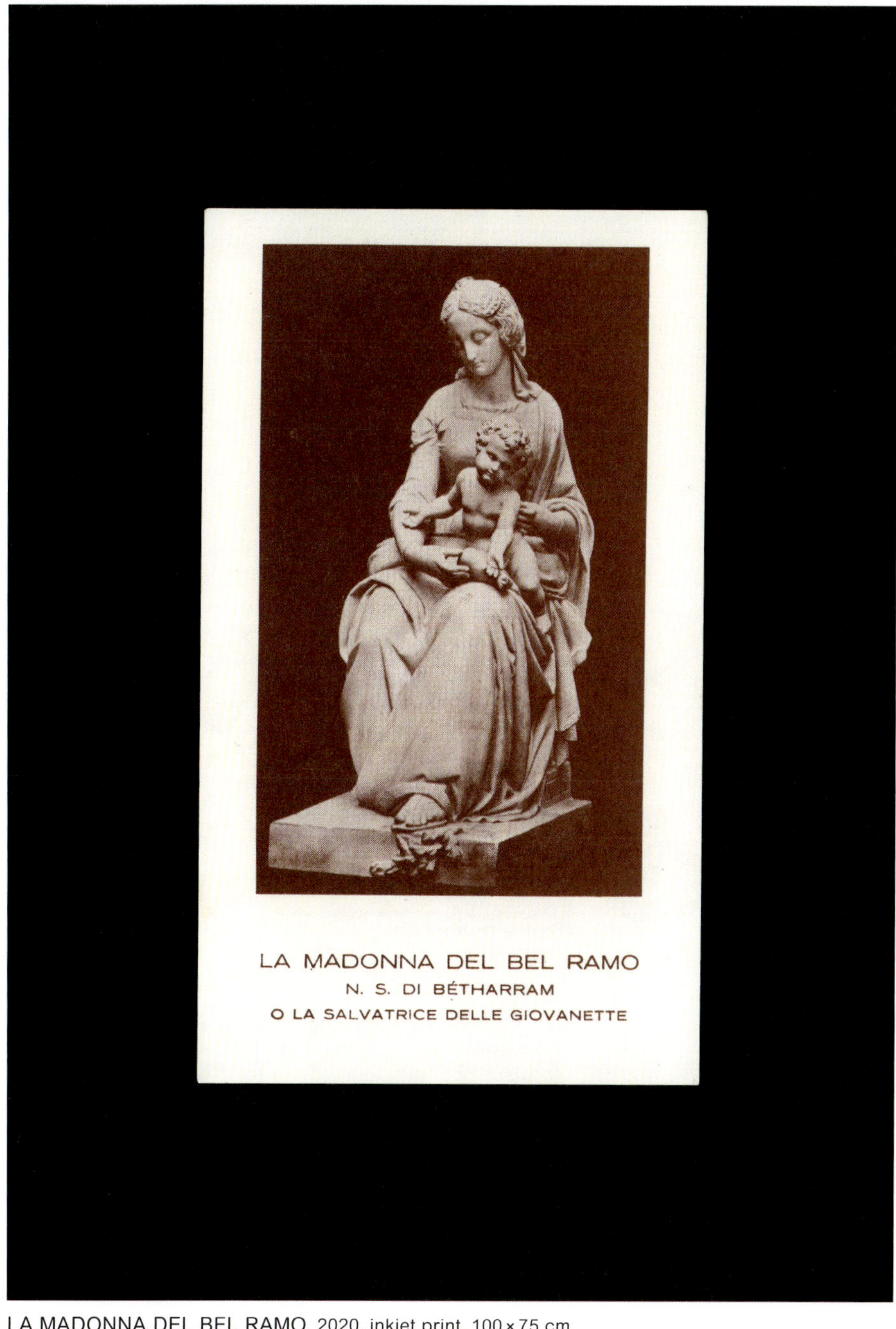

LA MADONNA DEL BEL RAMO, 2020, inkjet print, 100 × 75 cm

Candles at the Church of the Holy Sepulchre, Jerusalem, 2019

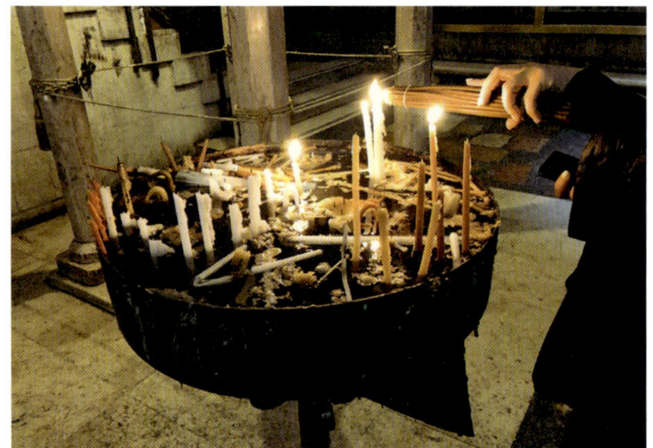

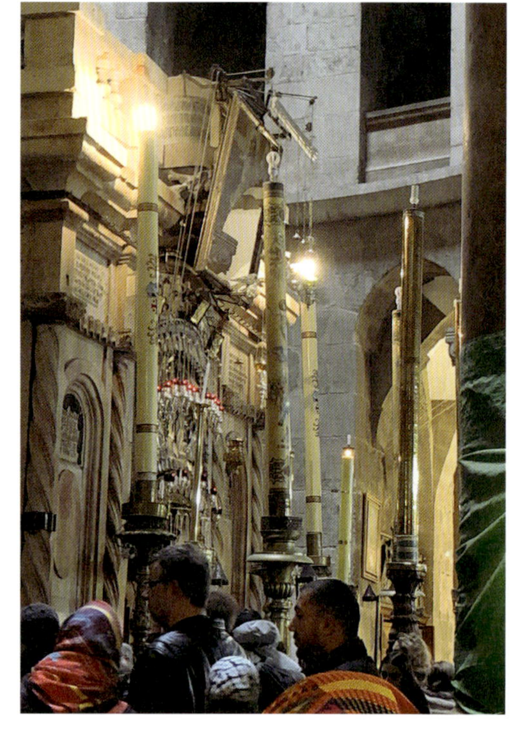

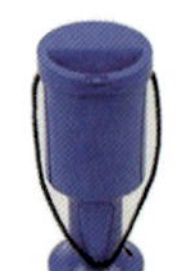

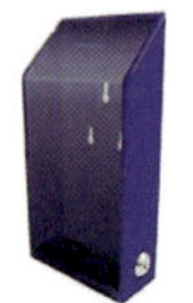

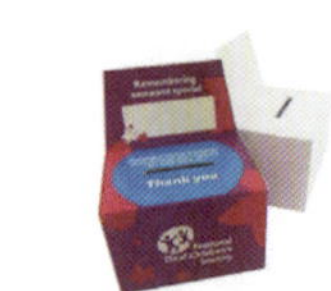

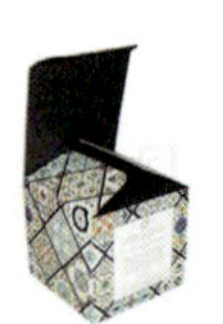

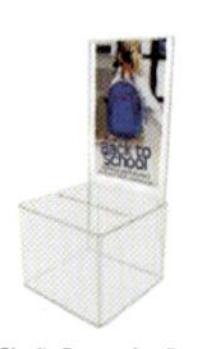

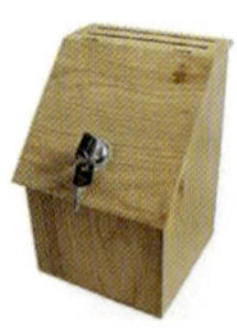

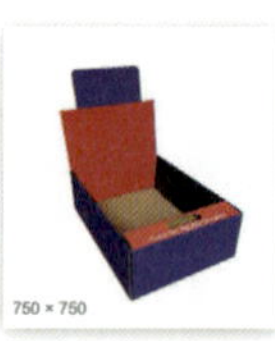

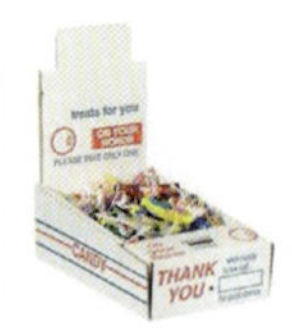

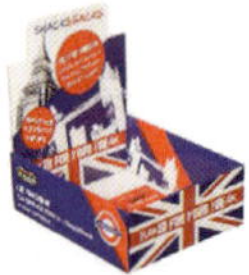

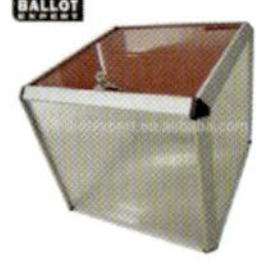

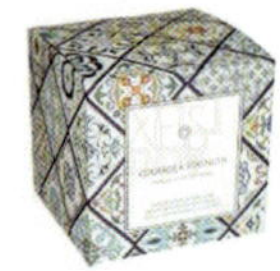

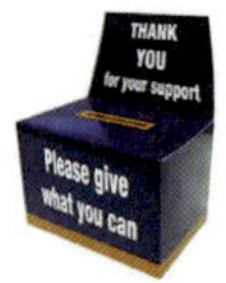

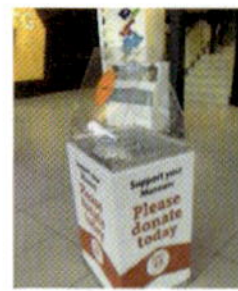

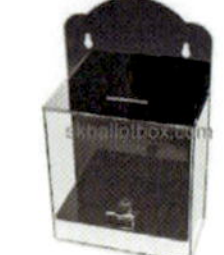

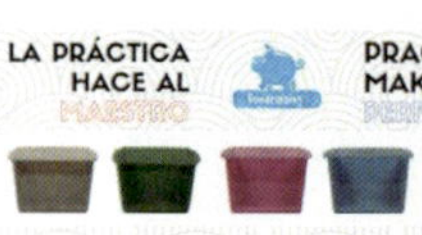

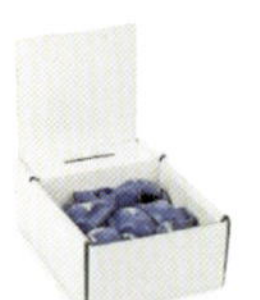

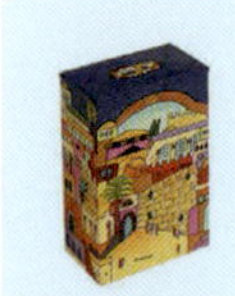

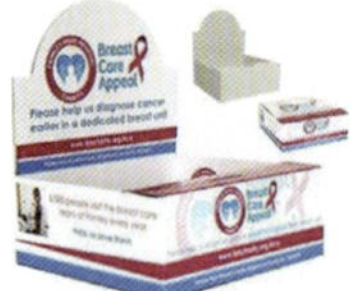

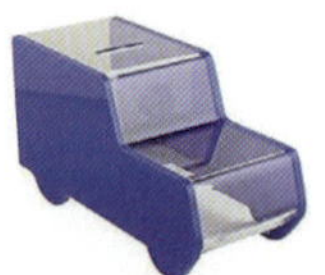

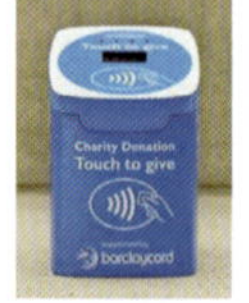

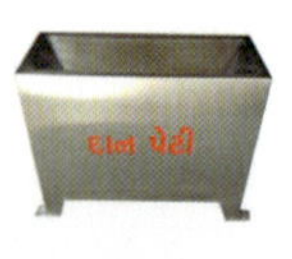

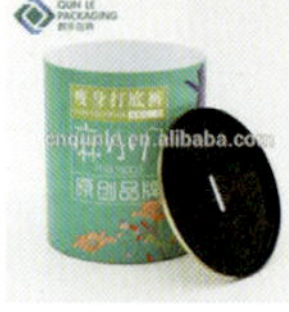

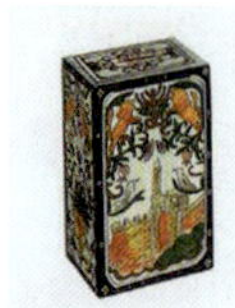

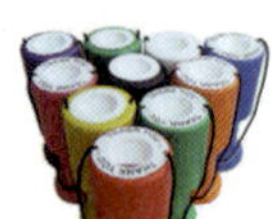

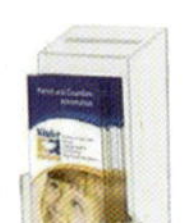

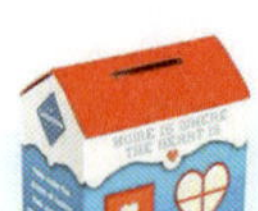

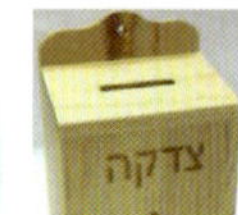

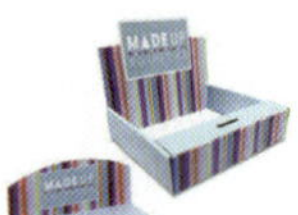

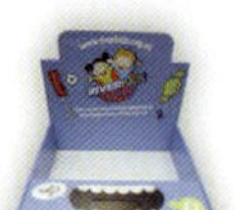

Charity boxes, web screenshot, accessed January, 2020

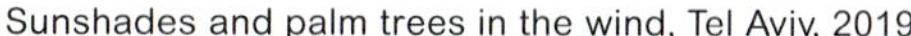

Sunshades and palm trees in the wind, Tel Aviv, 2019

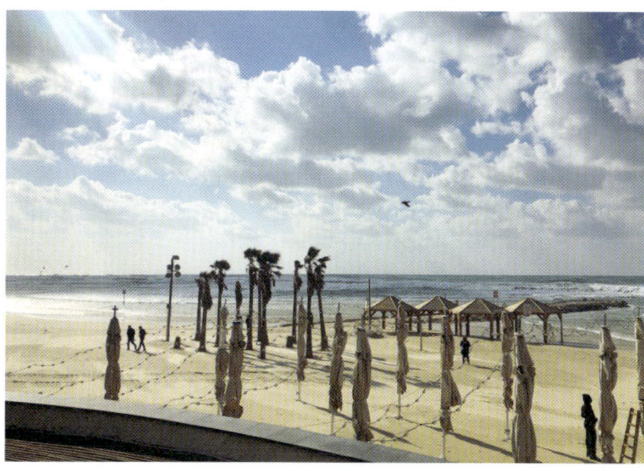

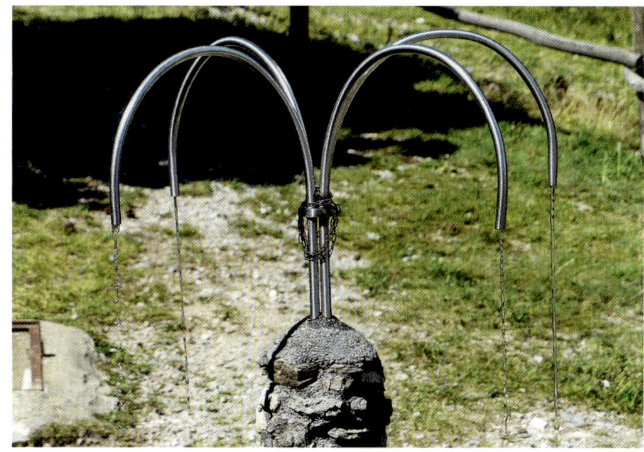

Construction of a fountain, web screenshot, accessed May, 2018

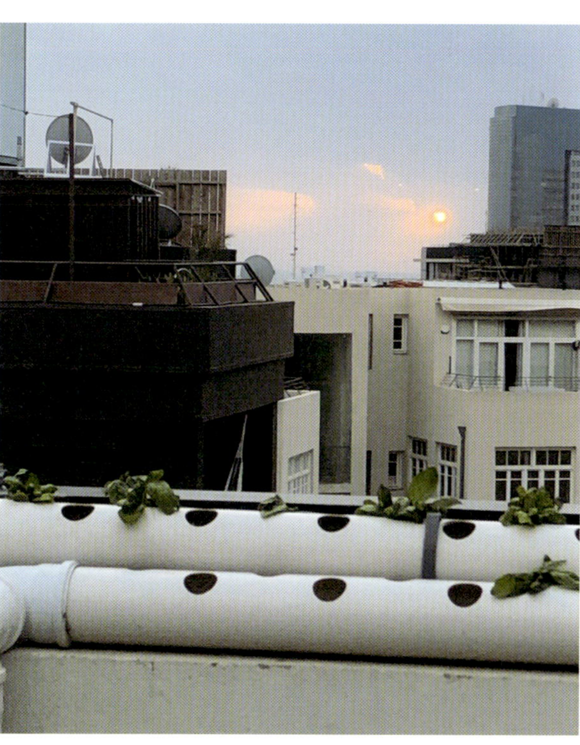

Growing plants in drainpipes, Tel Aviv, 2019

A semaphore or maybe just an accident (with bins), 2019,
PVC tube, styrofoam, expanding foam, filler, light bulbs, lamp holder, cables, bins, dimensions variable, SALTS, Birsfelden near Basel, 2019. Exhibition view: Gunnar Meier

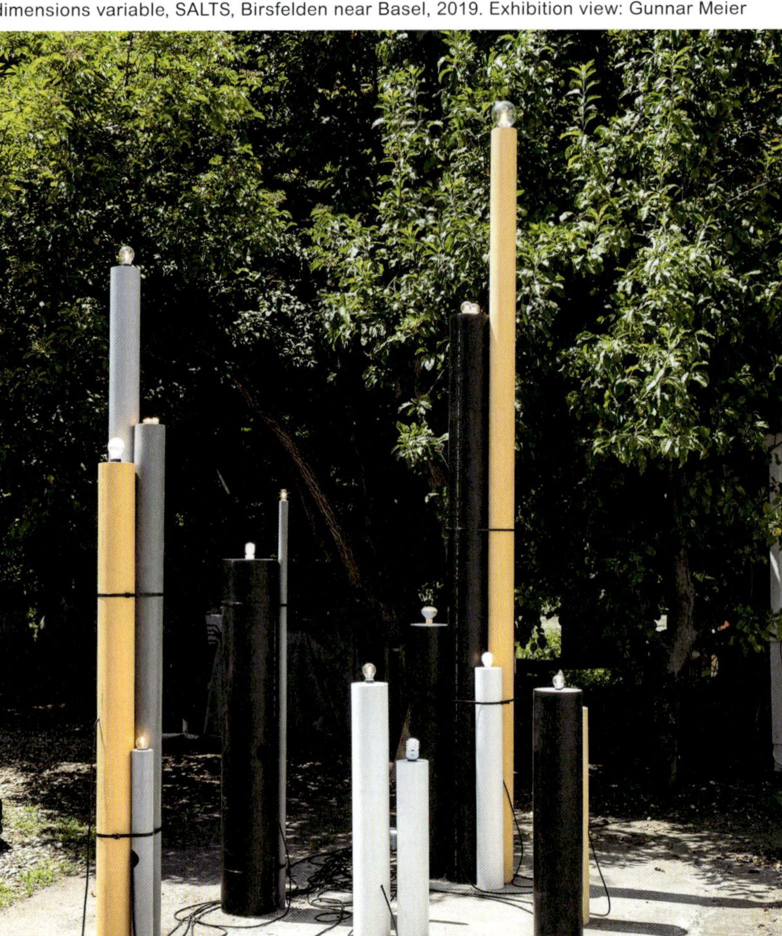

Detail of A semaphore or maybe just an accident (with bins), 2019, SALTS, Birsfelden near Basel, 2019. Exhibition view: Gunnar Meier

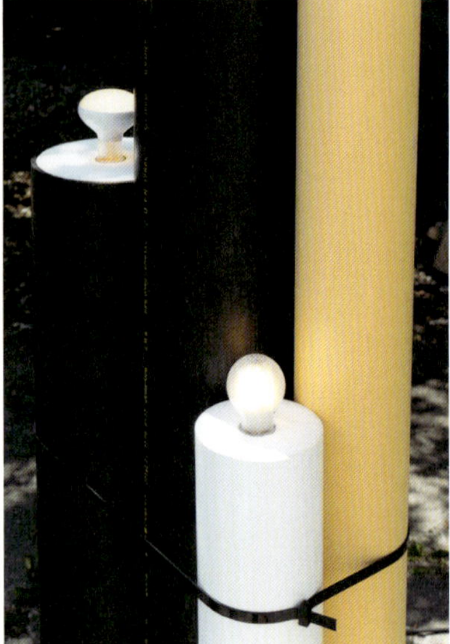

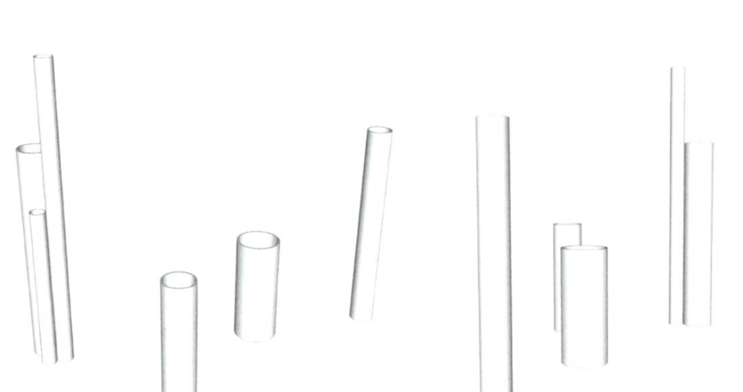

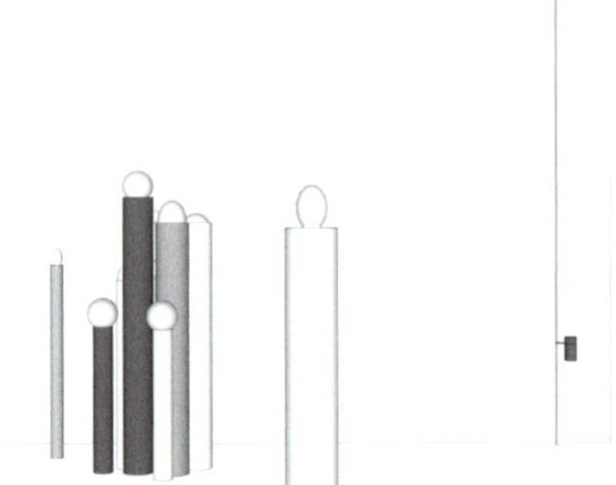

Renderings for A semaphore or maybe just an accident (with bins), 2019

Detail of A semaphore or maybe just an accident (organ, with bins), 2019, in Disposition, o.T. Raum für aktuelle Kunst, Lucerne, 2019

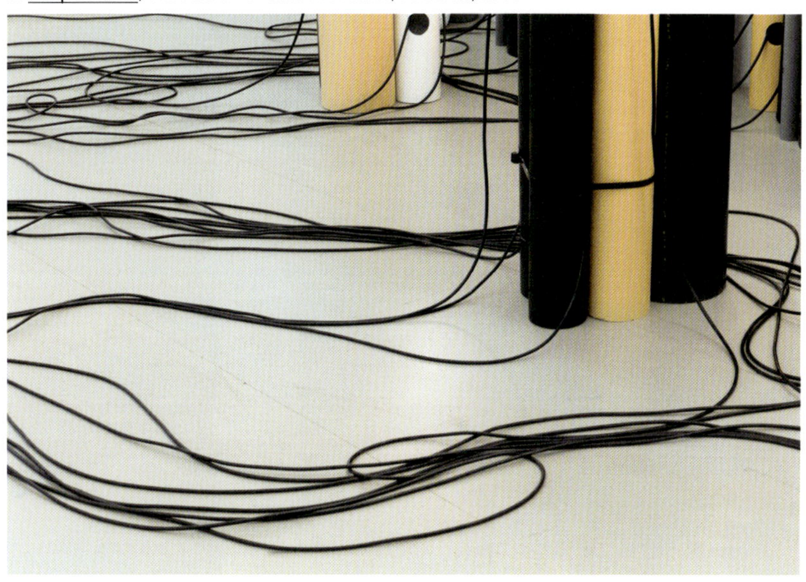

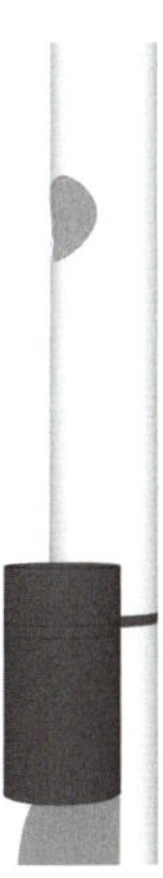

Rendering for A semaphore or maybe just an accident (with bins), 2019

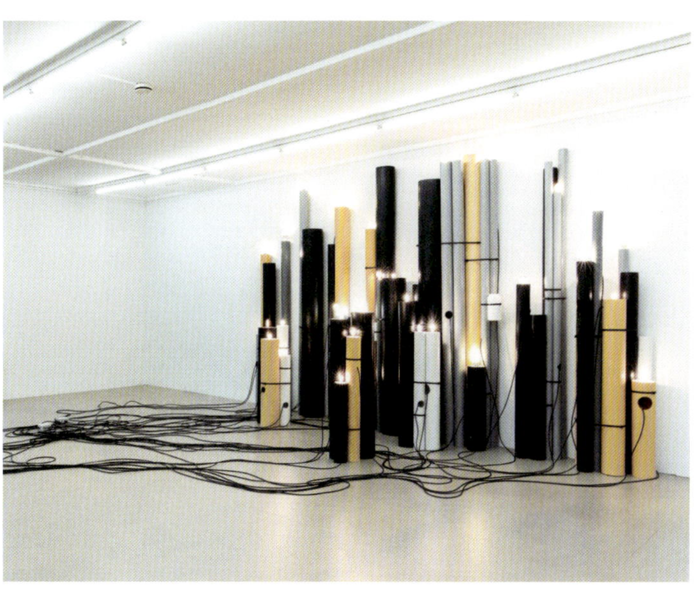

A semaphore or maybe just an accident (organ, with bins), 2019, PVC tube, styrofoam, expanding foam, filler, light bulbs, lamp holder, cables, bins, dimensions variable, in Disposition, o.T. Raum für aktuelle Kunst, Lucerne, 2019

Setting up A semaphore or maybe just an accident (with bins), 2019, SALTS, Birsfelden near Basel, 2019

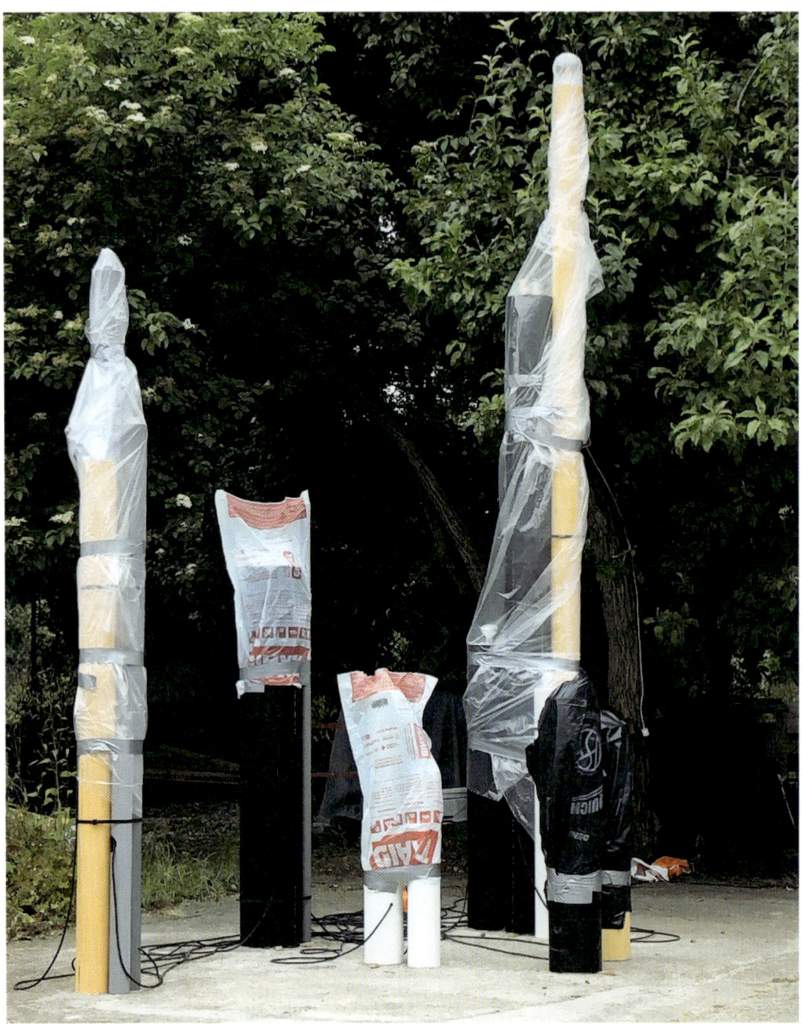

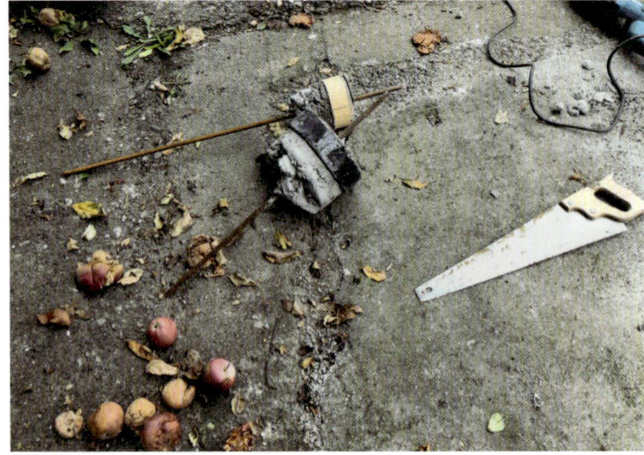

Dismantling A semaphore or maybe just an accident (with bins), 2019, SALTS, Birsfelden near Basel, 2019

Drainpipes at Dreispitz, Basel, 2019

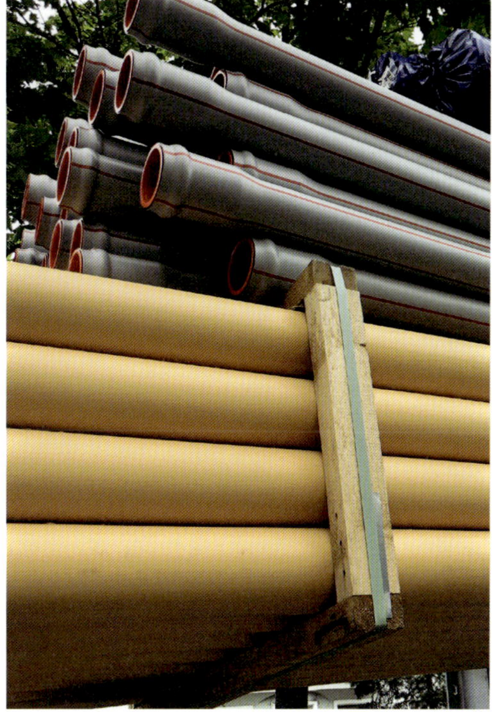

A semaphore or maybe just an accident (with bins), 2019, SALTS, Birsfelden near Basel, 2019. Exhibition view: Gunnar Meier

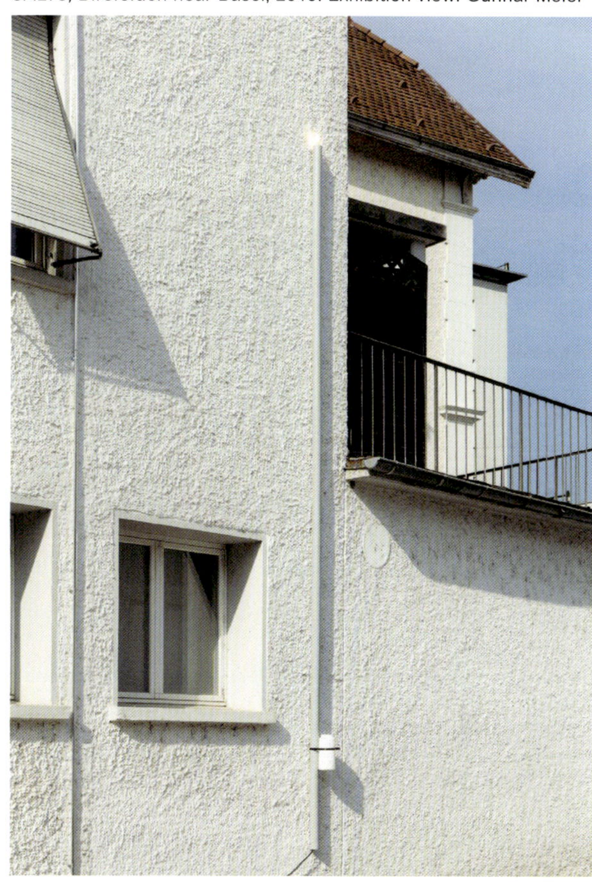

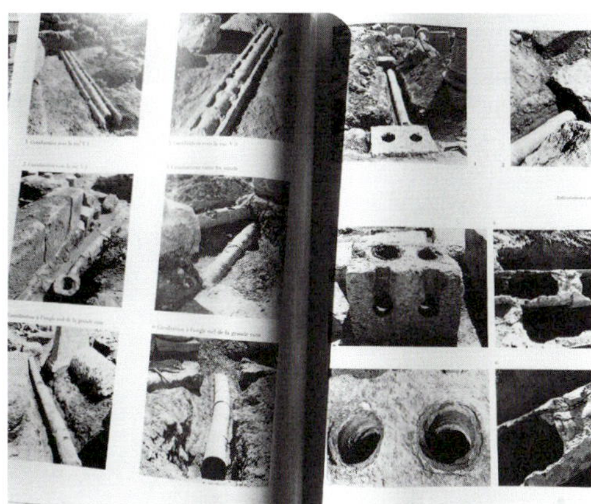

From Le sanctuaire de Baalshamin à Palmyre: Topographie et architecture by Paul Collart and Jacques Vicari (Rome: Istituto Svizzero, 1969), 57

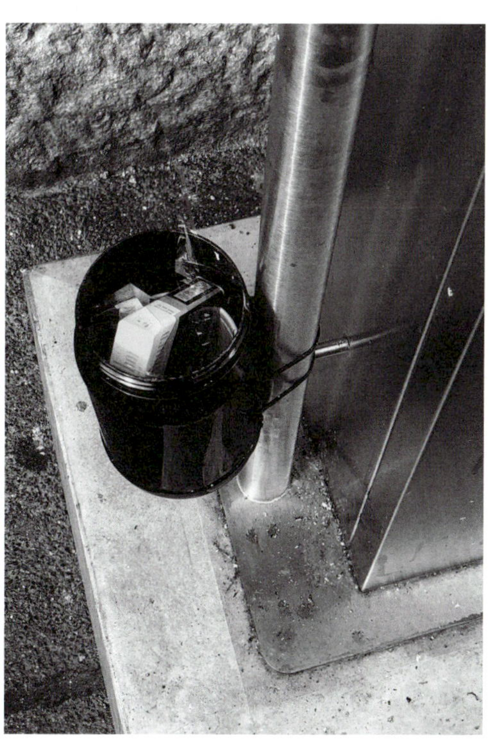

Improvised ashtray at Basel SBB railway station, Basel, 2018

View over the Bay of Tangier, 2020,
web screenshots, accessed August, 2020

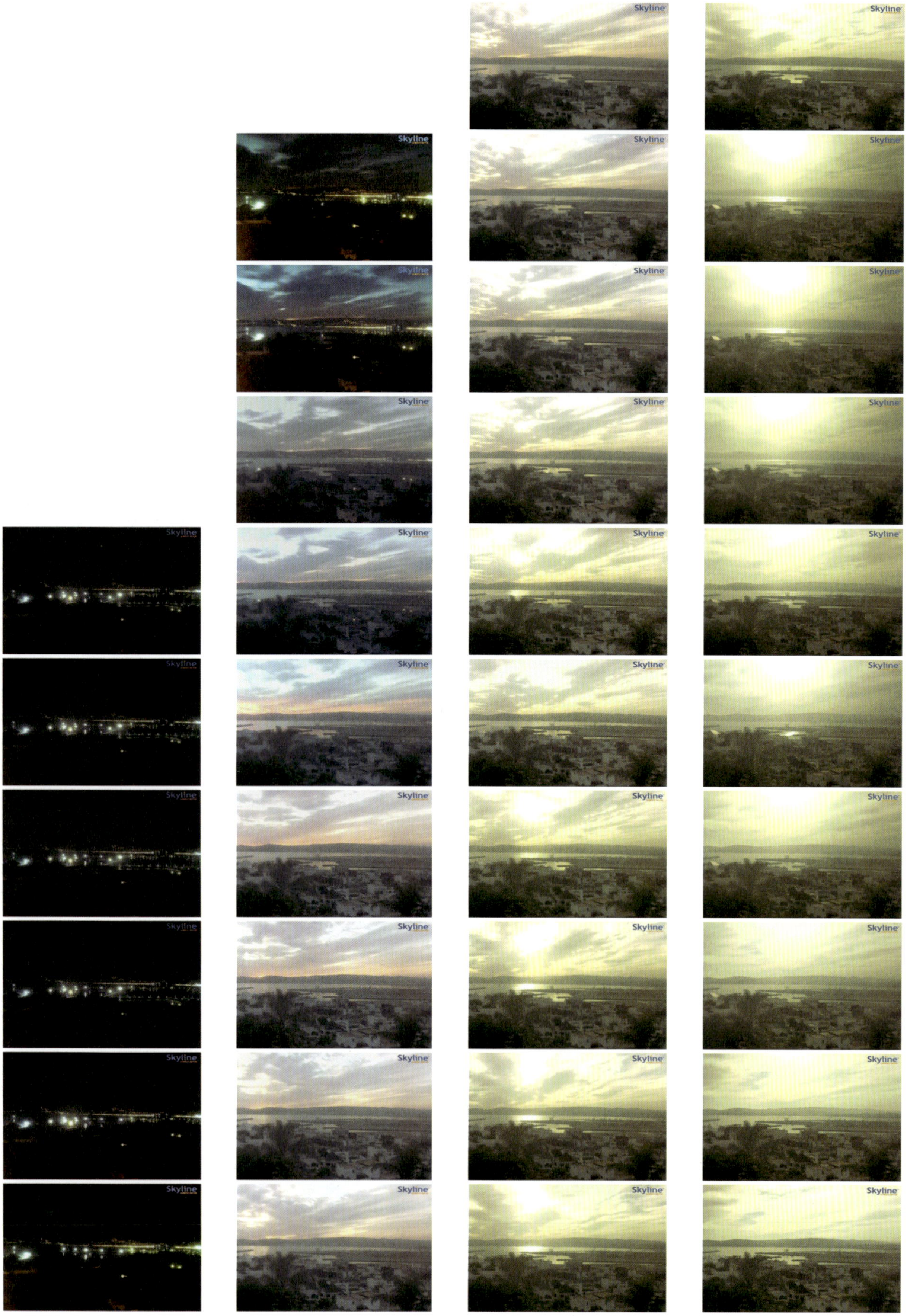

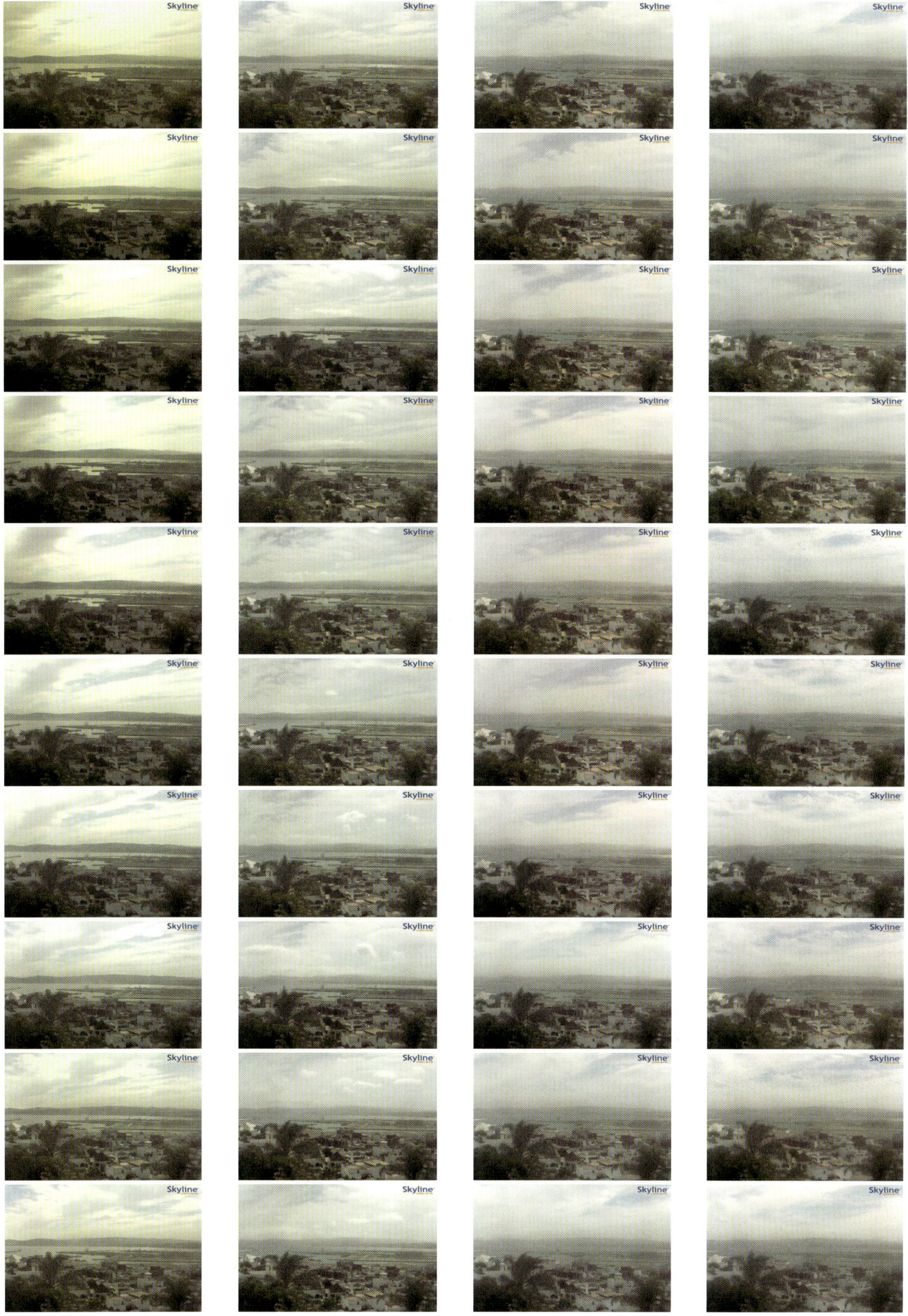
Skyline

View over the Bay of Tangier, 2020,
web screenshots, accessed August, 2020

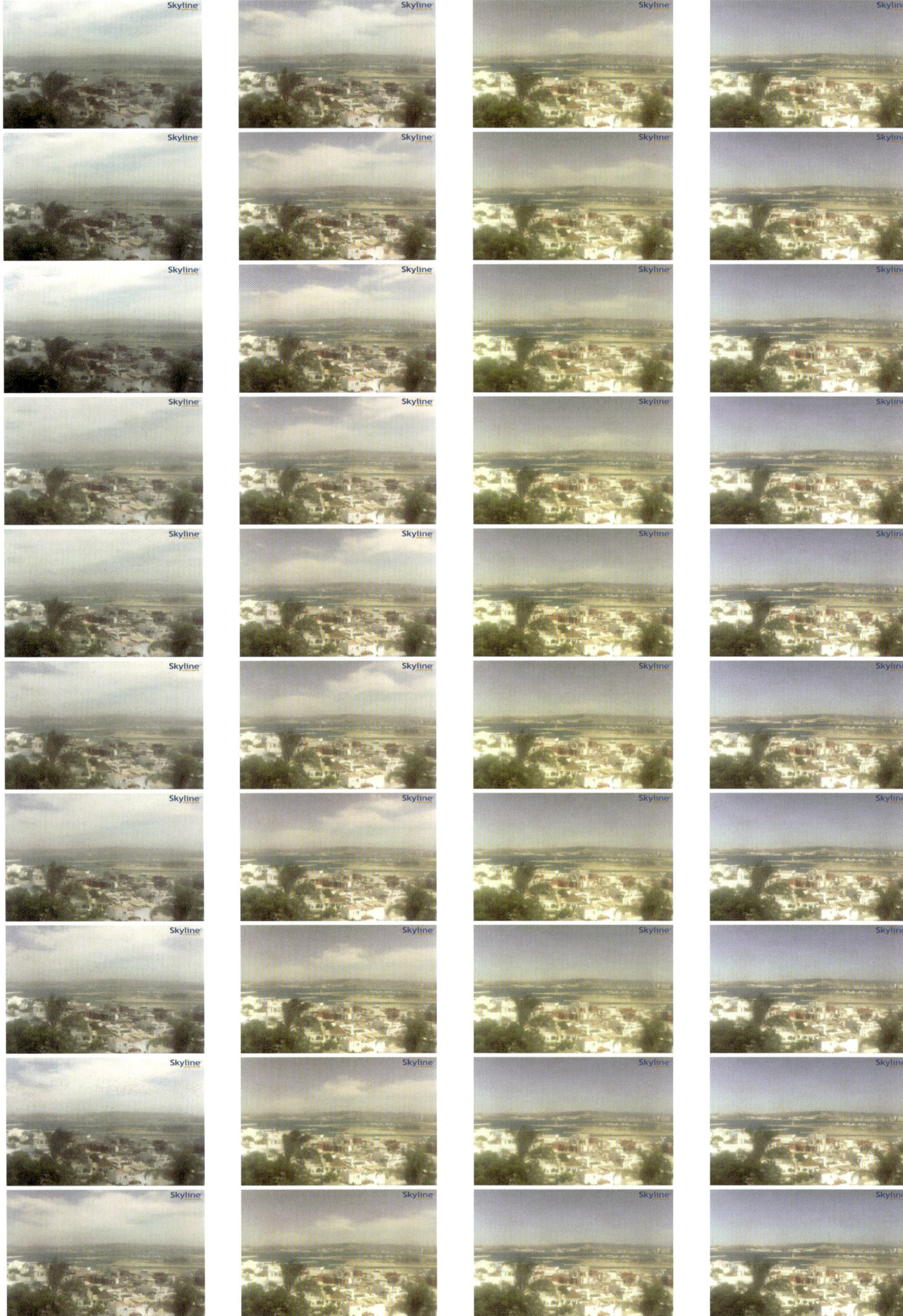

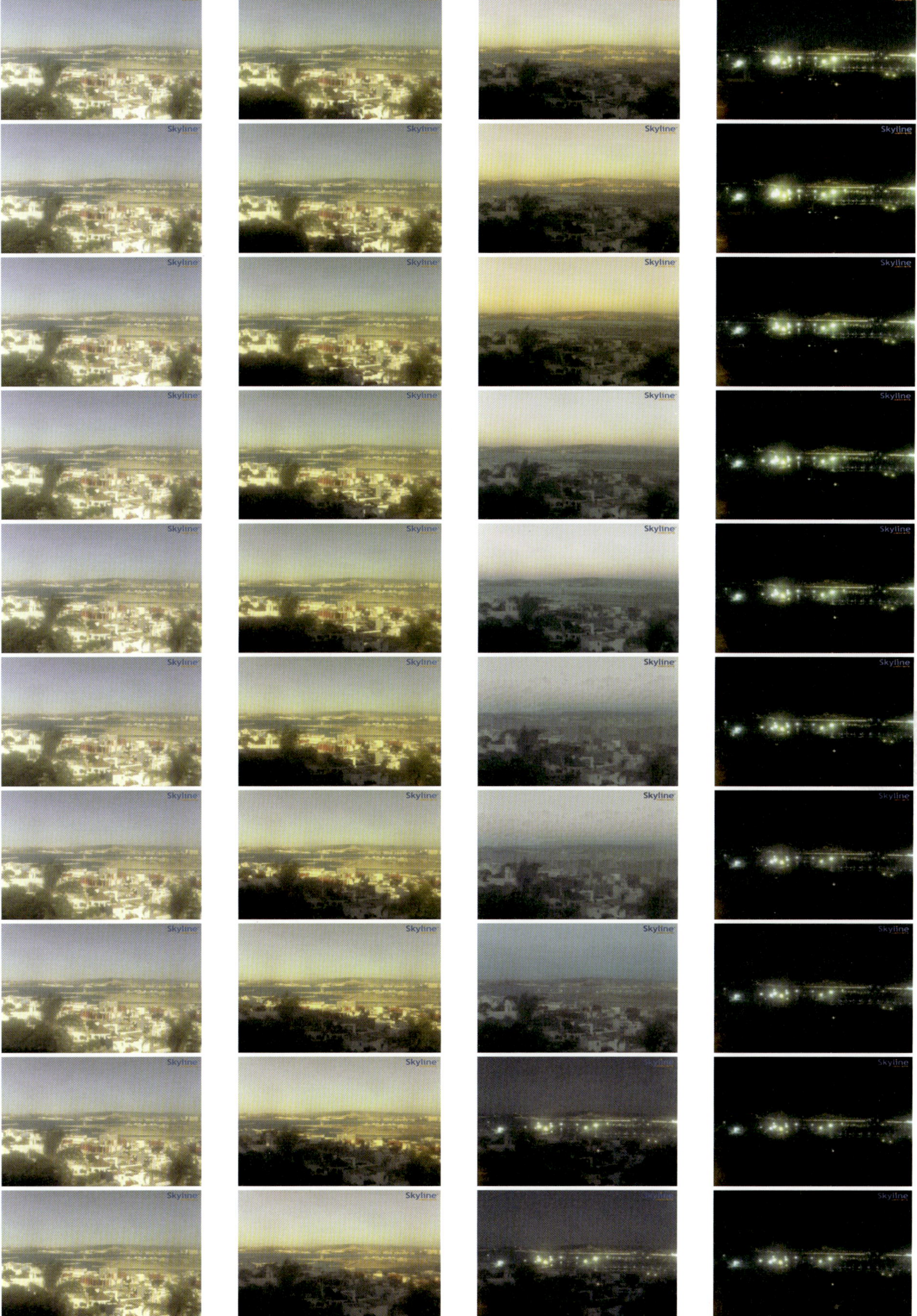
Skyline

View over the Bay of Tangier, 2020,
web screenshots, accessed August, 2020

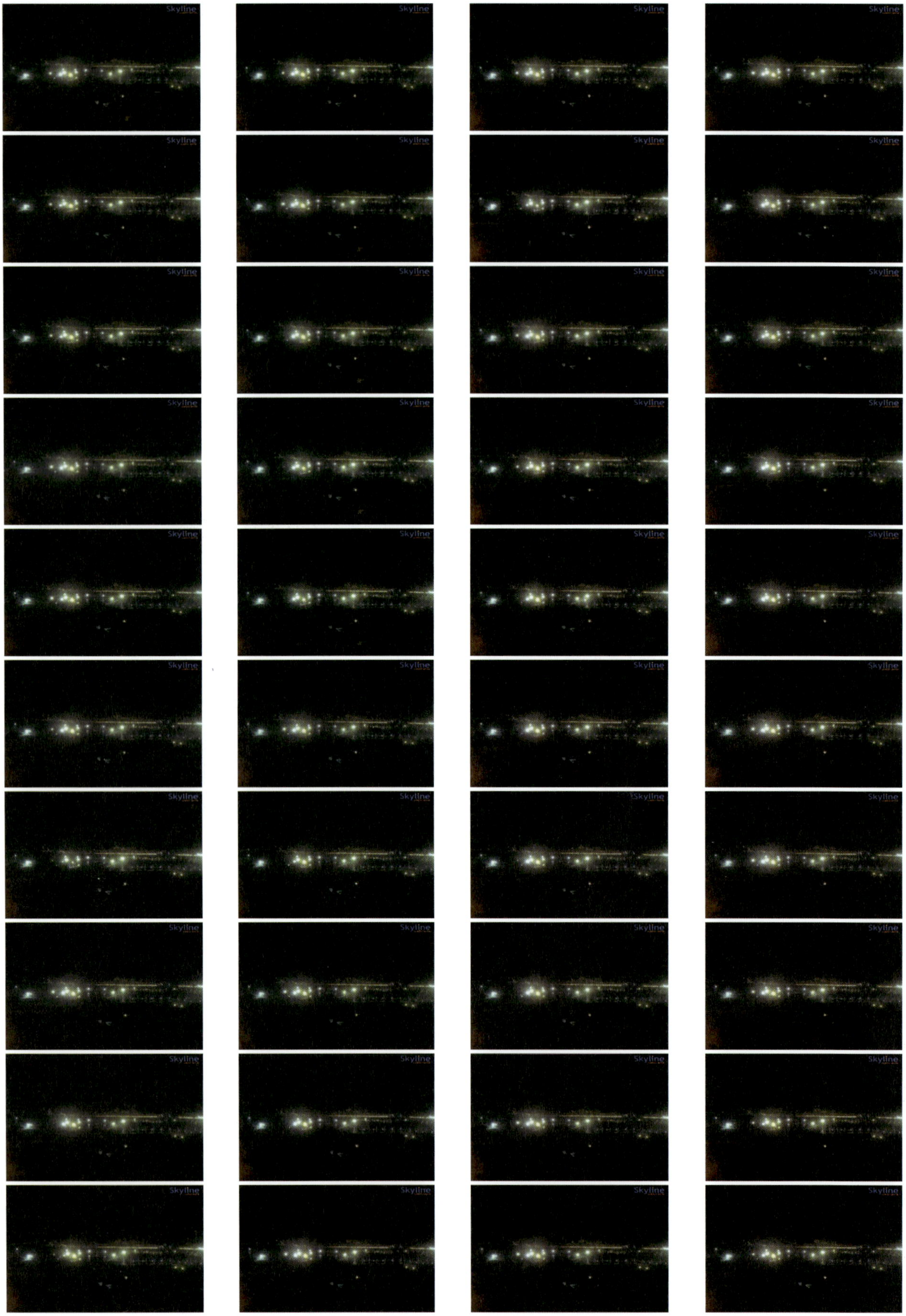

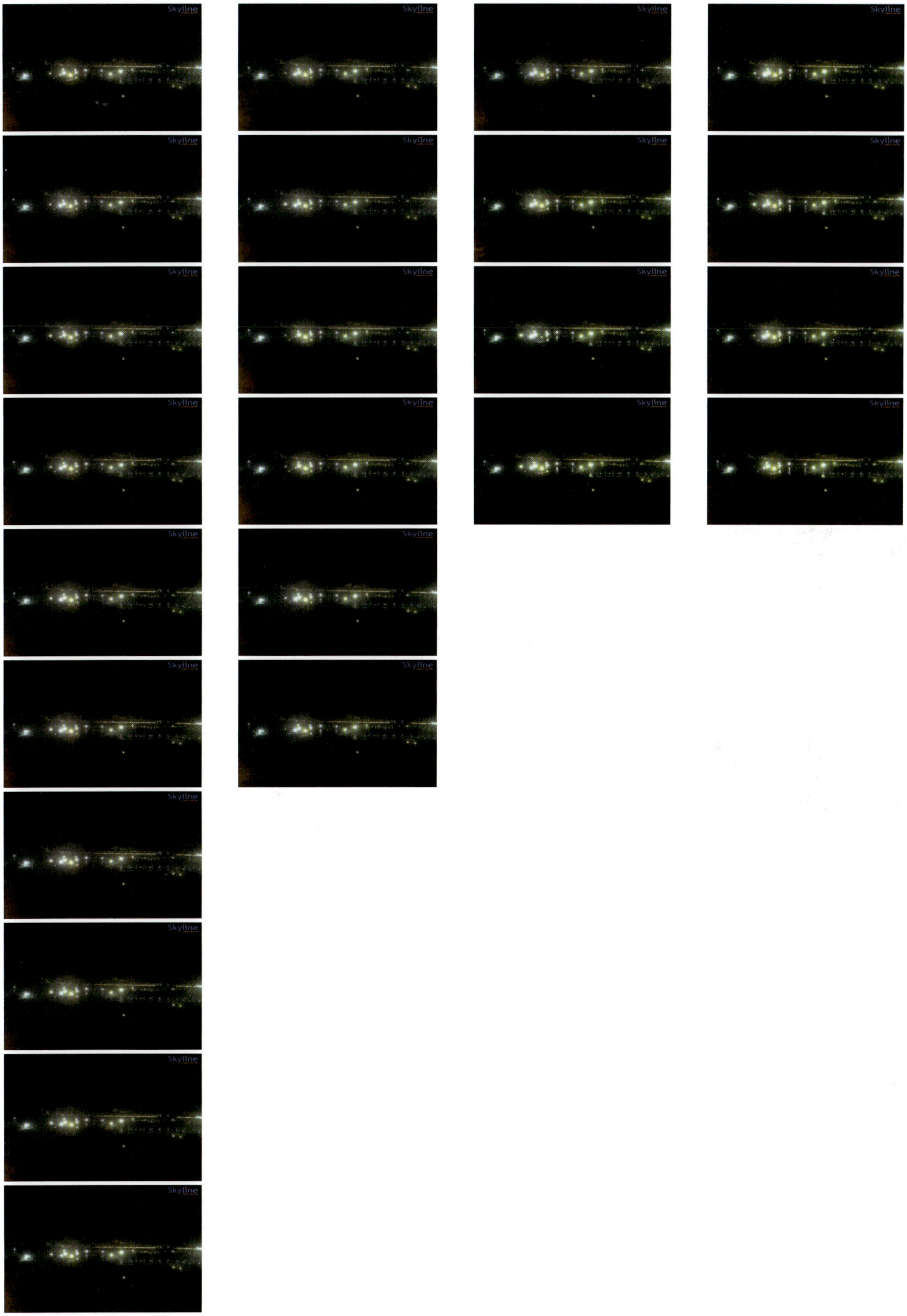

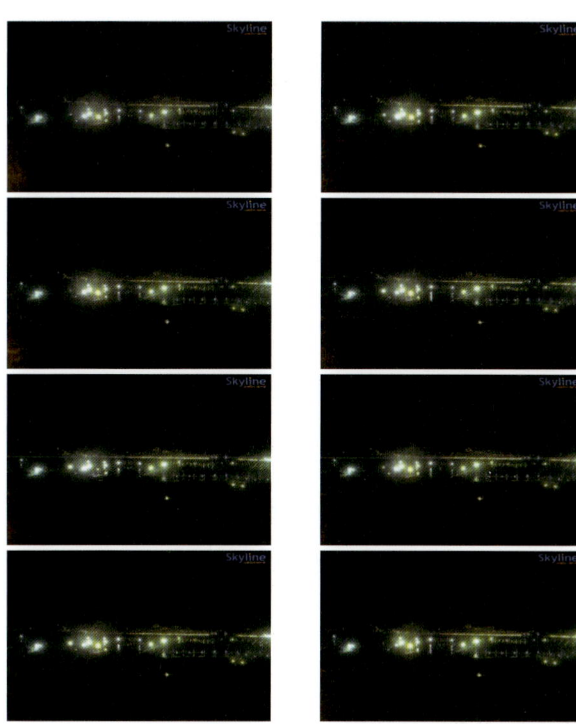
Skyline

This book is published on the occasion of the exhibition: Judith Kakon
Manor Art Prize Schaffhausen 2021
Museum zu Allerheiligen Schaffhausen
02.12.2021 – 27.02.2022

m' Museum zu Allerheiligen Schaffhausen

Editor: Isabelle Köpfli, Museum zu Allerheiligen Schaffhausen
Concept: Judith Kakon with Ronnie Fueglister and Yves Graber
Editorial coordination: Simone Neuenschwander
Copyediting: Isabelle Köpfli, Daniel Malone, Simone Neuenschwander
Authors: Quinn Latimer, Boaz Levin, Simone Neuenschwander, Sadie Plant
Translations: German–English: Alisa Kotmair (Text S. Neuenschwander), English–German: Nina Franz (Texts Q. Latimer, B. Levin), Meret Kaufmann (Text S. Plant),
German texts available at: https://judithkakon.com/stolen-language
Design: Ronnie Fueglister, Yves Graber
Production: Longo AG, SpA, Bolzano

Published and distributed by:
Mousse Publishing
Contrappunto s.r.l.
Via Pier Candido Decembrio 28
20137, Milan–Italy

Available through:
Mousse Publishing, Milan (moussemagazine.it)
DAP | Distributed Art Publishers, New York (artbook.com)
Vice Versa Distribution, Berlin (viceversaartbooks.com)
Les presses du réel, Dijon (lespressesdureel.com)
Antenne Books, London (antennebooks.com)

First edition: 2021
Printed in Italy by Longo AG, SpA, Bolzano

ISBN 978-88-6749-486-6
22 EUR / 25 USD / 25 CHF

Artist's acknowledgements:
My personal thanks go to my family and all the friends who have supported me in various ways over the past years. I would also like to thank all the people and institutions involved in the exhibition and the publication. My special thanks go to all the contributors, the many eyes, ears and minds that made this book project possible.

The publication has been generously supported by:

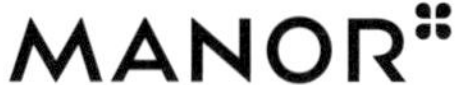

STURZENEGGER STIFTUNG SCHAFFHAUSEN

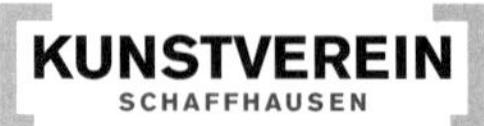

DR.GEORG UND JOSI GUGGENHEIM STIFTUNG

BASEL LANDSCHAFT
SWISSLOS

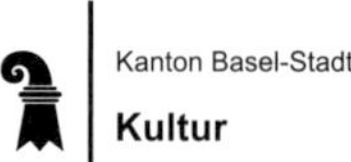

RUTH UND PAUL WALLACH-STIFTUNG

Scans of parcels received by post between November, 2020, and April, 2021

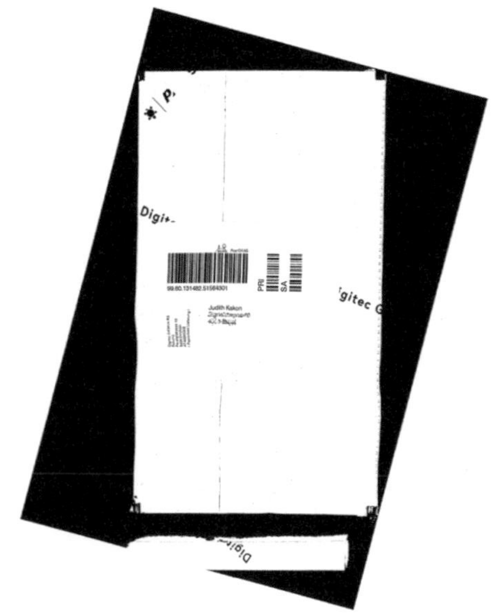

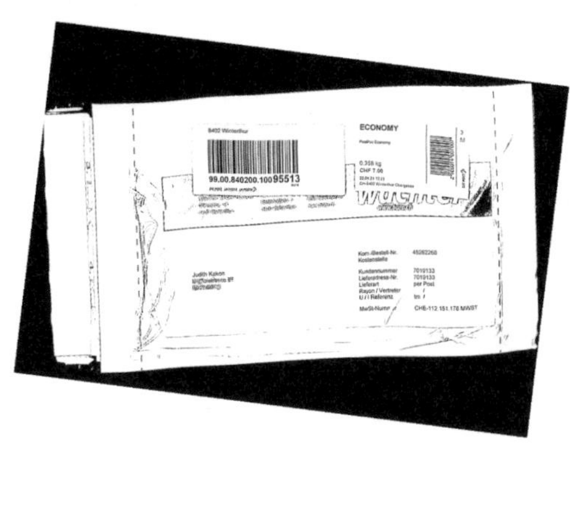

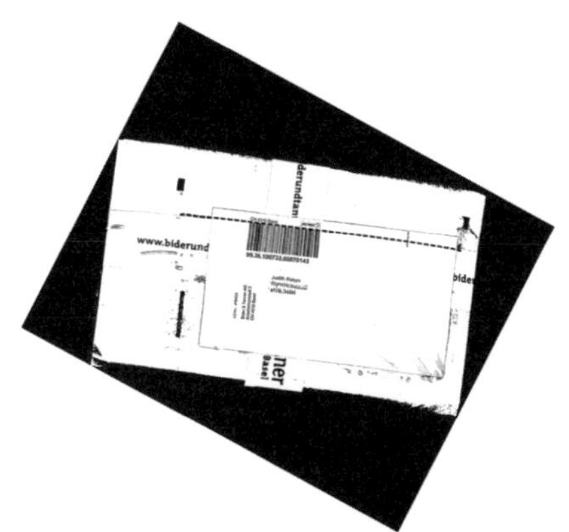

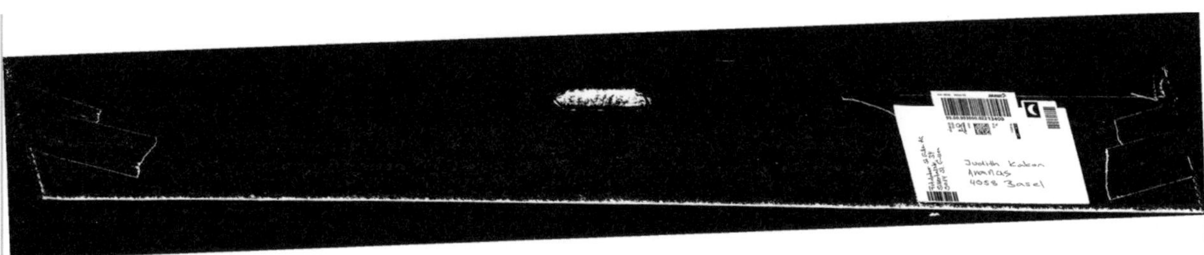

Scans of parcels received by post between November, 2020, and April, 2021

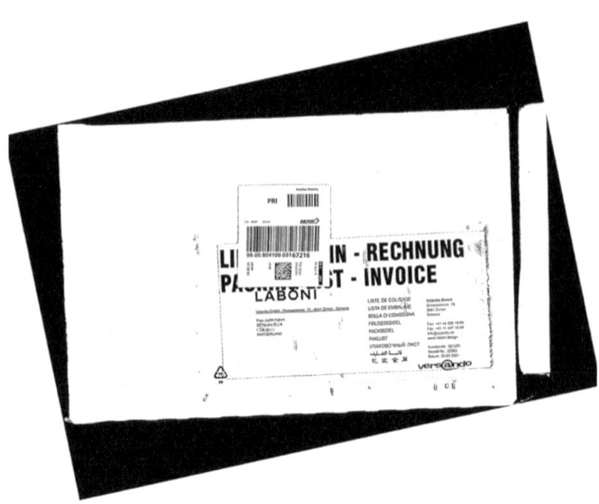

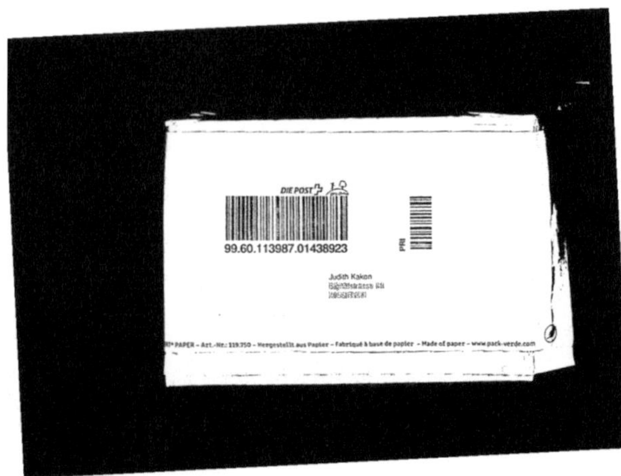

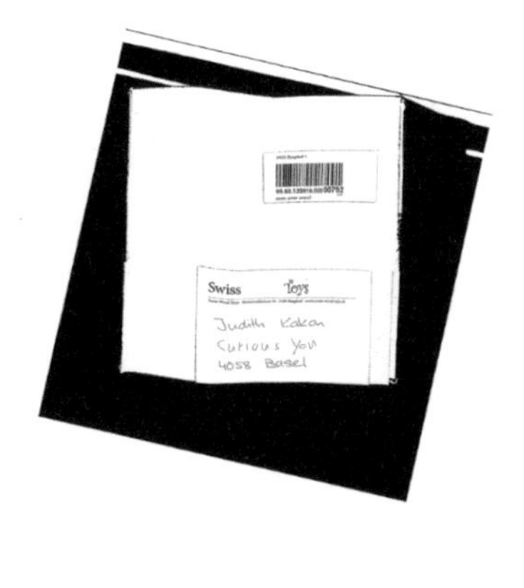
Swiss Toys
Judith Kakon
Curious You
4058 Basel

Hier öffnen
bergzeit
99.60.103421.00640847
Schweiz
Judith Kakon
PRI

99.60.006418.01340379
Judith Kakon

Scans of parcels received by post between November, 2020, and April, 2021

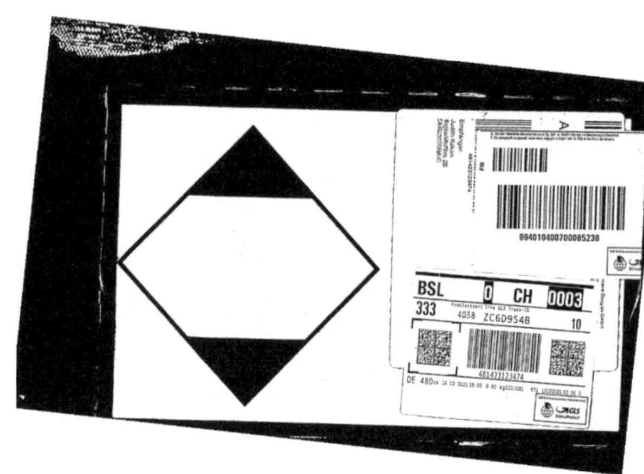

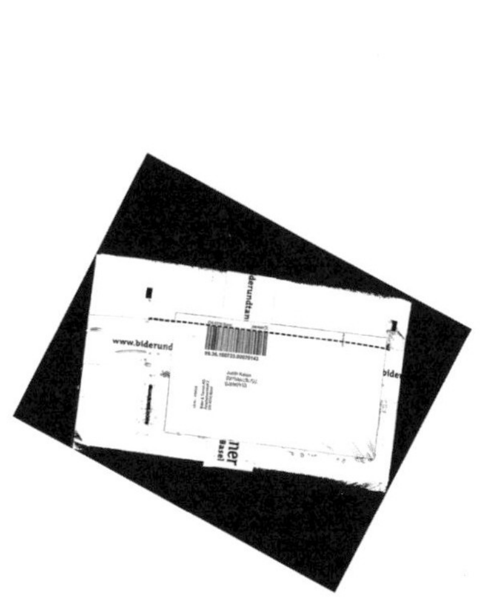

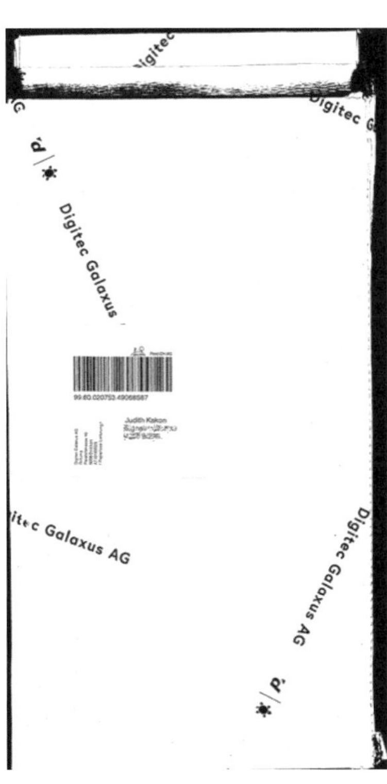
Digitec Galaxus
Digitec Galaxus AG

Mari (written by Nissar Makhdoomi), 2021

ماری ماری

ماری ماری

ماری ماری

ماری ماری